Praise for Sons of God – 1

"A *story of prehistory and the b*   ided
reading for anyone with an interest in antiquarian history and/ or the
history of religion, In *Sons Of God Daughters Of Men*, Edward F.
Malkowski pieces together a story of prehistory and the birth of
civilization from the myths of Genesis discovered through the revelations
of archaeology. Exploring the legends of history and various culture
folklore, as well as cities from Biblical times, the search to locate Eden,
the evolution of religious and spiritual thought since prehistoric times,
and so much more, *Sons Of God Daughters Of Men* offers a thoughtful and
thought-provoking wealth of insights into the gradual process of an
increasing cultural sophistication in humankind's attempts to grapple
with both real and spiritual dilemmas."

Midwest Book Review

What readers are saying…

"*Eye opening...* Thoroughly researched and well put together, it offers an
alternative view of history, not bound by religious or academic doctrine.
Every author should be as thorough and unbiased as Mr. Malkowski."

"*Fascinating Research...* It seems as though there is a faction who would
keep the truth from the masses. Scientists' egos prevent them from
expanding their minds and embracing the research contained in this
book. Publishers refuse to publish controversial findings such as this. The
research is solid and the conclusions are logical. I found it a fascinating
collection of information."

"*Excellent history and excellently resourced...* Malkowski has done his research
on this read. Meticulously resourced, he dives into the history of ancient
cultures to the modern."

The Nephilim were on the earth in those days–and also afterward–when the sons of God went to the daughters of men and had children by them. They were the heroes of old, men of renown.

Genesis 6:4

Sons of God
Daughters of Men

Genesis: A Clash of Cultures

Edward F. Malkowski

ISBN Number: 0-9743950-0-5

Library of Congress PCN: 203110479

Third Printing, 2006

Printed and bound in the United States

To Mom: For all the questions twenty years ago.

To Dad: For giving me a reason to write.

Acknowledgements

I extend a very special thanks to John Anthony West. Although we view history in slightly different perspectives, he has been a true inspiration as well as a friend. His insights have been valuable key in my search for ancient history; and to David Hatcher Childress, for his advice and photos.

I also wish to thank my editor, Ronda McBride, who has worked diligently for many months; Vi Malkowski, Jeff Masters, Tony Schutz, and Veronica Malkowski for their feedback, comments and questions. And my children Joe, Ronni, Thomas, and Chelsea for their patience and fair treatment of my ideas and conclusions, I am a lucky man to have such a fine family.

Preface

Twenty-five years ago as I read the biblical story of Noah's flood, I was captivated by its preamble. Like most young adults, I already knew the story from childhood, and even watched John Huston's epic film "The Bible" on its network debut. In the commercial versions of the story there was no mention of, what I call, the big mystery. According to the text, giants lived on the earth in those days. Making it more mysterious, these giants are mentioned in the same breath as the "sons of God" who took for wives the daughters of men. Furthermore, the *Genesis* author describes them as "heroes of old" and "men of renown." How could anything be 'old' if mankind was created a few generations before?

This enigma has prompted speculation of all kinds over the years. From demons and angels to spaceships and extra-terrestrials, a variety of theories have been put forth to explain this puzzle. Although interesting, they are difficult to believe. I have never found a reasonable answer from anyone. So, as a non-academic historian I decided to find my own answers.

I began my quest with a search for the physical evidence of giants. This led to the realization that ancient texts were in a mythical way, in fact, describing historical truths, which prompted a much broader search for civilization's origin.

The scientific evidence of mankind's past, I propose, must agree with ancient legends and myths. Created by religious, personal, and academic bias, there is a great chasm between scientific theory and religious doctrine. I believe I have bridged this gap in a fair way.

Sons of God – Daughters of Men is about history, and not theology, although it is difficult, at times, not to mention and discuss various theological ideas and trends. The scope of prehistory will be confined to the areas in and around Mesopotamia, the Near East, Europe and the Americas. Europe plays a material role in providing the evidence of mankind's first known organized societies. Surprisingly the Americas, I discovered, does also. Although the Far East and Egypt have a significant prehistory, their inclusion is beyond the topic and scope of investigation.

There is abundant archeological evidence regarding the prehistory of man. Although its interpretations are often debated among the scientists themselves, their factual basis is irrefutable. Those who wrote ancient texts assigned to history the traditions and stories of men who witnessed the events. Putting these two elements together provides a compelling picture of man's hidden history.

Table of Contents

Table of Contents

Introduction

The most mysterious book of the Bible can be no other than *Genesis*, and particularly puzzling is the story of creation. Until recently in Western society, the story of Adam and Eve, Cain and Abel has long been accepted as fact. However, with profound scientific discoveries of the nineteenth and twentieth centuries, especially in archeology and geology, all but the most reactionary now consider these stories to be more metaphorical than genuine; spiritual truths as opposed to actual truths. And it appears their philosophical opponents consider them more or less fact-less, spiritual or otherwise.

Peculiarities in the first ten chapters of Genesis raise important and fundamental questions concerning the believability and reliability of the text, which was written then handed down the generations, as the story goes, by Moses himself. There are questions, which are typically explained away by patterns of logic encouraging a self-perpetuating ignorance of history and unflappable allegiance to sightless doctrine. For example, if the great flood destroyed all people on the face of the Earth, then how could "giants [exist] in the earth in those days; and also *after that*"? Perhaps more importantly, who were these giants? And who were the "sons of God" somehow associated with these giants, which took for wives the daughters of men? And then there is the legendary Garden of Eden, fact or fiction? Why was the serpent chosen to beguile mankind? Did a snake really talk or was the author referring to something else entirely? And what fruit, after eaten, could possibly cause such an epiphany allowing man to distinguish between naked and clothed, good and evil?

Human events in ancient history did not occur in a vacuum and therefore, are not without a historical context. *Sons of God – Daughters of Men* hunts through the pages of history in search of facts, in an attempt to establish Genesis as a believable and literal text.

Our search begins in nineteenth century America when settlers moving into the Ohio River Valley unearthed the remains of a forgotten civilization, a society where giants lived among men, and a culture that encompassed the vast, eastern territories of North America. For their posterity, numerous county histories, and eventually the United States Geological Survey, documented the events of this almost forgotten chapter in U.S. history.

We follow the historical evidence of giants back to ancient Israel. From the legendary King David, to Joshua and the conquest of Canaan, then to Abraham and his flight from the Sumerian City of Ur; and finally to Noah and his great-grandfather, Enoch. We also visit the antediluvian world of Genesis, where a clash of cultures sparked the most famous fable of all. With scientific and historical evidence cast in complementary light we can see fact in myth and truth in tale. As we explore the past, it is our intent to discover a factual, but lost history.

We humans rationalize and justify and search for a better explanation of the world we live in. We do this to ourselves, in and about our own lives; as new memories form, older memories change. We also do this collectively as a society through arts, entertainment, and education. And our changing ideas are often a matter of opinion about the available facts and shifting circumstance. Here lies the reason the truths of ancient stories have been lost in myth.

Human culture has had a long history of conflict and order. Those who succeed tell their story, almost always as the *only* story. It is cliché though true, history is written by the victor. Nations, societies, movements and ideas that failed somewhere along the way are often depicted as inhuman or evil and in most cases were probably neither. Their vain struggle offers valuable insight into our past and our own way of thinking. To truly understand the triumphant, we must also understand the defeated.

Chapter 1
Unusual Skeletal Remains

- The Lovelock Nevada Mummies
- The Anakin of Niagara
- Tall Tales from County Histories
- The United States Geological Survey Steps In
- Mound Majesty

During the 1980s, the enduring scientific debate between evolutionists and creationists exploded along the banks of the Paluxy River near Glen Rose, Texas. The controversy focused around footprints overlapped by tracks of a dinosaur in the bed of the river. Several footprints were reported as gigantic. Originally cited as evidence for scientific creationism in *The Genesis Flood* by John Whitcomb and Henry Morris (1961), these footprints have been a source of controversy since then, with a long list of 'who's right' from both sides.

Roland Bird, a maverick fossil hunter, was first to excavate Glen Rose during the 1930s for the American Museum of Natural History. His crew excavated a large portion of the riverbed and divided it into three sections which are on display at the University of Texas, the Smithsonian, and the American Museum of Natural History. A number of other teams representing both sides of the controversy, and some with more objective views, conducted investigations during the next three decades.

One of the more sensational publications occurred in 1987 with Carl Baugh's *Dinosaurs: Scientific Evidence that Man and Dinosaurs Walked Together.* Director of the Creation Evidence Museum, Baugh began excavation at Paluxy in 1982 in an attempt to prove his convictions.

Besides the footprints he believes to be human, he claims to have uncovered the impression of a human hand and metal hammer (wooden handle included) embedded in the sandstone.[1]

With journalists invited as chaperones, Baugh's team removed a layer of cretaceous limestone to reveal the tracks of man and dinosaur side by side. It was an attempt to further proved his point. However, the media exposition was fruitless, and neither side has budged from their respective positions.

A less controversial anecdote from Baugh's book is the inspection of a human skeleton over seven feet tall. Geologist John Morris from Oklahoma University told one of Baugh's associates that a man living near Glen Rose held a giant skull in his collection. A meeting was arranged and, to the astonishment of the group, a Mr. Wayland Adams displayed a large skeleton on the hood of a car (Photographs of the event appear in his book).[2] According to the story, Wayland's father discovered the skeleton years ago, twelve miles from Paluxy at Panther Cave. The woman, from whom the skeleton came, apparently died in childbirth; the remains of a small infant were found at her side.[3]

Baugh makes no claims to the dating of the skeleton, except that it was prehistoric when discovered. He also makes no claim that the skeleton dates to the biblical flood or left tracks in the riverbed. His claim is fair; she was a giant who died in the company of others near the site of human and dinosaur tracks.[4]

The Panther Cave skeleton may be labeled an isolated incident. However, evidence exists throughout North America to suggest otherwise. Unusual skeletal remains have been found as far east as Niagara, New York and as far west as Nevada.

The Lovelock Nevada Mummies

In 1911, a group of workers from *Guano Mining* (a company founded in 1904 to harvest bat guano as fertilizer) discovered the mummified remains of several individuals in Lovelock Cave, seventy miles northeast of Reno, Nevada. Atypical of western Native American Indians, these mummies had red hair and ranged in height from six and a half to eight feet tall.[5] Other artifacts were found as well, including artfully modeled duck decoys.[6]

The site was never properly excavated, but one skull nearly twelve inches long (nine inches is today's average) is stored with other artifacts at the Humboldt County Museum in Winnemucca, Nevada. Other artifacts are also displayed at the Nevada State Historical Society in Reno.

The Anakin of Niagara

Originally published in *The Daily Telegraph* of Toronto, Ontario in 1871, another report heralded a similar discovery. Forty miles west of Niagara Falls (in the township of Cayuga on the banks of the Grand River), stone skimmers, axes, and large stone pipes were unearthed along with the remains of nearly two hundred individuals. Male skeletons were very tall, several measuring nine feet in height; few were less than seven. Several thighbones were reported to be twelve inches longer than those of an average man. One skull examined, it was said, would completely cover the head of an ordinary person. According to the Daily Telegraph author, local townspeople believed these skeletons belonged to a race of people who lived there before the region's occupation by Native Indians. The author of the article explained the discovery:

> The farm, which consists of 150 acres, has been cultivated for nearly a century, and was covered with a thick growth of pine, so that it must have been ages ago since the remains were deposited there. The skulls of the skeletons are of an enormous size and all manner of shapes, about half as large again as are now to be seen. The teeth in most of them are still in almost perfect state of preservation, though they soon fall out when exposed to the air.[7]

When the Daily Telegraph published this story, 'mound' sensationalism had already gripped North America – a phenomenon that had its beginnings in the heartland of Ohio. Eventually, this unknown culture from the past was referred to as the "Mound Builders" for their practice of burying their dead in earthen mounds.

Tall Tales from County Histories

At the end of the eighteenth century, expanding influence of the United States moved across the Appalachian Mountains into the Ohio Valley. With it came a throng of settlers. Most were families in search of land to farm. The early years were difficult, but by the turn of the century (with the Native Indian population sufficiently reduced) homesteaders began to establishment farms, townships, and (with a growing population of 5,000 to 60,000 by 1802) statehood.

In the progress of civilization, it was traditional to record events and place them into 'county histories.' Nearly every county had one. From county establishments, office appointments, and business enterprises – to the journeys of a popular preacher, these histories documented everything of importance in the county including oddities.

Ohio homesteaders discovered that some hills were tombs created by a prehistoric culture and sometimes included the remains of remarkably tall individuals. Ohio was not alone in their fascinating discoveries. From Logan County in Illinois to Erie County Pennsylvania, stories from these histories often describe amateur excavations of burial mounds and chance finds through ordinary labors.

Brown County, Ohio

One section in the *History of Brown County Ohio* reported that mastodon bones were occasionally unearthed and, at other times, ancient settlements were discovered and identified "by the appearance of gigantic skeletons."[8] Unlike Native Indians of the day, the remains were peculiar; high cheekbones, powerful jaws and a massive frame were the usual characteristics. According to a Brown County historian, those responsible for the remains left no other clues from the history of past ages.

Ashtabula County, Ohio

Stephen D. Peet, a contributing author of the *History of Ashtabula County Ohio*, wrote that Indian earthworks were more numerous than previously supposed. They were found in various townships, usually near streams or other frequented areas, and were often accompanied by beautiful scenery.

He describes one of the more remarkable structures of the area on the banks of the Conneaut River. It was as a burial place belonging to the ancient races of the region. Occupying nearly four acres, the cemetery was located just west of the village next to a stream. It was oblong in shape and laid out in lots with the order and propriety of modern burials. Nearly 3,000 graves were laid in straight rows with intervening spaces used as alleys. According to Peet, they were "examined as early as 1800, and were found to contain human bones, some of which were of a large size."[9]

Peet also describes the discovery of artifacts found while workers were cultivating a garden near the village of Ashtabula. The men conducted an excavation and found bones:

> ...which seemed to have belonged to a race of giants. This land at one time belonged to a Mr. Peleg Sweet, who was a man of large size and full features; and it is narrated that at one time he, in digging, came upon a skull and jaw which were of such size that the skull would cover his head and the jaw could be easily slipped over his face, as though the head of a giant were enveloping his. Other burial-grounds of an ancient people existed in the vicinity, – one on the very bank of the lake, near the mouth of the river.[10]

A similar account of the Conneaut mounds (published in 1888) is described in the *Historical Collections of Ohio* by Henry Howe.[11]

Marion County, Ohio

In Marion County, Ohio, evidence for regional occupation before the appearance of Native American Indians is found in almost every part of the county. While quarrying gravel for road construction, hundreds of human skeletons – some of giant form – were uncovered. Similar finds were also found in excavated cellars. One individual estimated there were almost as many skeletons in Marion County as there were current inhabitants.[12]

Monroe County, Ohio

According to the History of Monroe County Ohio, Chester Bishop unearthed a skeleton of unusual length while digging a cellar. Richard Kirkpatrick, a local doctor, carefully removed it. From his calculations, the height of the man when living would have been eight feet five inches tall.[13]

A mound existed at Marietta, Ohio "of a magnitude and height which strike the beholder with astonishment."[14] Its base diameter was 115 feet and it reached thirty feet high, surrounded by a ditch four feet deep and fifteen feet wide.

Medina County, Ohio

Nine human skeletons were found while digging a cellar in Medina County, Ohio. And, just as with specimens from other ancient mounds, these too were of large stature. Placement of the skeletons appeared random. Albert Harris is quoted in the History of Medina County, 1881: "It looked as if the bodies had been dumped into a ditch. Some of them were buried deeper than others, the lower one being about seven feet below the surface." He also stated that the skulls were so large one would fit over his head (while wearing a fur cap) with room enough to rest upon his shoulders. A genetic oddity was also apparent; the skull contain teeth that were described as "double all the way round."[15]

Morrow County, Ohio

According to the History of Morrow County and Ohio published in 1880, a nearby Indian mound was demolished to provide materials for the construction of a hotel near Chesterville in 1829. While digging, workmen found a large human skeleton but no measurements were taken. However, it was related to the press that the jawbone would easily fit over that of any citizen in the village. Local doctors examined the skull and found it proportionately large, with more teeth than people of today. The skeleton was taken to Mansfield but was subsequently lost.[16]

Erie County, Ohio

The *Firelands Pioneer* (of Vermillion Township in Erie County, Ohio) reported in 1858 that several mounds had produced bones and sometimes whole skeletons of a race of beings who were very large. Some of the inhabitants believed that they had belonged to a race much larger than the local Indians who were encountered by the first settlers. [17]

Noble County, Ohio

According to *Historical Collections of Ohio* (1872), in the Seneca Township of Noble County Ohio, one of many Indian mounds was excavated. This particular mound (known as the "Bates" mound) contained broken pieces of earthenware, a large quantity of flint points, and several stone instruments. The remains of three skeletons (whose size would suggest that in life they measured at least eight feet tall) were also recovered. The most remarkable feature of these remains was a double row of teeth in both the lower and upper jaws. After exposure to the atmosphere, the skeletons reportedly crumbled into dust.[18]

Lawrence County, Ohio

As reported by a newspaper in Lawrence County Ohio (the *Ironton Register*) on May 5, 1892, the site where Proctorville now stands was once part of a well-paved city. The *Ironton* author believed that the greater part of it is now located in the Ohio River. Only a few mounds are there, one of which was near the Wilgus mansion. It contained "a skeleton of a very large person, all double teeth."[19] Its jawbone was so large that it would fit over the jaw of a grown man. This common burial ground was filled with skeletons at a depth of six feet.

Erie County, Pennsylvania

On the John Pomeroy place in Erie County Pennsylvania (on the second flat of Conneaut Creek), traces of an ancient mound existed like those found at Girard, Springfield, Harbor Creek, Fairview, Wayne, and other townships of the county. The circular mound encompassed three-fourths of an acre. After the land around the mound was cleared, the embankment was found to be three feet high by six feet thick at the base, with large trees growing on it. A giant oak near the summit was removed. According to its rings, it had been there for five hundred years. Beneath the tree, a skeleton was recovered which "showed to a verity that giants lived in those remote ages." The Erie County author explained that:

> **The bones measured eleven feet from head to foot, the jawbone easily covered that of a man who weighed over 200 pounds, and the lower bone of the leg, being compared with that of a person who was six feet four inches in height, was found to be nearly a foot longer.**[20]

Adair County, Kentucky

On January 5, 1897, the *Adair County News* (a Kentucky newspaper) reported that an old Indian mound was opened on the Harrison Robinson farm – four miles East of Jackson, Ohio. Two skeletons of extraordinary size were recovered with a great quantity of trinkets. The find was surprising since, according to the paper, a party of relic hunters who worked for an archeological society had visited the farm years before and removed a large collection of stone hatchets, beads and bracelets.[21]

Gastonville, Pennsylvania

The American Antiquarian (issue 7:52) published an article in 1885 covering the Smithsonian Institution's excavation of mounds near Gastonville, Pennsylvania. The committee of scientists found that:

> At some depth from the surface a kind of vault was found
> in which was discovered the skeleton of a giant measuring
> seven feet two inches. His hair was coarse and jet black, and
> hung to the waist, the brow being ornamented with a
> copper crown.[22]

According to the article, the skeleton was remarkably well preserved and carved inscriptions were visible on stones covering the vault. Scientists believed that when deciphered, they would "lift the veil that shrouds the history of the race of people that at one time inhabited this part of the American continent." They were never deciphered. Artifacts from the site were shipped to the Smithsonian and said to be the most interesting collection ever found in the United States.[23]

Logan County, Illinois

Several other stories come from farther west in Illinois. Reported in the *History of Logan County* in 1886, it was said that it was sometimes difficult to distinguish between burial sites raised by the Mound Builders and more modern Indian graves. Tombs of the Mound Builders, the report advises, were generally larger than those of recent burials and usually contained a greater number of bodies. They also contained relics of art – evidence of a high-level of civilization. To some degree, modern Indians seized these ancient earthworks for their own use. But the skeletons of the Mound Builders could be distinguished from more recent burials by their greater stature.[24]

Lake County, Illinois

During the early history of Lake County, Illinois, it was discovered that Mound Builders had once occupied the region but left no written language or tradition. They erected piles of earth (usually from surface soil) and deposited the remains of their dead inside, along with pottery and crude instruments of husbandry and warfare. Indian mounds were numerous along rivers and near inland lakes with large trees having grown to maturity on their summits which suggested great antiquity. According to the Lake County author, excavations revealed the crumbling bones of a mighty race.

Samuel Miller, a resident of the county since 1835, described one skeleton he had assisted in unearthing as slightly more than eight feet long with a correspondingly large skull. Other skeletons measured at least seven feet. Extensive burial grounds were also found on the shore of Lake Michigan south of the Waukegan River and at various other points throughout the county. The graves in these primitive cemeteries were often found to contain beads, earrings, arrowheads, and silver trinkets. While workmen were digging a foundation for a sugar refinery in 1889, several Catholic and Masonic-style emblems were gathered and carried away by relic hunters. Skeletons found near the lakeshore were also of unusual size but were probably the remains of more recent burials.[25]

Virginia

Numerous Indian artifacts were found on the Wappatomaka River. Among them was a highly finished pipe, its bowl crafted in the image of a coiled snake. Also discovered (according to the *Historical Collections of Virginia*, 1845) was the lower jawbone of a human. According to a Mr. Kercheval who witnessed the event, it was of great size. The jaw contained eight teeth (also of enormous size) on each side. Even more remarkable was that the teeth stood transversely in the jawbone. The skull, it is told, would pass over any man's face with ease.[26]

Literary Uproar

The act of recording these 'groundbreaking' events in county histories typically occurred long after the event, likely written because of a cultural phenomenon that began earlier in the century. Although exaggerations of the original events may have occurred (given the overwhelming number of similar reports), it is likely that the essential facts of the stories are genuine.

These tall tales began when farmers found burial grounds while clearing land. The news of their discoveries spread east, and a sensation of speculation soon developed into national proportions. Knowing nothing of the burial mounds or the people who built them, it was a common understanding of the time that indigenous Indians (or their ancestors) could not be responsible. As viewed in stereotypical manner, Indian society was unorganized and formed of nomadic tribes who were spiritually ill equipped to build such impressive earthworks. Because of their lazy nature, some other culture had to be responsible. Although mistaken, this was their logic. Naturally the question was asked, 'Who built these grand tombs?' Imaginations went wild and theories were plentiful. Built with geometric precision and engineering complexity, approximately 10,000 mounds existed throughout the Ohio Valley. According to local lore, they must have been the remnants of a grand, lost civilization.

One author, William Pidgeon in *Traditions of Dee-coo-dah and Antiquarian Researches*, credited the Adam of biblical fame as being the first mound builder. Still others believed that either the lost ten tribes of Israel, Vikings, Welshmen or Phoenicians were the builders. Ignatius Donnelly, a statesman and the famous author of *Atlantis: the Antediluvian World*, proposed that survivors from the lost continent of Atlantis created them.[27] There was a sensational literary uproar akin to the "year 2000 bug" of modern times. The rational and scientific man begged for a logical explanation.

The United States Geological Survey Steps In

In 1881, a group of influential archeologists persuaded congress to appropriate $25,000 of the United States Geological Survey budget for mound research. The USGS Director, John Wesley Powell of Grand Canyon expedition fame, was furious. He preferred the study of languages, arts, institutions, and myths of existing Indian tribes. Nevertheless, he obliged Congress and named Cyrus Thomas to work directly under the newly formed archeology division.

Thomas began excavation in 1881. It was a monumental task that involved several teams moving to different parts of the country according to the seasons – northern sites in the summer, southern in winter. His first report, a small paper entitled *Exploration in Mounds*, was published in 1884 and included in the 3rd *Annual Report of the Bureau of Ethnology*. It covered excavations in West Virginia, Ohio, Tennessee, Arkansas, and Florida. Approximately 4,000 artifacts (including pipes, pendants, polished stones, hammers, and axes) were recovered and brought to the National Museum in Washington.

Several years later, a more lengthy report was published in the 5th *Annual Report of the Bureau of Ethnology*. Thomas explained that according to his preliminary conclusions, there was no evidence the mound builders were an ancient lost civilization. Indeed, he agreed with Harvard Peabody Museum Curator, Frederic Putnam; they were the work of several tribes of Indians, although the connection between the tribes was not yet clear. Peabody suggested the mounds were the result of two tribes: a long, narrow headed people of the north, and a short, broad-headed people of the south. After these two tribes came the Indians of today. Before them there was an unknown tribe whose roots go back 8,000 years.

Thomas decided the ancestors of current Indians had built the mounds in Wisconsin, Illinois, Iowa, and New York. On the other hand, Ohio mound origins were more elusive. He embraced a theory created by John Heckewelder that the Talligewi Indians (also known as the Alligewi or Allegheny) were responsible for their construction. These people had moved or were forced out of the area into the Carolinas to become the Cherokee. Georgia mounds were even more mysterious. Although their art was similar in style to the Mexican Aztec, too many differences between them prevented any link. Nor were they like other mound peoples. Their art was savage yet sophisticated, bizarre and striking. It sometimes included trophy skulls.[28]

His final work was published in the *12th Annual Report of the Bureau of Ethnology* in 1894 (a 730-page paper entitled *Report on the Mound Explorations of the Bureau of Ethnology*). After four years of excavations – covering twenty-four states, 2,000 earthworks, and 40,000 artifacts,[29] Thomas and his research corroborated on the fact that the mound builders were native to America. *Report on the Mound Explorations* proved to be a thorough debunking of popular, sensational literature. Science had its explanation.

Yet the Bureau of Ethnology research proved more than was originally planned. Although only a footnote in history, Thomas's work agreed with the amateur excavations performed by early pioneers. He also found unusual skeletal remains, evidence that giants had lived among the mound builders. In three separate sections of his report, Cyrus Thomas described the unearthing of unusual skeletal remains [author emphasis added]:

Underneath the layer of shells the earth was very dark and appeared to be mixed with vegetable mold to the depth of 1 foot. At the bottom of this, resting on the original surface of the ground, was a very large skeleton lying horizontally at full length. Although very soft, the bones were sufficiently distinct to allow of careful measurement before attempting to remove them. *The length from the base of the skull to the bones of the toes was found to be 7 feet 3 inches. It is probable, therefore, that this individual when living was fully 7½ feet high.* At the head lay some small pieces of mica and a green substance, probably the oxide of copper, though no ornament or article of copper was discovered

(Explorations in Roane County, Tennessee) [30]

No. 5, the largest of the group was carefully examined. Two feet below the surface, near the apex, was a skeleton, doubtless an intrusive Indian burial... Near the original surface, 10 or 12 feet from the center, on the lower side, lying at full length on its back, was one of *the largest skeletons discovered by the Bureau agents, the length as proved by actual measurement being between 7 and 8 feet.* It was clearly traceable, but crumbled to pieces immediately after removal from the hard earth in which it was encased.

(Mounds at Dunleith, Illinois) [31]

The outer layer consisted in sandy soil, 2 feet thick, filled with slightly decayed skeletons, probably Indians of intrusive burials. The earth of the main portion of this mound was a very fine yellowish sand which shoveled like ashes and was everywhere, to a depth of 2 to 4 feet, as full of human skeletons as could be stowed away in it, even to two and three tiers. Among these were a number of bones not together as skeletons, but mingled in confusion and probably from scaffolds or other localities. *Excepting one, which was rather more than 7 feet long,* these skeletons appeared to be of medium size and many of them much decayed.

(Pike County, Illinois) [32]

Modern investigations have not found skeletons over seven feet tall. But Robert Silverberg, one of today's leading authorities on the subject, recognizes (in his work *The Mound Builders*) that these aboriginal people were unusually tall and that bones of women over six feet in height and men approaching seven feet have been discovered. [33] He also cites that according to the nineteenth century missionary, John Heckewelder, there was apparently a tradition of giants among them.

Based upon the evidence, it is clear that unusual skeletal remains existed and giants lived among the Mound Builders. Of course, this raises several questions. Who were these Mound Builders? What was their origin? Although work has continued in the field and much detail has been gained, more recent findings cannot improve on Cyrus Thomas' original conclusions. Part of the difficulty is that most mounds were destroyed years ago under progressing civilization.

Mound Majesty

What we do know about the Mound Builders is that they were an agrarian society that existed between 2,000 BC and 500 AD, and were native to America. Although mounds and earthworks were concentrated in the Ohio Valley, their territory spanned the eastern half of the North America. They built different types of mounds for ceremony than for fortification and burial. We also know that two different mound-building peoples occupied the area – the Adena and Hopewell Indians, at different times.

The earlier people, the Adena, were named from the estate of Thomas Worthington from which many artifacts were excavated. The Hopewell people were named in honor of Captain M.C. Hopewell of Ross County

Ohio whose estate supplied a fantastic collection of artifacts for the *1893 Chicago World's Fair.*[34]

Although many of the Adena and Hopewell mounds and earthworks were destroyed during midwestern settlement, some of the more monumental sites remain to this day. The grand Cahokia Mounds in western Illinois, a few miles west of Collinsville, is one of the largest sites. In Ohio, there are the mysterious Great Serpent Mound in Adams County and the Octagon Earthworks in Newark.

The Cahokia mound complex is vast, covering 2,200 acres. At one time, it consisted of hundreds of platform mounds supported by a population numbering in the thousands. Since it was strategically centered at the juncture of the Missouri, Illinois, and Mississippi rivers, some believe it was part of a regional trade network stretching from the Great Plains to the South Atlantic. Artifacts discovered there have led some to speculate that Cahokia represented a vast social, religious, and political complex that exerted a major regional trade influence.

Many artifacts (including pipe fragments and five ceremoniously destroyed figurines) were discovered during the construction of Interstate 270. Researchers and historians originally believed materials for the artifacts originated in quarries located in Arkansas, Oklahoma, and Minnesota. However, mineralogical and geochemical analyses show that only Missouri flint clay deposits could have been the source. In addition (given the similarity of the figurines' chemical and mineralogical composition), the carvers may have selectively quarried their raw materials from a single site or from nearby and closely related sites of the mound complex. Other highly crafted figurines have prompted scholars to believe the site may have been of more local importance.

Northeast of Columbus, Ohio, the Octagon Earthworks occupy fifty acres and are enclosed by another twenty acres of circular embankments. The intricate geometry of the Newark earthworks, originally mapped in 1848 by Ephraim Squier and Edwin Davis under the auspices of the Smithsonian Institution, has today been largely destroyed by decades of agriculture and indifferent development. However, the most striking features of the complex (the "Octagon" and the "Great Circle" mounds) have been preserved.

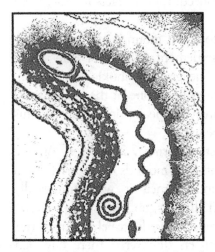

Sketch of the Great Serpent Mound

The *Great Serpent Mound* of Adams County, Ohio is perhaps the most mysterious. The mound itself is in the shape of a snake. The head and tail are clearly identifiable, with its body slithering in several "S" curves. According to Native American Indians, it is the wisdom of a world symbol and a great, powerful *Manitou* (or spirit) existing for a purpose that has mystified its investigators. According to local folklore, it is an ancient symbol of a celestial dragon and serpent. As we shall discover later, the Great Serpent was common in other regions of the northern hemisphere during prehistoric times. Whether the design of the serpent mound effigy originated in the Americas is unknown.

Just as mysterious and perhaps more intriguing is the *Great Hopewell Road* which stretches sixty miles from the Octagon Earthworks to another mound now barely visible, near Chillicothe, Ohio (due south of Columbus). The ancient road is defined by earthen mound walls which are lined with ceremonial circles. It is a magnificent phenomenon of engineering skill requiring massive organizational efforts. The straightness of this ancient road (which is nearly 70 yards wide) has never been explained.

No one can say with confidence where the Mound Builders originated. Some scholars believe it was Mexico, but there is insufficient evidence to draw any conclusions. Our only other source in finding their possible origins and history is through the stories of Native Americans.

Chapter 2
Giants of Native American History

- Legend of the Allegheny
- Other Eastern Legends
- Western Legends

Traditions of Native American tribes are rich with myth and legends explaining everything from the creation of the world to why a specific mountain range looks a certain way. Although their stories sometime sound like children's fables, their themes are true and often represent historical events or instructional information for their audience. As in other cultures around the world, Native Americans remember a great flood. It is a common theme. Some stories even reflect biblical causes; the flood cleansed the land of evil. Tribes from different areas of the country tell flood stories which feature endless rain as the disaster's source[1] – a western counterpart to the biblical deluge.

The general understanding of Native American beliefs is that they were primitive, pagan, and wrong. Nothing could be further from the truth. Although there is no evidence that Native Americans believed in a personalized Hebrew-Christian style God, they did believe in one God who was often referred to as the 'Great Spirit', 'Old One', or 'Man in the Sky'. They also believed other 'spirits' existed. Overall, their beliefs were not all that different from Jewish and Christian traditions.

In a general way, some Indian stories parallel those of the biblical Genesis. According to the Okanogan tribe of Northwest Washington, man was created from the soil and animated by the breath of God. The Old-One made mud balls, the first of which became the animals, and the later ones, he rolled over and over and shaped like Indians. When he blew on them, they came to life.[2]

According to these ancient American traditions, long-ago there was a golden age throughout the land. Life was lived without privation. Many animal species roamed the land before any ice existed on the continent. These ideal conditions were remembered in many societies, but were forever changed when an environmental catastrophe occurred that triggered a vast amount of rainfall in more temperate regions.[3] Numerous intriguing stories refer to a spiritual being called the 'Changer' (often named 'Coyote') as the source of the catastrophe. He was also a helper of mankind changing the way the world was then to what it is now.

Texts describing a detailed history of specific tribes are rare. However, at the beginning of the nineteenth century, one Tuscarora Indian decided to preserve the oral traditions of his people in writing. Despite the handicap of a poor education, David Cusick took on the task of recording a history of the Iroquois Nation. The result was a short book entitled *Sketches of Ancient History of the Six Nations* published by Recorder Print of Fayetteville, New York in 1827. Another author, John Heckewelder (a Moravian missionary who lived among the Delaware Indians between 1772 and 1786) wrote *History, Manners, and Customs of the Indian Nations, Who Once Inhabited Pennsylvania*, published in 1819. Neither book directly chronicles a history of the Mound Builders, but they do offer intriguing insight into the possible histories of the Adena and Hopewell nations.

Cusick's Iroquois history begins around 1,000 BC with the proto-Iroquois nation of the Great Lakes region, and how the *Eagwehowe* (the original tribe of one language) separated into the Mohawk, Oneida, Onondaga, Cayuga, Seneca, and Tuscarora tribes. Most of his text refers to the Five Nations (or five families) because of the Tuscarora Indians' early withdrawal and nonparticipation in the confederacy until the eighteenth century. Cusick also notes that all of his dates are estimates because of the oral manner in which the stories have been remembered.

Early in Iroquois history, he alludes to a "vast empire" to the south with a capital referred to as the "Golden City" which an Iroquois prince once visited. According to Cusick, settlements of this vast southern empire infringed on the borders of the Iroquois in the year 700 BC. Alarmed that these people were erecting fortifications near their southern border and would possibly deprive them of their county, war was declared that lasted one hundred years. No details exist of the war. But because of their skillful use of the bow and ability to endure hardship, the Iroquois Nation was eventually triumphant.[4]

Since no account of their culture is given, it can never be known for certain if Cusick's southern empire is the mound-building Adena but no other vast nation has ever occupied the region. The geography and time period seem correct, as well as the described vastness of the empire. Heckewelder describes a more elaborate but similar encounter as the Delaware Indians migrated east from western lands.

Legend of the Allegheny

Originally native to the western lands of North America, the Delaware Indians (an Algonquian language family) called themselves the *Leni-lenape* which literally means "original people."[5] Although the precise time period is unknown, their history describes an eastward migration that includes an encounter with a powerful nation just east of a great river (presumably the Mississippi).

When the Leni-lenape reached the river, they stopped at its western shores and sent scouts east to survey the land. On their return, they reported that a great nation occupied the land with many large towns, a people called the Talligew or Tallgewi (in later traditions the "Alligewi"). From the eighteenth century, when European colonists first heard of this tradition, there were no surviving Alligewi Indians spoken of in these Delaware legends.

There also is no historical basis for the name 'Allegewi' except that it is a conclusion of a man named Colonel Gibson who had learned it from the Delaware Indians. They referred to the Allegheny River and Mountains as the Alligewi (presumably a forerunner to the word Allegheny). Allegheny, an Algonquian Delaware word, simply means the Alle River, and includes the river from its fork at the Mississippi to its origin in New York (in other words, the complete Ohio River Basin). Henry Schoolcraft, a nineteenth century explorer, Indian agent, and historian,[6] believed the Alligewi was the oldest tribe found in the United States.[7]

According to the legend, these Alligewi were "tall and stout;" so tall the head of a Leni-lenape man would not reach their arm and their women were taller than the biggest Leni-lenape man. They liked to wear red and black paint, built fortifications and entrenchments,[8] had a shrill war-whoop, and enjoyed the strife of the spear.[9]

The Leni-lenape sent a message to the Alligewi seeking permission to settle in their land. Although denied, they received consent to pass through. It was a trick. Ambushed by Alligewi warriors on the other side of the river, they retreated and remained on the western banks for some time. Now distrustful of their new neighbors, the Leni-lenape formed an alliance with the "Mengwe" people that lasted for many years (as did their war with the Allegewi). Eventually they were triumphant.

The Leni-lenape, who bore the brunt of the fighting, moved through the heartland of the Alligewi. They followed the streams eastward and occupied the country from the Hudson River to the Chesapeake Bay, thus making the country of the Delaware the center of their vast possessions. This territory included the shores of four great rivers: the Hudson, Delaware, Susquehanna, and Potomac. The Mengwe moved north and occupied the areas bordering the Great Lakes and, in time, separated into five distinct tribes: Mohawk, Oneida, Onondaga, Cayuga, and Seneca. As for the Alligewi, they are said to have escaped down the river to the south and were never heard from again.[10]

One conclusion to this fascinating story is that the Mengwe and the Iroquois Nation are one and the same. In *The Prehistoric World: or Vanished Races*, A.E. Allen expresses the idea that this confederation between the Mengwe and Leni-lenape is what Cusick spoke of in his book concerning the hundred-year war:

> This is perhaps the Confederacy of [sic] Cusic. A long war resulted, but in the end the Alligewi were defeated and, as the tradition states, "all went southward." We see no reason to doubt but what we have here is a traditional account of the overthrow of the Mound Builders. The remnant that fled south found the country inhabited by

mound-building tribes, and doubtless became absorbed among them. In confirmation of this view it may be said that the languages of the tribes of the Gulf States, which belong to one stock language, [The Chata-muskoki family. (Brinton)] have all been greatly influenced by words derived from a foreign source. [Hale: American Antiquarian, April 1883].[11]

Allen adds a footnote to his statement that all went south. There is a connection, he states, that is at least interesting. Several authors (Squier, MacLean, and others) have contended that, judging from the fortified hills and camps, the pressure of hostilities on the Mound Builders was from the northeast.

He also takes the 'absorption' theory one step further and cites other references in support of the idea that an escaping Alligewi remnant was the origin of the Natchez Nation. He suggests that this remnant was large enough to form a new tribe and, according to their own tradition, the Natchez were once the most powerful nation in North America,[12] boasting sixty villages and eight hundred princes.

Archeological evidence suggests the Natchez culture started about 700 AD and lasted through the first third of the eighteenth century. The Natchez were indeed mound builders and seem to have been influenced by northern cultures (that is, north of the Middle Mississippi River Valley).

Their government was despotic, a class of elite lived on top of mounds and ruled over the commoner who spoke a different dialect. Almost like slavery, the role of the common class was to serve royal leaders in every way. Their society dwindled over the years and was finally crushed by the French at Natchitoches in 1732. The remaining Natchez merged into the Chickasaw and other tribes.

Common histories of the Delaware (originally the Leni-lenape), Iroquois, and Mengwe, suggest a basis for fact in their encounter with the Alligewi. The probable time period stated by Cusick suggests that if the meeting occurred in the Ohio Valley, it had to occur with the Mound Builders. These histories loosely agree with accepted archeological fact that the Adena Indians, being the original mound building people whose roots go back 4,000 years,[13] were replaced by the Hopewell sometime around 200 BC. Cusick places the date of the prince's trip to the golden city at 700 BC. With no reason to believe they were not, it can be assumed somewhat speculatively that the Adena were the Alligewi.

But there are inconsistencies. Add a hundred years of war to the date in which the prince visited the golden city and we have 600 BC. A difference of 400 years exists between the end of the war (according to Cusick) and the modern date for the origin of Hopewell culture. Yet by using words such as 'approximately' and 'about' when referring to dates, Cusick is plainly unsure and may be wrong. We also must remember that, as with most ancient stories and cultures, dates are far less important than the substance of the story. It is amazing the Iroquois tradition included dates at all.

A more problematic date, however, is the origin of the Natchez (700 AD). This is at least seven hundred years later than one would expect if Cusick's chronology were correct. It could be that the Alligewi (or proto-Natchez Indians) slowly migrated southward after their defeat over a long period of time. We simply do not know.

Cyrus Thomas (in his 1889 publication for the USGS, *Problem of the Mounds*) favors a slightly different interpretation. He concludes that the Mengwe were the Hurons or the Huron-Iroquois Nation before separation. The Great River was not the Mississippi but the Upper St. Lawrence, which connects Lake Huron with Lake Erie (commonly referred to as the Detroit River). As for the Alligewi, they moved south to become the Cherokee.

According to Thomas, this case is more agreeable with tradition than any other theory that has been offered. The country from which the Lenape migrated was *Shinaki* or 'land of fir trees' and was not in the West but in the far North, probably a forest region north of Lake Superior. The similarity between the names Tallgewi (Alligewi) and Cherokee or Chellakee, and the "character of the works and traditions of the latter, furnish some ground for assuming that the two were one and the same people."[14]

In further support of this theory, he also states that according to Heckewelder, desperate conflicts took place near the river just west of Lake St. Clair and just south of Lake Erie. Hundreds of the slain Tallgewi were buried under mounds. This agrees with Cusick's statement that the people of the great southern empire had penetrated the countryside close to Lake Erie when the war began. As for the variation in the interpretations, he states that:

> ...in coming to the Detroit River from the region north of Lake Superior, the Algonquins would be advancing from the west to the east. It is quite conceivable that, after many generations and many wanderings, they may themselves have forgotten which was the true Messusipu, or Great River, of their [sic] traditionary tales.[15]

Despite the two different approaches to the legend, Thomas advises it is important to bear in mind that, when the tradition was first made known to the people, these ancient earthworks were virtually unknown to the investigative minds of the country. It negates any possibility the tradition was altered to fit a theory in regard to the origin of the mounds. He believes there is at least a basis of truth to the story.

Other Eastern Legends

A creation myth exists for almost every ancient culture, and the Iroquois are no exception. Cusick's Iroquois account of creation, *A Tale of the Foundation of the Great Island, Now North America*, is in much the same manner as the author of the biblical *Genesis* (although not divided into days). God made the universe, the world, and its people from dust of the earth and animated man with a soul by his breath. It could be that Christianity influenced Cusick's tale of creation. Nonetheless, we must accept his word according to his preface as "authentic Iroquois tradition:"

> When he [God] had made the universe he was in doubt respecting some being to possess the Great Island [North America]; and he found two images of the dust of the ground in his own likeness, male and female, and by his breathing into their nostrils he gave them the living souls, [sic] and named them Ea-gwe-howe, i.e. a real people; and

he gave the Great Island, all the animals of game for their maintenance...[16]

Next, in *A Real Account of the Settlement of North America and Their Dissensions*, Cusick explains again (in summary) the creation of the world, but adds, "..after a time some of the people become giants and committed outrages upon the inhabitants."[17]

The Ronnongwetowanea

Cusick's account of giants only occurs early in Iroquois tradition, soon after the Eagwehowe reach the St. Lawrence Valley. Although he does not state what year, based on his chronology of subsequent events, their arrival occurred sometime before 1,000 BC. A tribe of giants called the *Ronnongwetowanea*, whose origin was in the north and of considerable population, launched raids against the Eagwehowe, typically to pillage.[18] It is likely that this tribe previously existed and was molded into their creation story once they were encountered.

The Ronnongwetowanea were depicted as a fair people and not as bloodthirsty savages hungry for conquest. They were a strange, almost quiet lot who apparently attacked only to meet their own corporeal needs. They would wait until the males of the village were away hunting, plunder the people's houses and make captives of those who were found, then hastily retreat to their home in the north.[19] Cusick describes their method of attack as "slily" [slyly], for they would not do so unless success was assured.[20]

The practice of abduction was common among Native American tribes. Captives were usually taken for one of several reasons: 1) as slaves (those who were already mature), 2) to be raised as tribal children to add stock to the clan, or 3) to barter for materialistic items. In some instances, infants were taken to replace a recently deceased Indian infant and given to a grieving Indian mother to be raised within their tribe as her own.

One specific story told by Cusick involves the abduction of a princess who in turn fell in love with her giant abductor. After returning from a day's hunt, her brothers realized she was missing and, after searching well into the night, assumed the enemy (the Ronnongwetowanea) had taken her. The eldest brother set out and, after a three-day journey, he found her gathering sticks for a fire. He tried to persuade her to return home but she refused. The giant (who was nearby) noticed her brother, invited him in for the night, and offered him food and the pipe. However, the giant had plans to murder him. To amuse and pacify his ill-fated guest, the giant began singing. After he was asleep, the giant killed him and deposited his body in a nearby cave.[21]

After the first brother failed to return, the second brother, Donhtonha, ventured out. Like his brother, he found his sister in the company of the giant. As his brother went before him into the giant's house, so did he. To fool the giant, he lay in a manner in which the reflecting light from the fire made him appear to be awake while he slept. The next morning Donhtonha began looking for his brother. Knowing he would soon find his brother's body, the giant protested. A long argument escalated into a mortal fight with Donhtonha being the victor. He set fire to the house with the giant's body inside. Consumed with despair, his grieving sister fled into the wilderness and died. Her spirit, it is believed, became one of the northern stars.[22]

At another time, the Ronnongwetowanea attacked a small village on the banks of the St. Lawrence, waiting until the village was vacant except for an old chief and an attendant named Yatatonwatea. At the sight of the giants, Yatatonwatea fled, but one of them gave chase. Hiding behind rocks and under the bank of the river, he tried to lose his pursuer but to no avail. Finally, he ran towards the region where warriors were hunting, hoping to gain assistance. He did and two warriors killed the giant.[23]

Having grown weary of Ronnongwetowanea raids, "about two thousand five hundred winters before Columbus discovered America" (or 1,000 BC), a convention was held by the chieftains to decide how to defend their country. Since the Ronnongwetowanea were not so numerous at that time, a few hundred warriors were sent on a mission to search and destroy. Afterwards, the Eagwehowe enjoyed peace for many winters.[24]

Stone Giants

The *Otneyarheh*, or Stone giants, were a savage tribe from the wilderness and understood the language of the five nations. According to Cusick, about 1250 years before Columbus (242 AD), they invaded and subdued the people for many years:

> The people have been reduced so often they could not increase. Stonish Giants were so ravenous that they devoured the people of almost every town in the country.[25]

Whether the Stone giants practiced cannibalism or the people were engaged in a siege is unclear. It is assumed that since Cusick had not fully mastered the English language, the latter is true in the context of the story.

Cusick supplies a footnote to this story that bears light on the possible origin of these Stone giants. According to Shawnee tradition, these giants descended from a family of the Tuscarora Indians (Cusick's sixth family). They journeyed to the northwest after being separated from their main tribe east of the great river (a reason why they would understand the Iroquois language). Living in the wilderness, this family lost all sense of humanity and would eat the raw flesh of animals. They became giants, in a mythical sense, by rolling in the sand:

> At length they practiced rolling themselves on the sand, by means their bodies were covered with hard skin these people became giants and were dreadful invaders of the country. It is said that Sir William Johnson, the Superintendents [sic] of the Six Nations, had a picture of the giant. Probably the English have recorded in the Historian respecting North America.[26]

It is likely that these people wandered northward and encountered (or were absorbed into) another tribe living in the upper regions of North America. Many Indian legends contend that the north was known to be a land where giants lived.

At this point, with no hope of saving themselves from the giants, the "Holder of the Heavens" (assumed to be God) intervenes. He transforms himself into a giant, talks them into an all-out assault on the people, and begins a march to Fort Onondaga. On the first night of the march, he orders them to sleep in a hollow. The next morning he scales the hill above and pummels the giants with rocks. A few giants escape and seek asylum in the north. Others say the giants retreated by way of Mountain Ridge and crossed below the Niagara Falls.[27]

Cusick's final tale concerning the Stone giants explains how an Onondaga hunter wandered north into an area where beaver dams were numerous. Unfortunately, he wandered into the giant's territory, was captured and forced to run a long race with a giant. Initially the hunter was leading, but when the giant whooped to scare him he fainted, giving the giant opportunity to take the lead. At that point, the hunter tries to escape by hiding in a large basswood stump. As the giant approached the stump, he stopped to examine it and:

> ...at length the giant exhibited a curious instrument, which he called a pointer, and possessed a power of the nature; [it] directed him where to find game; the giant could not live without it.[28]

The hunter then jumped from the stump and grabbed the instrument. Dismayed by the loss of his pointer (most likely a divining rod of some kind), the giant offered the knowledge of medical roots in return for it. The hunter obliged, so the giant retired and the man returned home to become a doctor.[29]

There is another interesting feature in Iroquois traditions of Stone giants. The Iroquois practiced the tradition of the False Face Society. This society performed ceremonial dances where the participants wore masks. Two Seneca and three Mohawk stories explain the origin of the different masks: doctor, dancing, beggar, and secret. One story relates the origin of the society with the Stone Giants.[30] Arthur C. Parker, author of *The Code of Handsome Lake - the Seneca Prophet*, claims to have obtained the mask of a Stone giant from a woman purporting to be the keeper of these secret masks.

Tsunil'kalu of the Cherokee

In James Mooney's *Myths of the Cherokee*, based on the *19th Annual Report of the Bureau of American Ethnology 1897- 98*, a western Cherokee named James Wafford tells the story of a tribe of giants which was told to him by his grandmother. A party of giants came to visit the Cherokee:

> They were nearly twice as tall as common men, and had their eyes set slanting in their heads, so that the Cherokee called them Tsunil'kalu, "The Slant-eyed people," because they looked like the giant hunter Tsunil'kalu. They said that these giants lived very far away in the direction in which the sun goes down. The Cherokee received them as friends, and they stayed some time, and then returned to their home in the west.[31]

James Wafford was born in Georgia in 1806. His grandmother probably lived in the middle of the eighteenth century. According to Wafford, she heard from the "old people" that this occurred long before her time.

Stone Heart Giants of the Winnebago

A long time ago, before the oldest tribe was created there lived giants to the North of Wisconsin where it's always cold. Called the *Wonga-Rouskah-Podarouhuh-Poruh-Wah-Roughe-a-ga*, their name means "those who eat people and have hearts of stone." They were cruel. So cruel, the legend says, that they had ice in their stomachs.

One day a beautiful Indian maiden went to the stream for water and noticed a giant on the other side. Her first impulse was to run and warn the people. But he did not attack her, just watched. So she watched him. Since this happened several days in a row, she lost her fear of him and wondered why he wasn't fierce like the others. Later, she fell in love with him and prayed to the Great Spirit to cast out his heart of stone. He did so, and the maiden and giant became man and wife.

Western Legends

Tales of giants were not confined to eastern tribes; western Indian nations also had their stories. Piute, Pawnee, and Shoshone legends, as well as stories from the Pacific Northwest, all tell of a race of giants. Some were even more ferocious than the Stone Giants and Ronnongwetowanea.

Rocky Mountain Giants

In *Sketches of Ancient History of the Six Nations*, David Cusick describes a legend of giants in the Rocky Mountains. Six hundred years before Columbus discovered America (800 AD), King Ototarho VII, with the authority of the Iroquois senate, sent an expedition west to explore the country. The expedition consisted of two captains and fifteen men from the five nations. As they began their march west, they stopped at Sandusky where two Ottawa warriors joined them. When they reached the banks of the Mississippi, the duke of Twakanah called the towns together to greet them by singing and beating on drums. Later that night, a ceremony for them was held at their national house.

After crossing the Mississippi, they continued west and discovered a curious animal they call a "winged fish" that flew about the trees and moved like a hummingbird. Farther west, they met and were astonished by the "Dog Tail Nation" (a people who had short tails like apes; holes were dug into their seats to fit their tails). The Dog Tail Nation made the party welcome and amused them with dancing at the chief's house. Later, they were received by another nation even further west where the people didn't eat meat but only drank soup. And as they approached the Rocky Mountains, they were stopped by a giant and compelled, by whatever the giant said or did, to return home.[32]

The story does not explain further concerning the Rocky Mountain giants. Oddly enough, he only mentions one giant, not a tribe. It is unlikely that one man (even a giant) would be able to arrest a party of nineteen. Speculatively, the giant must have warned them that harm would come to their party if they continued.

In *Life Among the Piutes*, Sarah Winnemucca (c. 1844-1891) tells a legend among her people that a savage tribe of 2,600 strong lived near their land along the Humboldt River in Nevada. According to the legend, this tribe had a taste for human flesh. Not only did they dig pit traps on trails to catch their human prey, they also ate their own and would exhume recent Piute graves. The Piutes simply referred to them as the "people-eaters."

Occasionally they made war on the Piute. Their women would carry away those that were killed from either side. When fighting they would jump up after the arrows over their heads and shoot the same arrows back. For this they were considered very brave. One time, several of these cannibals were taken as members of the Piute tribe but they could not be civilized. [33]

After growing weary of these savages, the Piutes waged a war on this tribe that lasted for three years. Near the war's end, a remnant of the people-eaters sought shelter in the bush near Humboldt Lake. After being rooted from the bush, they then sought refuge on the lake. Eventually they came ashore and as they did, the waiting Piute warriors killed them.

One night, the entire remnant landed on the east side of the lake and went into a cave near the mountains, a most horrible place. The Piutes watched at the mouth of the cave, and would kill all that came out for water. They were asked to "be like us, and not eat people like coyotes or beasts" but they refused to give up. (They spoke the same language.) After all attempts to negotiate had failed, the Piutes filled the mouth of the cave with brush and set it on fire, crying out to them, "Will you give up and be like men, and not eat people like beasts? Say quick and we will put out the fire."[34] No answer came. (The cave, according to Winnemucca, was unknown to the Piutes, and must have been deep.) A final chance was given. They called out to them as loud as they could, "Will you give up? Say so, or you will all die."[35] But no answer came. Once the fire had died and when the cave was again accessible, it was reported to the chief that a horrible smell filled the cavern and all must be dead.

Who was this tribe? Sarah Winnemucca's only description is that they had red hair:

My people say that the tribe we exterminated had reddish hair. I have some of their hair, which has been handed down from father to son. I have a dress, which has been in our family a great many years, trimmed with this reddish hair. I am going to wear it some time when I lecture. It is called the mourning dress, and no one has such a dress but my family.[36]

Although there is no reference from Piute tradition for the "people-eaters" being giants, their location and red-haired description coincides with the mummies found in Lovelock Cave.

Traditions of the Pawnee

The Pawnees believed the earth was first inhabited by a race of giants so large that they could carry buffaloes on their backs. These people did not accept Ti-ra'-wa, the invisible yet ever-present Creator, and grew more and more wicked. The Creator was angry and caused the water to rise and the ground to become soft, and the giants sank into the mud. Large bones, found at different times, were thought to be their skeletons (most likely large animals from the ice age). Then a new race was created from which all nations sprang.[37]

Baya-Vid-Eetso of the Navaho

The Navaho creation myth explains that the world was created in five stages. In the third stage, one woman bore the Big Birds of Tsa bida'hi and others gave birth to giants and monsters which later destroyed many people. Their legend says two women gave birth to two babies that grew more rapidly than all others. They were clumsy, dirty, lazy, and half-wit children whose hair stuck out roughly, and when they grew up they became cannibals. When these giants would find people, they would capture them and carry them home to eat at the east end of Top Mesa.[38]

Tsawhawbitts of the Shoshone

Today's Native American Indians refer to Idaho's Sawtooth Mountains as the *Coapiccan Kahni*, which means the Giant's House. Shoshone legend has it that the giant Tsawhawbitts occupied this land near the headwaters of the Bruneau River. These beings were believed to be evil spirits in superhuman form with a thirst for human blood. According to their legend, they terrorized the Shoshone. After a hunt, they would carry their human prey in a large basket to their mountaintop homes for a cannibal feast.

They also claim that these giants sometimes had only one eye, could cross over creeks in a single step, had supernatural powers, and could be seen digging in the ground for unknown objects. They could freeze a man with a stare from their glowing red eyes, then impale him with a harpoon, and could only be killed with fire or ice. If one was found to live in a cave, the mouth of the cave was filled with timber and set on fire until the giant was consumed. Because of their wickedness, they were swept away by a great flood. Most perished although some survived to settle in other parts of the world.[39]

Giants of Mount St. Helens

According to Indian legends of the Pacific Northwest, in the snow-covered areas on Mount St. Helens above Spirit Lake there lived a race of man-stealing giants. During the night, these giants would approach the lodges while the people were asleep, kidnap them, place them beneath their skins, and return to their mountaintop. In the morning when the kidnapped people awoke, they would find themselves lost not knowing which way home was.[40]

These giants also came in the night to steal salmon. If anyone were awake when the giants approached, they would smell a strong, unpleasant odor in the air. Sometimes there would be three whistles and then stones would hit the lodges. By this they knew the giants were returning.[41]

Natliskeliguten of the Salish

Ancestors of the Salish Indians reported that there was a time when giants inhabited most of the earth. These giants were terrible and killed everyone they met. For this they were called the *Natliskeliguten*, which means "killers of men."[42]

Sinchlep was a prairie wolf, a coyote. To man, he was viewed as the most powerful and favorable of all animals. For the smaller people, Sinchlep went throughout the earth killing every giant and turning them into large stones. In later times, when Flathead Indians were crossing the mountains and saw a basaltic rock standing upright, they would say to one another that it was a Natliskeliguten that was killed by Sinchlep.[43]

Nearly half of all Flathead Indian stories address these giants and more than sixty percent mention them. According to the stories, they had amazing strength. One time while walking through the forest, a small hunting party happened on a sleeping giant. Using ropes of buffalo hair, they tied him down and beat him until he awoke. When he opened his eyes, he laughed thunderously, broke the ropes that bound him, and sent the men flying through the air. One man was seized by an ankle and tossed across the Missoula River.[44]

The Indians occasionally saw these giants, but they usually avoided being seen. They gradually decreased in number, some say, because there was not enough food for such large creatures.[45]

Giants in the Coeur d'Alene Country

Giants were common in Coeur d'Alene country. They emitted a strong odor, like that of a burning horn. Their faces were black, although some say they were painted black. These giants were said to be taller than the highest tepees. When they saw a lone tepee or lodge, they would crawl on the ground to it, rise up and peer down the smoke hole. But if several lodges were nearby, they would not be so bold.[46]

Most of them wore bearskins as clothing and lived in caves among the rocks. They had a taste for fish and would steal fish from the people's traps. Otherwise they left the Indians alone. Other nearby tribes say they were known to steal women occasionally, but there is no tradition of this among the Coeur d'Alene country.[47]

Man-Eaters of The Kutenains

The Kutenais are the remnant of a once brave and powerful tribe who lived along the Columbia River and its northern tributaries.[48] According to their legends, there are several tales about giants. These giants lived along the large streams and whenever they would find Indians, they would kill and eat them. As a result, the Indians lived by the smaller streams near the mountains.[49] According to Ella Clark in *Indian Legends in the Northern Rockies*, a skeleton of one of these giants was found buried, in a sitting position, near Lake Superior.[50]

Indian Nations of Canada also have stories concerning giants. According to the Assinibine tribe, long ago when the world was very young, giants also lived in their country.[51]

Considering Legend as History

To some degree, archeological evidence from the nineteenth century corroborates the Native American Indian stories of giants. Whether specific stories of encounters are true, obviously we will never know. It is reasonable to accept that at one time they existed and lived alongside the Indian Nations of North America, typically as their enemies and, perhaps in certain instances as their friends or possibly masters. It is also possible the giants of the Adena culture were, as it was in Natchez society, a ruling class. They disappeared, but not without a trace, obvious by unusual skeletal remains found during the nineteenth and early twentieth centuries.

How can we explain so many different, Native American tribes having such similar stories of giants when added to the material evidence found by modern civilization? Although it is considered mostly "legend," there must be enough fact to accept it also as history.

North America is not alone in producing historical evidence of giants. The cradle of civilization also has its own stories. Interestingly, a similar tale on the other side of the world parallels the fate of the Shoshone's Tsawhawbitts.

Chapter 3
Men of Renown - Heroes of Old

- Moses and the Exodus
- The Anakim
- The Sons of God
- Divine Council of the Most High
- The Biblical Enoch

One of the most popular stories concerning giants is the account of David and the Philistine giant named Goliath. Goliath's height was said to have been six cubits and a span or about nine feet tall. (An alternative description of Goliath's height states that he was 6' 9".) He wore a bronze helmet and a coat of bronze armor weighing five thousand shekels – 125 pounds. His spear shaft was like a weaver's rod with an iron point weighing six hundred shekels (15 pounds). The sight of him in front of the Philistine ranks terrified the Hebrew army. A standoff ensued for forty days until a young David boldly stepped forward with his sling.[7]

The Philistines engaged the Israelites several more times during the reign of King David and giants were always on the point. First there was *Ishbibenob*, one of the sons of a giant whose spear weighed three hundred shekels (7½ pounds). At Gob there was another giant's son, *Saph*. And at Gath there was yet another man of great stature. He had six fingers and toes on each hand and foot.[8]

Biblical text offers little insight into Philistine culture and none into their relationships with giants. Modern scholars, however, have discovered much. The Philistines were a cultured, as well as militant, people. They were experts in metallurgy and lived in the choicest land of Canaan, an agriculturally rich coastal strip from Gaza in the south to Tel Qasile, near modern Tel Aviv in the north. Their society was comprised of a loose federation of five city-states: Ashdod, Gaza, Ashkelon, Gath, and Ekron.[9] These city-states engaged in trade throughout the Eastern Mediterranean. Their origins, however, are still a mystery. Philistine pottery, handsome as it was, suggests a possible Aegean source. Some scholars believe they may have been refugees from Thera (modern day Santorini), an island destroyed by a volcanic blast in 1626 BC. Others reason that, as shown by many Egyptian inscriptions, they originated in Crete.[10] However, the Philistines were not the only giants encountered by the Hebrewa.

Moses and the Exodus

Unarguably, the most prevalent Bible story is the Exodus, how Moses led the Hebrew people out of Egypt for God's 'Promise Land,' sometime around 1300 BC – although some evidence suggest it may have occurred as early as 1600 BC. It is in this chapter of Judeao-Christian tradition where God's Ten Commandments, etched in stone, were given to Moses atop Mount Sinai. According to the story, for their disbelief, symbolized in the erection of a golden calf in favor of God, the Hebrew people were forced to wander in the desert for forty years, ostensibly to purge this unfaithful, rogue element from the ranks of the people.[1] For their sins, the story goes, that generation of Hebrews and, unfortunately, Moses, would never enter the Promised Land.

Its popularity wanes at that point, but the story continues and the Hebrew people enter the Promised Land, the land of Canaan. To lay claim to their territory, however, a military conquest was in order. As any respectable military organization would do, a scouting party, comprised of a man from each of the twelve Hebrew tribes, was sent on a mission to survey the land. From the wilderness of Zin to Rehob and to the entrance of Hamath, then south to Hebron, the party observed Canaan's inhabitants.

After the exploration was complete and they were in an assembly of the Hebrew encampment, the twelve scouts reported the results of their fact-finding mission. The land was as God promised, rich and fertile, flowing with milk and honey. Joshua, full of confidence and a rising leader-to-be, motioned to continue and move into the promised land. His comrades objected and for good reason. At Hebron, they observed an unusual race of beings, the sons of Anak: Ahiman, Sheshai, and Talmai, giants whose "bodies [were] so large, and countenances so entirely different from other men, that they were surprising to the sight, and terrible to the hearing."[2] Those that were frightened explained:

> We are not able to go up against the people; for they are stronger than we. And they brought up an evil report of the land which they had spied out unto the children of Israel, saying, The land, through which we have gone to spy it out, is a land that eateth up the inhabitants thereof; and all the people that we saw in it are men of great stature. And there we saw the Nephilim, the sons of Anak, who come of the Nephilim: and we were in our own sight as grasshoppers, and so we were in their sight.[3]

After Moses' death on Mount Nebo, leadership passed to the ever-confident Joshua. Three days later, he led the Hebrew armies across the Jordan River into Canaan. Their conquest – a long, grueling task for any army at any time – found early success in three major campaigns. First they took Jericho and Ai, marched through the southern alliance of kingdoms to Debir, and finally north along the Jordan to Kadesh and Mount Hermon. Hebron was taken and all of its inhabitants, including the giants, were slain. Interestingly, corpses of giants were presumably kept as trophies or oddities. According to the first century Jewish historian, Flavius Josephus (37-100 AD), "The bones of these men are still shown to this very day, unlike to any credible relations of other men."[4]

Although the conquest was successful, not all lands were fully conquered. It was not a crushing, blitzkrieg-style operation. Only three cities were actually destroyed: Jericho, Ai, and Hazor.[5] The Canaanites still controlled some inland towns and another people, known as the Philistines, freely occupied the coastal plains. By the time Joshua was very old, there were still many lands unconquered.[6] Occasional battles with the Philistines would continue for the next 300 years. As the story of the thriving Israelite Kingdom continues, we discover a tradition of giants also living among the Philistines.

There is no direct proof that Moses existed. However, what archeologists and Egyptologists have discovered is that the story is historically plausible. Historical parallels for episodes in the epic saga exist and there is evidence of cataclysmic events, which may lie behind the stories of the plagues and the parting of the Red Sea. Particularly the volcanic eruption on the island of Thera in 1600 BC, which places the Moses story earlier than traditionally believed. Its eruption and the ensuing tsunami would have created the conditions for the crossing of the Yam Suph, the "Sea of Reeds," which has been mistranslated as the Red Sea. As the tsunami neared the shore the giant wave pulled the water out and away revealing the sea's bottom. Later, a wall of water came crashing down.

Mount Sinai has been misidentified as well. At the foot of Mount Kharkom, near today's border between Egypt and Israel, there exists an arrangement of twelve large, standing stones on the floor of a desert valley. Ironically, the name of the mountain means "Mountain of God" and at its base there exists evidence of an ancient settlement. Rock carvings have also been found depicting the traditional idea of the ten commandment, single tablet separated in to ten distinct compartments.

The war between the Hebrews and Canaanites is also suspect. While it is likely they moved into region there is no archeological evidence of war. Some historians believe that the situation was more amicable and that the migrating Hebrews were welcomed by the Canaanites relatives. Yet there were other cultures in the area not associate that may have been the source of the exaggerated war story.

The Anakim

Precisely who were these giants referred to as the Anakim, the sons of Anak? It is clear from biblical text that they already inhabited the land when Moses and the twelve Hebrew tribes arrived. Certainly they were not viewed as Canaanites. Those tribes were clearly identified as Hittites, Jebusites, Amorites, Girgashites, Hivites, Arkites, Sinites, Arvadites, Zemarites, and Hamathites. They were the descendents of Ham, the son of Noah,[11] and, in general, all were referred to as Canaanites.

Five hundred years earlier, Abraham also discovered aboriginal peoples living in Canaan, though during his time they were referred to as the Rephaim, Zuzim, Emim, and Horites. Yet Canaanites are often mistakenly considered the first peoples of Palestine. Semitic descendants of Canaan (from which they took their name) were viewed in this way in part because they were of a traceable civilization. Migrating from their original home, they reached the Persian Gulf and remained there for some time before spreading west across the mountains to the shores of the Mediterranean. They occupied the land as far north as the Taurus Mountains.

Canaanites occupied the lowlands, plains, and valleys,[12] the richest and most productive parts of Palestine. Their golden age lasted from 1450 to 1200 BC. During this era, they produced palaces, temples, shrines, and libraries. Their cultural centers of Tyre and Sidon attracted commerce. Textiles, ivory, weapons, and silver were traded with cities of the Mediterranean, Mesopotamia, Egypt, and Asia Minor, possibly through their naval power and knowledge of navigation. The name itself became synonymous with trader or merchant,[13] but was also used to describe non-Hebrew inhabitants in general.

Aboriginal Palestinians

As every scholastic textbook explains, life (as we know it) and civilization started on the Mesopotamian Plain 5,000 years ago and spread to other regions of the greater Near East. (Egyptian culture is a close second.) However, the way history is written it is easy to believe that relatively little in the ways of culture occurred before those first cities that grew into the ancient kingdom of Sumer. History seems to dive into obscurity before then. In sublime ways, the mythology of those first 'modern' civilizations, through tales of creation, often adds to our belief. Facts concerning prehistoric cultures are discussed but are often construed in our minds as part of a different world. There is nothing to relate to; no stories, fables, or documents (or at least none we can assign as such and decipher). All we can perceive is skeletal remains and stone tools provided by the discipline of archeology. Their culture often remains, at best, speculative.

Archeology is what provides us with our main clues to the past and can sometimes be complemented with historical records. It confidently states that the Middle East has been occupied for a very long time. The first known burials occurred there some 100,000 years ago. Jericho, one of the oldest cities in the world, predates the war between the Israelites and Philistines by thousands of years. A "plastered" skull (excavated from Jericho now in the British School of Archeology at Jerusalem) has been dated to be 9,000 years old.[14] This suggests that people settled in the area before 7,000 BC – more than 5,000 years before the Hebrews arrived and 2,000 years before the first settlements in the Mesopotamian Valley.

With this is mind, the stories of unknown prehistoric cultures may be easier to relate to, accept, and view as our history just as much as Egypt, Sumer, and Judea. Those giants (aboriginal Palestinians), who in vane defended their lands against triumphant Hebrew armies, may become more than just a name.

The Rephaim

Genesis tells a tale of similar conquest five hundred years before the campaigns of Joshua. Fourteen years after Abraham settled in Hebron,[15] an alliance of kings led by Chedorlaomer of Elam marched on the southeast region of Canaan just east of the Jordan River which is biblically known as Edom and Moab. (Elam is a great plain north of the Persian Gulf and east of the lower Tigris.) There they destroyed the Rephaim in Ashteroth-karnaim, the Zuzim in Ham, the Emim in Shaveh-kiriathaim, and the Horites of Mount Seir.[16]

The identities of the conquered people and cultures are unknown but through translation some insight can be provided. Typically the names of tribes assigned by the Hebrews, were defined by lineage. For example, Canaan was a man and all of his descendents were referred to as Canaanites. Yet he gave birth, through his sons, to many other tribes (Jebusite, Amorite, Girgashite, Hivite, etc.) as we have seen. Descriptive names were given for an unknown culture. And, according to the Jewish Encyclopedia, Rephaim is the Hebrew term for "giants" and Zuzim is translated as "the strong" (ha'izzuzim) or "the mighty" (ha-'ezuzim). Emim are also considered giants. The author of *Deuteronomy* describes these tribes as people that "dwelt there in times past, a people great, and many, and tall, as the Anakims; which also were accounted giants (Reph'aim in Hebrew), as the Anakims; but the Moabites called them Emims."[17] The name Horite comes from the nature of aboriginal dwellings in Idumaea and is confirmed by excavations in the mountains of Edom. In other words, they were cave dwellers.[18]

The author of *Deuteronomy* also provides the link between these people, specifically the Emim and Rephaim with the Anakim. Although some aboriginals were referred to by other names which were more suitable, they were considered giants (Reph'aim) and of non-Semitic lineage. Rabbinical literature explains that the Anakim are the same race as the Rephaim, Nephilim, Gibborim, Zamzummim, and Emim, and in Hellenistic literature – Titans.

The Anakim were great and tall.[19] They were initially observed by Joshua and the other scouts in southern Palestine, around Hebron. The author of *Joshua* later describes how the Israelites destroyed them and their cities in the hill country of Hebron, Debir, Anab, Judah, and Israel. It appears that they were a large population living throughout the land. Unlike Canaanites, they lived in the hills.

There is also evidence that they were not uncivilized barbarians. Joshua tells us they built "great fortified cities."[20] Hebron, their cultural center, was also called the city of Arba, named after the greatest Anakim leader and father of Anak[21] (although the Septuagint states that Arba was Anak's brother).

As the Hebrew words Rephaim, Emim, Zuzim, and Horite describe the people they are naming, so does Anakim. Anak (singular) means "neck," suggesting they wore neck-chains, were long-necked, or perhaps thick-necked. It can also mean "to press" or "force" as they seized the solar disk and cried, "Send us rain" or that "they squeezed their heads into the sun." Joshua and the Hebrew scouts also referred to the Anakim by another name, the "Nephilim," and it meant something to them. Implicit in their dialog, whether from experience, tales, or fables, Nephilim is a name they already knew and understood among themselves. For them, it was a name synonymous with the word giant. This name provides a connection to the story of Noah and the flood. Its introduction is one of the more mysterious passages of the Bible:

> When men began to increase in number on the earth and daughters were born to them, the sons of God saw that the daughters of men were beautiful, and they married any of them they chose. Then the Lord said, "My Spirit will not contend with man forever, for he is mortal; his days will be a hundred and twenty years."

> The Nephilim were on the earth in those days-and also afterward-when the sons of God went to the daughters of men and had children by them. They were the heroes of old, men of renown.[22]

This passage creates several intriguing questions. Who are the sons of God? And, except for being giants, precisely who or what are the Nephilim? Perhaps a more sober question: How did the Nephilim survive the flood if it was, indeed all encompassing, since they were on the earth in those days *and also afterward*? How it is written assumes the reader already knows, as if a chapter of biblical history is unwritten or missing from Canon.

To explain this passage, the *Matthew Henry Bible Commentary* suggests the sons of God are "professors of religion who were called by the name of the Lord and called upon that name" and the daughters of men are "those that were profane, and strangers to God and godliness." Other interpretations contend that the sons of God were men in the lineage of Seth; a legacy that leads to King David and Jesus and everyone else are simply "men." Both theories are a meager attempt to explain the inexplicable. For a moment, let's suppose that this is the case and the sons of God are nothing more than "believers." This makes the introduction to the flood story, verses one through four, meaningless, and the chapter's introduction should begin with verse five and end with verse eight: "The Lord saw how great man's wickedness on the earth had become..." Why bother with two odd irrelevant paragraphs?

Curiously, the sons of God are never mentioned again in the flood story. Yet Noah and his sons, by definition being believers as well as descendents of Seth, are very much sons of God but are never referred to as such. Why is this? Why bother with such an introduction when the subjects of the introduction, the Nephilim and the sons of God, are never explained forthright?

If the *Matthew Henry Bible Commentary* is correct and these sons of God were "heroes of old" and "men of renown," why would they become corrupt so easily by simply taking a wife? This is, in fact, the first command given to man according to the Bible, "be fruitful and multiply" (*Genesis* 1:28). Since it was socially acceptable to have more than one wife, why would there be such a problem with marriage? And, according to scripture, at no time before or after the Flood has God destroyed or threatened to destroy the human race for "mixed" marriages.

Another difficulty in understanding the passage is the use of the word Nephilim. It is Hebrew and is sometimes translated as "giant" because of the size of the people it describes. (It only occurs twice in the Bible.) Its literal essence is something entirely different and means "those who fell" or "were fallen." The root word itself is Aramaic (naphal), and was incorporated into Hebrew text.

Of course, all this leads to even more questions. Why are these tall and seemingly frightful people (and only these people) called the "fallen ones?" From what or where did they fall? Before addressing this matter any further, we must pursue the mysterious "sons of God" who somehow connect to the Nephilim.

The Sons of God

With obvious implications, "Son of God" is a very special phrase used forty-three times in the New Testament, always referencing Jesus. It is never used in the Old Testament. Although Jesus was referred to as the "Son of God" thirty-nine times by other people, he referred to himself as the "Son of God" only four times, all in *The Gospel According to John*. A more common reference was the "son of man" (sometimes capitalized). It appears eighty-six times in the New Testament and one-hundred-sixteen in the Old Testament. Jesus more often referred to himself in this manner.

The phrase "sons of God," being plural, is especially curious. It only appears in the Bible eleven times, six in the Old Testament and five in the New Testament. In the Old Testament, it occurs only in *Deuteronomy* and *Job*, other than the two times used in Genesis 6:

> When the Most High gave to the nations their inheritance, when he separated the sons of men, he fixed the bounds of the peoples according to the number of the sons of God [or "Sons of Israel" in most translations]. For the Lord's portion is his people, Jacob his allotted heritage.
>
> *Deuteronomy 32:8-9*

> Now there was a day when the sons of God came to present themselves before the Lord, and Satan also came among them.
>
> *Job 1:6*

> Again there was a day when the sons of God came to present themselves before the Lord, and Satan also came among them to present himself before the Lord.
>
> *Job 2:1*

> When the morning stars sang together, and all the sons of God shouted for joy.
>
> *Job 38:7*

There is some difference among translators whether to use "Angels" as opposed to "the sons of God" in the verses from Job (as the *New*

International Version does). But this is a purely interpretive matter. There is no debate; the Hebrew word for sons of God is *bene elohim*.

A more controversial point is the use of "the sons of God" instead of "the sons of Israel" in *Deuteronomy* 32:8. Most translations prefer "the sons of Israel" or "the children of Israel," unlike the *Revised Standard Bible*, which uses "the sons of God." At the center of debate is which original text to use. Several originals do exist: the Hebrew Masoretic, the Septuagint, Manuscripts of Aquila, Symmachus, and fragments from Qumran. Older texts typically support the use of "sons of God" and later ones, the "sons of Israel." On the surface, it seems, this controversy is an academic quarrel among textual scholars, but not all think so.

Michael Heiser, a Hebrew scholar at the University of Wisconsin, believes "The debate over which text is to be preferred is more than a fraternal spat among textual critics."[23] There is no scholarly argument that *Deuteronomy* 32:8 is referring to *Genesis*, chapter ten, where the descendants of Noah spread throughout the world and formed nations. However, at that time in the *Genesis* stories the nation of Israel did not yet exist and therefore, cannot be the basis of separation. A common argument would be that God, being omnipotent and timeless, was already planning the nation of Israel and had every right to do so.

Heiser's theological rebuttal to this supposition is difficult to refute. "Even if one contends that the correlation was in the mind of God prior to Israel's existence and only recorded much later, what possible point would there be behind connecting the pagan Gentile nations numerically with the children of promise?"[24] If the interpretive use of "the sons of Israel" in *Deuteronomy* 32:8 is wrong, and we must accept the use of "the sons of God" from earlier texts, then what is the author of *Deuteronomy* referring to? Similarities between the Hebrew and Ugarit cultures offer insight.

The Ugarits were a Semitic people and descendents of Shem. Most likely they were proto-Phoenicians. An independent kingdom from the eighteenth century BC, the city of Ugarit (modern Ras Shamra on Syria's Mediterranean coast) reached its political, religious, and economic zenith during the twelfth century BC. This coincides with the entry of Hebrew people into Canaan. They were the first to compose an alphabet based on atomic sounds of which all phonetic languages stem from: Hebrew, Latin, Sanskrit, Aramaic, Arabic, and Greek. (Herodotus, in his Histories, admits the Greeks received their alphabet from the Phoenicians.)

There are striking similarities between Ugarit and Hebrew literature. Several Psalms appear to be adapted directly from Ugaritic sources. The story of Noah's flood has an almost perfect counterpart. Since they held similar beliefs and shared the same land, they must have been culturally close.

Heiser offers a good explanation for this biblical "sons of God" concept based on biblical parallels with Ugarit literature. Ugarit mythology believes that God (Hebrew, *El*), also referred to as Most High (Hebrew *El Elyon*), was head of a pantheon and fathered seventy sons.[25] It is with this idea the author of *Deuteronomy* wrote that God separated men into nations according to the number of the sons of God. In other words, in Ugarit beliefs, God divided the earth according to the number of heavenly beings who existed from the time of creation.

So was Israel polytheistic? Most would argue that they were not. But did they accept the notion that other divine beings existed, subordinate to God the Most High? Other scriptures clearly support Heiser's idea, suggesting there is more to the story.

Divine Council of the Most High

A passage in *The Gospel According to John* raises suspicion of shared mythical values between the Hebrew and Ugarit cultures. Jesus himself refers to a scripture, which in turn cites a Psalm not only supporting the "sons of God," but also a much ignored and mysterious idea of a council of gods.

Judea had been looking for their promised savior. Governed by Rome during the first century, they were looking for a great man in the tradition of King David, a warrior to set them free from foreign rule. This is certainly understandable and may be one reason Jesus did not openly proclaim himself as Christ.

One winter, during the Feast of Dedication, Jesus was walking in the Temple near the portico of Solomon. A crowd had gathered and someone asked him if he was Christ. As the story goes, he dodged the yes-or-no answer and eloquently explained that he and his Father (God) were one. Outraged, the crowd accused him of blasphemy and attempted to stone him. He intensified the situation by arguing and eventually escaped. How he answered their allegations of blasphemy, and how he philosophically defended himself, deserves a closer look:

> The Jews took up stones again to stone him. Jesus answered them, "I have shown you many good works from the Father; for which of these do you stone me?"
>
> The Jews answered him, "It is not for a good work that we stone you but for blasphemy; because you, being a man, make yourself God."
>
> Jesus answered them, "Is it not written in your law, 'I said, you are gods?' If he called them gods to whom the word of God came (and scripture cannot be broken), do you say of him whom the Father consecrated and sent into the world, 'You are blaspheming,' because I said, 'I am the Son of God?'
>
> *John 10:31-36*

In saying "I said, you are gods," Jesus was quoting Psalm 82:6 and using it as a precedent for his divine nature. It can be suggested that Jesus was using the general notion that every man is a "Son of God" simply because mankind was created by God, but this is clearly not the case of Psalm 82, as we will see. It has much greater implications.

Psalm 82 - *A psalm of Asaph.*

1 God presides in the great assembly;
he gives judgment among the "gods":
2 "How long will you* defend the unjust
and show partiality to the wicked?

Selah

3 Defend the cause of the weak and fatherless;
maintain the rights of the poor and oppressed.

4 Rescue the weak and needy;
deliver them from the hand of the wicked.

5 "They know nothing, they understand nothing.
They walk about in darkness;
all the foundations of the earth are shaken.

6 "I said, 'You are "gods";
you are all sons of the Most High.'

7 But you will die like mere men;
you will fall like every other ruler."

8 Rise up, O God, judge the earth,
for all the nations are your inheritance.

The Hebrew is plural.

The setting for the Psalm is Heaven, where God has taken his place in "The Great Assembly, among the gods." Clearly the author is referring to a "Divine Council." Although he never tells precisely who these other 'gods' are, he does refer to them as "sons of the Most High." He hears a case put forth for the weak and fatherless, the afflicted and destitute, and then passes judgment on other gods. He speaks to them: "You are gods, sons of the Most High; all of you, nevertheless, you shall die like men, and fall like any prince."

His judgment of them (to die like men) would be meaningless if they were not immortal. The sentencing here is not an execution as it would be for a man, but a revocation of immortality. Sentencing a man to die like a mere man seems pointless. On the other hand, to a god it is severe. If this Psalmist was referring to a human court with human judges, then Jesus' argument of divine precedence would also be meaningless because all men would be sons of God. It seems clear that Jesus was reminding the people that there are other divine beings, and he is one of them but different – "consecrated and sent forth into the world."

There is more. We find the Psalmist again referring to this council in Psalm 89 [author emphasis added]:

> For who in the skies can be compared to the Lord? Who among the heavenly beings is like the Lord, a God feared in the *council of the holy ones*, great and terrible above all that are round about him? O Lord God of hosts, who is mighty as thou art, O Lord, with thy faithfulness round about thee?
>
> *Psalm 89:6-8*

We see a similar idea in Isaiah's mount of assembly. The obvious implication here is that multiple beings are needed for an assembly:

> "How you are fallen from heaven, O Day Star, son of Dawn! How you are cut down to the ground, you who laid the nations low! You said in your heart, 'I will ascend to heaven; above the stars of God I will set my throne on high; I will sit on the *mount of assembly* in the far north; I will ascend above the heights of the clouds, I will make myself like the Most High.' But you are brought down to Sheol, to the depths of the Pit.
>
> *Isaiah 14:12-15*

Deuteronomy, written before *Isaiah*, also speaks of a mount of assembly in a blessing to the children of Israel: "The Lord came from Sinai, and dawned from Se'ir upon us; he shone forth from Mount Paran, he came from the ten thousands of holy ones."[26]

If early Hebrew theology solely embraced the idea there is only God and no other divine beings exist, the term assembly would not be used. It would simply be referred to as the Mount of God, which sometimes it is. A traditional argument is that an assembly is referring to angels; God's messengers, but as we shall see this cannot always be the case.

Isaiah's prophecy is equally interesting in a different approach. Theologians have identified a passage in this prophecy as the origin of

Satan. In Isaiah's prediction against Babylon he draws a parallel between the King of Babylon and the sin of a being who fell from heaven. The name of the fallen one is "Day Star;" in other translations, "morning star" or "shining star," and in the King James Bible, "Lucifer". His goal, his sin, and why he fell was for his ambitions to "sit on the mount of assembly" and make himself "like the Most High". (It is noteworthy to state that pre-Christian Judaism had no concept of Satan, at least as has been defined during the Christian era. The Hebrew word translated as Satan literally means 'accuser'.)

Apparently, "Day Star" was a member of this heavenly host before his fall, although subordinate to the "Most High." It must be the case that these beings had their own free will with the ability to think, feel and aspire or there would be no fall. This suggests that interaction existed among heavenly beings. In *First Kings*, chapter 22 we find just such an interaction:

> And Micai'ah said, "Therefore hear the word of the Lord: I saw the Lord sitting on his throne, and all the host of heaven standing beside him on his right hand and on his left; and the Lord said, 'Who will entice Ahab, that he may go up and fall at Ramoth-gilead?' And one said one thing, and another said another. Then a spirit came forward and stood before the Lord, saying, 'I will entice him.' And the Lord said to him, 'By what means?' And he said, 'I will go forth, and will be a lying spirit in the mouth of all his prophets.' And he said, 'You are to entice him, and you shall succeed; go forth and do so.'
>
> 1 Kings 22:19-22

Again we have a scene implying a divine council. We also have a possible clue to its purpose. God asks his assembly for someone to volunteer and entice Ahab. An entity, though not an angel, steps forward and volunteers to be a 'lying spirit.' It appears their role is to work with God and for Him. Micaiah's description comes eerily close to a scene from Greek mythology where the gods, with Zeus as chairman, meet to discuss a proposed action against man.

Were there really "sons of God?" Or, perhaps more correctly, were there lesser gods engaging in a Divine Council? Were they free to roam and work within a certain system provided by God "Most High?" Are they angels according to the doctrines of modern Christianity? Or are they something else entirely? There are over two hundred references to other gods in the Old Testament. The question is: Were they real, were they inventions of man's imagination to explain the unexplainable, or were they simply leftover ideas from an earlier time?

The blaring question is, what is the origin of this seemingly forgotten or suppressed idea of a council of gods? For Jesus himself to reference such a tradition, at one time in Hebrew history the idea must have been prevalent. So when and where did early Hebrew culture get this concept? And whom did they get it from? Jesus hints that, like himself, these "sons of God" were human beings, the argument for his bold claim in the face of criticism. However, biblically, there is little to go on.

We are left with a clue from that seemingly out of place introduction to the story of Noah and the giants who struck such fear into the hearts of the Hebrews. From *Genesis* 6:14, we recognize the "Sons of God" as mighty, renowned men of an ancient origin. They were famous and infatuated with women. Since they produced offspring, they were indeed physical beings. As for the Nephilim, these mysterious "fallen ones" that existed before and after the flood, we can infer very little. It is only by referring to *Numbers* 13:33 that we know they were the Anakim, the Rephaim, the giants, and from obscure passages in *Genesis*, *Deuteronomy*, and *Joshua*, that they were indigenous to prehistoric Palestine. If it were not for a patriarch named Enoch, the story would end here.

The Biblical Enoch

Two different men named Enoch are recorded in the pages of *Genesis*. The first was born to the infamous Cain, the son of Adam who murdered his brother and was banished from paradise to wander in the land of Nod. There is nothing of consequence of this man except that his father built a city named after him. Another Enoch appeared four generations later, born to Jared, the great-great-great grandson of Seth who was the third son of Adam.

The *Book of Jubilees* is a Midrashic commentary on the *Book of Genesis* as well as part of *Exodus* written between 135 and 105 BC. It is in the form of an apocalypse, containing the views, legends, and religious practices of the most rigid Pharisaic school during the reign of John Hyrcanus. According to this text, Enoch was born in the year 3238 BC.

He is probably the most mysterious character named in *Genesis*. The only information that scripture tells us is that at age sixty-five he fathered Methuselah (who fathered Noah), walked with God another 300 years, and then "he was not, for God took him."[27] The implication is that he bypassed death and was transfigured in someway from mortal to immortal.

It seems odd, given the extraordinary righteousness of this man, that there is very little information concerning his deeds and accomplishments. Only through the unknown author of the *Letter to the Hebrews* and the *Letter from Jude*, both written during the first century, do we find a hint of his character:

> By faith Enoch was translated that he should not see death; and he was not found, because God translated him: for he hath had witness borne to him that before his translation he had been well pleasing unto God.
>
> *Hebrews 11:5*

> It was of these also that Enoch in the seventh generation from Adam prophesied, saying, "Behold, the Lord came with his holy myriads, to execute judgment on all, and to convict all the ungodly of all their deeds of ungodliness which they have committed in such an ungodly way, and of all the harsh things which ungodly sinners have spoken against him."
>
> *Jude 14-15*

The author of *Jude* quotes from the first chapter of a sacred text called the *Book of Enoch*, not included in the Canon of Scripture.

Chapter 4
Enoch the Scribe

- Nephilim - The Fallen Ones
- Angels or Sons of God
- Judgment
- The Real Watchers
- Watchers and The Day of Atonement
- The Real Enoch

The Ethiopian Christian Church has long accepted the *Book of Enoch* as principle. Although not included in Orthodox Christianity, it was a widely recognized part of the Apocrypha –meaning hidden or secret texts – and much referenced among early theologians. Some early church fathers approved and supported Enochian writings, such as Justin Martyr (100-165), Tatian (110-172), Irenaeus, Clement of Alexandria (150-220), Tertullian (160-230), Origen (186-255), Lactantius (260-330), as well as Methodius of Philippi, Minucius Felix, Commodianus, and Ambrose of Milan. Yet others did not, and it failed to gain enough support for inclusion in Christian Canon.

The book disappeared during the Dark Ages and only fragments in Greek and Latin were preserved in the West. By the late 1400's, rumors began to spread that somewhere a copy of this lost *Book of Enoch* might still exist. In 1773, a complete manuscript of the Enochian text was discovered in Abyssinia, Ethiopian by the famous explorer James Bruce.

In 1821, Richard Laurence published the first English translation. Since then, it has become widely available.

Because of similarities with Christian terminology and teaching, its origin was once believed to be after the start of Christianity. The discovery of scroll fragments at the Essene community at Qumran during the 1950s has since proven the book was in existence before the time of Christ. Enoch, without a doubt, was part of the Essene library but evidence is lacking to suggest it was part of their Canon.[1]

Today, the academic consensus is that the *Book of Enoch* was written during the first or second century BC and probably involved several authors. Obviously this late date expounds that the stories are not the authentic words of Enoch, since he lived several thousand years before its first appearance. Nonetheless, it is a determined part of Jewish tradition.

According to the *Jewish Encyclopedia*, it is one of the most important pieces of apocalyptic literature, significantly contributing to the knowledge of Jewish folklore. It depicts apocalyptic literature in its early stages, as well as the Hebrew people during the time of the Hasmoneans (Maccabees of the first and second century BC). It is also a valuable source of information for religious ideas of Judaism, especially about the Messiah.[2]

Stories in the *Book of Enoch* attest to both Jewish and Christian sources: The *Book of Jubilees*, scroll fragments from Qumran (the *Dead Sea Scrolls*), the *Book of Daniel*, the *Works of Josephus*, the *Second Letter of Peter*, and the *Letter from Jude*. Although Enoch is called a book, it is really a collection of five books. Book I parallels the early stories of Genesis, particularly creation and the deluge. Book II tells of Enoch's visions about the coming deluge and describes some history of the Israel nation. Book III claims to give a prophetic vision of the events of the "world-weeks" centered on Israel, and is distinguished by a conflict between the righteousness of the nation and their wicked opponents both within and outside Israel. Book IV consists of three parables: the secrets of heaven, the Elect One (or Son of Man), the great Judgment and the secrets of nature. Book V is a text on celestial physics or astronomy, relating to the movements of the heavenly bodies as provided by the angel Uriel. Its final chapters are taken from the lost *Book of Noah*.

The books of Moses (*Genesis*, *Exodus*, *Leviticus*, *Numbers*, and *Deuteronomy*) predate the *Book of Enoch*, as evidence currently suggests. And it is questionable whether the early stories of *Genesis*, up to the flood, were based, at least in part, on the ancient traditions of Enoch. Chronologically, Enoch lived twenty-four generations before Moses, and if oral traditions of his deeds existed and were handed down through the generations, as it seems they were, surely they would be the basis for any other story before the flood.

Nephilim - The Fallen Ones

The *Book of Enoch* fills the literary gap in the peculiar introduction to the biblical story of Noah's flood, with an explanation of the sons of God and the Nephilim. It tells a story about how the sons of God, called "Watchers," long ago brought the methods and tools of civilization to the first peoples of the greater Mesopotamian area. It tells the story of how these Watchers fell from heaven, civilized mankind, took daughters of men as wives (according to the tradition this is an unforgivable sin against God and man), and how they became the Nephilim.

The Enochian tale of the flood begins in much the same way as the *Genesis* version, with a commentary on the state of mankind:

> And it came to pass when the children of men had multiplied that in those days were born unto them beautiful and comely daughters. And the angels, the children of the heaven, saw and lusted after them, and said to one another: "Come, let us choose us wives from among the children of men and beget us children."[3]

Similarities end there. Enoch elaborates with the leader of the "children of heaven;" Semjaza is in fear of receiving all blame, and seeks an oath from his companions:

> Semjaza, who was their leader, said unto them: "I fear ye will not indeed agree to do this deed, and I alone shall have to pay the penalty of a great sin." And they all answered

him and said: "Let us all swear an oath, and all bind
ourselves by mutual imprecations not to abandon this plan
but to do this thing." Then sware they all together and
bound themselves by mutual imprecations upon it. And
they were in all two hundred; who descended in the days of
Jared on the summit of Mount Hermon, and they called it
Mount Hermon, because they had sworn and bound
themselves by mutual imprecations upon it.[4]

Clearly, Semjaza and his tribesmen wanted wives from the culture of
which Enoch belonged. But in fear of his companions' withdrawal at the
last minute, he requested that they give their word. They did so on Mount
Hermon. Enoch continues the story of Semjaza, explaining the acts and
deeds of the Watchers, their marriage to women, the resulting offspring,
and its consequences. It brought a "great wickedness on the earth."

Angels or Sons of God

Although referred to as angels throughout the story of the Watchers –
chapters 1 through 17 – in chapters 69 and 71 of the Parables, the author
of Enoch refers to these same beings as "sons of God." This inconsistency
is most likely because of different authors as well as the concept of angels.
There is a close linguistic association between "angels" and "sons of God."
The Hebrew word for angel is *mal'ak* which means "according to
derivation" or simply "messenger." By adding God's name to angel,
further signification is gained: "angel of the Lord," or "angel of God," or
"Sons of God," and "the Holy Ones."[5] Perhaps early in Hebrew history,
the distinction between angel and sons of God was less clear and became
more defined as their beliefs developed. If the oral tradition of Enoch was
his basis, the interpretation by the *Genesis* author is clearly "sons of God."
Nevertheless, it is clear the author is referring to the same beings.

The statement that "angels took wives among the children of men"
appears as nonsense but this is because of our modern views and accepted
doctrines. The modern definition of angels, which has developed over the
last 2,000 years, is that they are incorporeal beings whose role it is to aid
God and man. Although there are different types of angels, in general

they are messengers of God taking human form when necessary for the task assigned and returning to the spiritual upon completion. They fade in and out of the physical world spontaneously and when necessary. This understanding was most likely not the case in the ancient Near East.

By taking wives and begetting children, clearly the Watchers were not angels in our traditional sense of the word. Taking a wife means much more than simply appearing, impregnating, and disappearing. It implies establishing a household and a lasting, permanent relationship and usually involves love. In fact, if we are to believe there is any kernel of truth in the story, it implies they were not angels at all. By creating a composite description from *Enoch* and *Genesis*, we can see this is the case.

The *Book of Genesis* explains that these beings were "mighty men of old," "men of renown" and referred to as "sons of God." The *New International Version* explains that they were "heroes of old." In later chapters, the author of *Enoch* states that "men were created exactly like the angels."[6] This seems contradictory, but in earliest Hebrew beliefs angels were viewed differently. They were superhuman but were of human form. It may be the case that the author of *Genesis* is being more accurate and less mythical in his telling of the story. These "superhuman" angels called Watchers, are simply an elaborate description for the heroes of old and men of renown. It is likely that ancient peoples would adopt the moniker "angels" or "sons of God" to people possessing a greater knowledge. Although we are never told in the *Genesis* version, they must have had advanced knowledge in the ways of life that they are so famous for. This is precisely what the author of Enoch tells us.

The *Book of Enoch* directly credits the civilization of mankind to these Watchers. Their teachings cover a long list: knowledge of the clouds, signs of the earth, sun and moon (calendar systems), observation of the stars, astrology, science of the constellations, the bitter and the sweet (spices), sorcery, enchantments, the use of paint, and beautifying the body (cosmetics and jewelry). They also instructed in the supernatural with the smiting of spirits and demons, and the medical with smiting of the embryo in the womb (abortion).[7] And the most defining qualities of civilization the Watchers are credited with teaching is that which we are now so famous for, the art of war and the methods of writing.[8]

Judgment

The Watchers were said to have descended on mankind during the days of Jared (two generations before Enoch) and began to intermarry and spread their knowledge of civilization. By the time Noah was born four generations later, wickedness had spread throughout society. Ironically, it is by this conveyance of civilization to mankind that their descendents "fell" to become the Nephilim. Enoch writes that it was "through [sic] this their knowledge they are perishing."[9] The legacy they left behind for future generations (their offspring) threatened to consume mankind. According to Enoch's story, they were large and conducted their lives in a horrible way:

> [the daughters of men] became pregnant, and they bare great giants, whose height was three thousand ells: Who consumed all the acquisitions of men. And when men could no longer sustain them, the giants turned against them and devoured mankind. And they began to sin against birds, and beasts, and reptiles, and fish, and to devour one another's flesh, and drink the blood.[10]

The quality of life was reduced to the point where blood and unrighteousness filled the earth.[11] *Genesis* explains, "the wickedness of man was great in the earth, and that every imagination of the thoughts of his heart was only evil continually" and adds that, "the earth is filled with violence through them."[12] Violence is the key word in understanding just what this particular wickedness and evil constitute. It designates the use of physical force to injure, damage, and destroy; or the unjust, callous violation of another's rights and sensitivies, the mental image of which conjures thoughts of social barbarism and anarchy.

As a result, a judgment was pronounced on the Watchers and their descendents. The archangel Gabriel was ordered to proceed against the children of the Watchers and "send them one against the other that they may destroy each other in battle: for length of days shall they not have."[13]

Enoch sought out the Watchers. Finding them on Mount Hermon, he proceeded to tell them this news. He spoke first to their leader, Azazel, and told him and then the others all together. They were to be put in bonds for the unrighteousness they imparted. In response, they trembled with fear. Knowing that their plans and desires had resulted in disaster, they called on Enoch to petition the Lord and seek forgiveness. Enoch obliged by writing each request individually to be read before the Lord. Later, resting near the waters of Dan, he fell asleep while reading their petition. He envisioned the Lord's answer in a dream and it was "No." There would be no forgiveness and the sentence would go forth. Upon waking, he returned to the Watchers to explain God's answer. He found them sitting together and weeping with their faces covered.

Later, a second judgment went forth. A deluge would come to cleanse the earth of all impurities. As does *Genesis*, *Enoch* describes how Noah was chosen to survive the coming judgment:

> **The Most High, the Holy and Great One spake, and sent Uriel to the son of Lamech, and said to him: "Go to Noah and tell him in my name 'Hide thyself!' and reveal to him the end that is approaching: that the whole earth will be destroyed, and a deluge is about to come upon the whole earth, and will destroy all that is on it."[14]**

The Enochian texts clearly state that intermarriage between the "sons of God" and the daughters of men produced giants of questionable conduct and dubious morality. It seems reasonable that there must have been a poor cultural match between these ancient "heroes of old" and the tribe of Enoch, which, if left alone, would eventually destroy their society. Something else to consider is: could there have been a genetic problem between them? What was written concerning the character of Noah, besides his righteous standing with God, suggests there may have been something to this:

> **But Noah found grace in the eyes of the Lord. These are the generations of Noah: Noah was a just man and perfect in his generations, and Noah walked with God.[15]**

The Hebrew word *tamiym* is translated into the word "perfect" in verse eight. This same word is used to describe what an offering to the Lord should be in *Leviticus*, chapter 22; a whole lamb, a physically perfect specimen, without blemish. Strong translates this word to describe integrity, truth, without blemish, complete, full, perfect, sincere, sound, without spot, undefiled, upright, whole. Its meaning is physical as well as spiritual. Could it be that Noah and his family were chosen just as much for genetic purity as for spiritual righteousness? Was Noah chosen (according to tradition) to survive the flood because he was genetically pure, perfect in his generations so "his seed may be preserved for all generations of the world?"[16] It may have been the opinion of the people of that time.

The Real Watchers

Watchers are mentioned only twice in the Old Testament, once in Job and three times in Daniel. Job, a contemporary of Abraham, was a righteous man. Thoroughly tested by God and stripped of his wealth and health, he cried out in lament, "If I sin, what do I do to thee, thou watcher of men? Why hast thou made me thy mark?" (Job 7:20). He was referring to God, a single reference. Daniel, however, writes in a much different context. As a captive in Babylon, he interprets King Nebuchadnezzar's dream of a Watcher coming down from heaven to pronounce a sentence over his powerful reign. Why would a Babylonian King dream of watchers, a Hebrew concept? From this fourth chapter of *Daniel*, clearly the Babylonians held similar beliefs.

In their creation mythology, *The Enuma Elish*, Babylonians recognized a being known as a watcher. King Marduk divided the gods into two sets, one for heaven and one for earth with three hundred in each set. They were called "watchers of heaven" and "watchers of the law of Anu." In the *Magian* version, they were the guardians of gates (entranceways to other lands), and were spiritual as well as physical. (Gate was generally used to describe a mountain pass.) The Watcher, Ninnghizhidda, was a horned, plumed serpent of the deep.

This Babylonian creation myth was written no later than the reign of Nebuchadnezzar in the twelfth century BC. There is also little doubt that this story was written much earlier, during the time of the Sumerians. Drawing some new light on the ancients, Henry Layard found within the ruins of the library of Ashurbanipal in Nineveh, texts that were not unlike the *Genesis* creation in the Bible. George Smith first published these texts in 1876 under the title *The Chaldean Genesis*. It seems likely the source of creation mythology, as well as the idea of watchers, originated on the Mesopotamian Plain and was not specific to the Hebrew culture.

The *Book of Enoch* provides the most thorough and least mythological answers of all the creation stories. There is no evidence to suggest the Watchers were anything other than another tribe or race of humans, despite their reference as "angels" or "sons of God." Their main purpose was simple: take a wife and create a family. Each of them had names and some specific talents. *Semjaza* taught enchantments and root-cuttings. *Azazel* taught the arts of war and beautifying the body through cosmetics and jewelry. *Amazarak* taught sorcery and divider of roots. *Armaros* taught the solution of sorcery and resolving of enchantments. *Baraqel* taught observation of the stars and astrology. *Kakabel* taught the science of the constellations. *Ezekeel* taught knowledge of the clouds. *Arakiel* taught the signs of the earth. *Shamshiel* taught the signs of the sun. *Sariel* taught the course of the moon. *Penemue* taught the bitter and the sweet, and the use of ink and paper. There was also *Kasdeja* who directed in the smiting of spirits and demons, and smiting the embryo in the womb that it may pass.

So why were they called Watchers, angels, and "sons of God?" Perhaps it is because they lived in the mountains (which was higher in the sky, therefore closer to God) and descended into the valleys to interact with those living on the plains. The name itself, Watcher, lends credence to this idea. Living high in the hills they had the position to "watch over" the inhabitants of the valley below. It was common belief in ancient times that God lived high on his mountain. For example, Moses climbed Mount Sinai to receive the Ten Commandments, Elijah went to Horeb, the Mount of God, Isaiah refers to his Mount of Assembly, and so on. Indeed, the stories of Abraham and Joshua both reveal that the aboriginals they encountered (the Rephaim, the Anakim, etc.) lived in the hill country.

According to the *Book of Jubilees*, their initial role was to watch over mankind and direct him in the ways of judgment and uprightness.[17] It seems at one time that they were highly regarded. So what happened? It must be the case that they were considered mystical beings (in perception only), rarely encountered, and anyone who lives on the mountain must be closer to God so they must be "sons of God" or angels. Brief encounters with these mountain people, who were strange and different, reinforced their mystical ideas. As time went on societies grew, and soon the mountains could no longer support the expanding population of those who lived there. Maybe disease or some other form of bad luck reduced the number of women, or perhaps they were, quite simply, attracted to the people on the plains; maybe they were just curious. Whatever the cause, everything was fine as long as they stayed in their mountain home. When they left and took the daughters of men from the valleys below, social conflict spread among those on the plain. Yet, in their day of trouble, Enoch himself acted as an arbitrator and approached them in their lofty home.

As we have seen, the Watchers understood the ways of civilization. They married, raised children, wept, and trembled with fear. Obviously they were human, but what did they look like? A fragment from the lost *Book of Noah* (included in the *Book of Enoch* as chapter 106) provides the only explanation. An unnerving story, it tells of Lamech's reaction to the birth of his son Noah:

> And after some days my son Methuselah took a wife for his son Lamech, and she became pregnant by him and bore a son. And his body was white as snow and red as the blooming of a rose, and the hair of his head and his long locks were white as wool, and his eyes beautiful. And when he opened his eyes, he lighted up the whole house like the sun, and the whole house was very bright.[18]

Noah is described as being a normal, healthy baby with white skin and blond, curly hair. Undoubtedly this was an oddity for the early people of the Near East. The author's description of an infant's white complexion is accurate, in that a red tint is common among Caucasians, especially when exposed to cool temperatures. His eyes shone for two reasons; they are of a lighter color (a color other than dark brown) and were enhanced by a happy disposition. Certainly everyone has, at one time or another, seen the glowing eyes of happy baby. The story continues:

> And thereupon he arose in the hands of the midwife, opened his mouth, and conversed with the Lord of righteousness. And his father Lamech was afraid of him and fled, and came to his father Methuselah. And he said unto him: "I have begotten a strange son, diverse from and unlike man, and resembling the sons of the God of heaven; and his nature is different and he is not like us, and his eyes are as the rays of the sun, and his countenance is glorious. And it seems to me that he is not sprung from me but from the angels, and I fear that in his days a wonder may be wrought on the earth."[19]

The Genesis Apocryphon, found in cave #1 at Qumran (scroll 1Q20), elaborates on Lamech's reaction to the birth of his son Noah. In fear that the "conception was [due] to the Watchers and the Holy Ones ...and to the Giants,"[20] he accuses his wife, Bathenosh, of infidelity. She becomes angry, and insists:

> "O my Lord, O my [brother, remember] my pleasure! I swear to you by the Holy Great One, the King of [the heavens] ... This seed is yours and that [this] conception is from you. This fruit was planted by you... and by no stranger or Watcher or Son of Heaven... [Why] is your countenance thus changed and dismayed, and why is your spirit thus distressed... I speak to you truthfully."[21]

If Lamech's wife was a typical Mesopotamian, his paranoid reaction is understandable. The baby should have been born with dark hair, eyes, and skin. Why would she have given birth to a baby with Caucasian traits? One possibility is that Noah was born with a genetic alteration, which interferes with the enzyme tyrosinase (a melanin precursor). In other words, he was an albino which also provides an explanation for his glowing eyes. They would have been pinkish in color. Or perhaps, both

Lamech and Bathenosh had Caucasian ancestors and carried those genes which could, by chance, produce a white baby. Regardless of how or why Noah was born white, the crucial point is that he was thought to be a child of the Watchers, "the Sons of Heaven," because of his skin, hair, and eye color. We can therefore deduce that Watchers were generally of a light complexion, as well as tall, since they were commonly referred to as giants.

Watchers and The Day of Atonement

There is a strange connection between the Hebrew Day of Atonement and the Watcher Chief, *Azazel*. On the Day of Atonement, the tenth day of Tishri, the Hebrew high priest would present a ram for a burnt offering and two young goats for a sin offering. After bringing them to the door of the tabernacle, he would cast lots for the goats, one for God and the other for Azazel. The goat that was cast for God became the subject of a sin offering; the other, for Azazel, became the subject of a strange ceremony. The high priest would lay his hands on the goat, confess the sins of the people, and hand it over to a man standing nearby who would then lead the goat into the wilderness. From *Leviticus*, chapter sixteen:

> And Aaron shall present the bullock of the sin offering, which is for himself, and make atonement for himself, and for his house. And he shall take the two goats, and set them before Jehovah at the door of the tent of meeting. And Aaron shall cast lots upon the two goats; one lot for Jehovah, and the other lot for Azazel. And Aaron shall present the goat upon which the lot fell for Jehovah, and offer him for a sin offering. But the goat, on which the lot fell for Azazel, shall be set alive before Jehovah, to make atonement for him, to send him away for Azazel into the wilderness.[22]

The word "Azazel" has been translated differently depending on the translator. The *New International Version* of the Bible translates Azazel as "scapegoat," but footnotes it as "the goat of removal, Hebrew Azazel." (It seems as if our definition of the word scapegoat has its origin in ancient Hebrew tradition.) Why a goat? And why would a goat be blamed for the sins of the people?

Some believe the source of this scapegoat tradition has to do with Jacob and Esau (the sons of Isaac, grandsons of Abraham), physically similar but different in their essence, a contrast of good and evil. The tradition is said to reflect how Jacob was instructed to go to the herd and bring two good goats.[23] Azazel, in this interpretation, represents the duality of man in which God made evil as well as good. It seems logical enough, but fails to consider that at one time the Hebrew people were sacrificing to goats. We find in the next chapter of *Leviticus* (chapter 17) there is an odd reference to goat worship [author emphasis added]:

> **And the priest hath sprinkled the blood upon the altar of Jehovah, at the opening of the tent of meeting, and hath made perfume with the fat for sweet fragrance to Jehovah; and** *they sacrifice not any more their sacrifices to goats after which they are going a-whoring;* **a statute age during is this to them, to their generations.**[24]

Why would they make sacrifices to goats of which they go awhoring? The word "goat" is a mystery. Literal translations use "goat," but the King James Version uses "satyrs." The Hebrew word that is translated into goat or satyrs, is "sair" also spelled "saiyr." It means shaggy; as a noun a he-goat; and, also, devil, goat, kid, hairy, rough, and satyr.[25] The *Amplified Bible*, which seeks to present a full interpretation, explains that these goats are "goat-like gods or demons or field spirits." If this passage is taken literally, it could have been the case that the author of *Leviticus* was referring to "the daughters of men" and their desire for the "sons of God." But why were they referred to as goats? As we shall see later in Chapter 18, prehistoric beliefs often involved shaman-like values and practices of which animals were an integral part.

If we look at the Day of Atonement rituals based on Enochian writings, it reflects the sentence carried out on Azazel as ordered by God. According to Enoch, he was banished to the desert, bound hand and foot, and place on jagged rocks:

And again the Lord said to Raphael: 'Bind Azazel hand and foot, and cast him into the darkness: and make an opening in the desert, which is in Dudael, and cast him therein. And place upon him rough and jagged rocks, and cover him with darkness, and let him abide there forever, and cover his face that he may, not see light. And on the day of the great judgment he shall be cast into the fire. And heal the earth which the angels have corrupted, and proclaim the healing of the earth, that they may heal the plague, and that all the children of men may not perish through all the secret things that the Watchers have disclosed and have taught their sons. And the whole earth has been corrupted through the works that were taught by Azazel: to him ascribe all sin.' [26]

The connection between Enoch's story and the Hebrew ritual is obvious. The two young goats are a sin offering for all people. One is slain and the other sent into the desert "away for Azazel," just as the Chief Watcher Azazel is "ascribed all sin" and sentenced to be bound hand and foot in the desert. It is a more direct and powerful understanding of the tradition than the story of Jacob and Esau.

The Real Enoch

According to the *Book of Jubilees*, Enoch was born in the year 522 AM. During the twelfth Jubilee [588-82] he married Edna, the daughter of Danel, and fathered Methuselah. (AM is an abbreviation for Anno Mundi, which is Latin and means the year of the world, corresponding to 3,760 BC. A Jubilee is a period lasting 12 years.)

The author of the *Book of Enoch* refers to Enoch as a scribe[27] or a scribe of righteousness.[28] *The Book of Giants*[29] refers to him as the "noted scribe" and interpreter of dreams. *The Book of Jubilees* also states that he was the first among men who "learnt [sic] writing and knowledge and wisdom."[30] He wrote down the signs of the heaven according to their months so men could know the seasons of the year. In the mystical sense of the word, he was also a visionary:

> And what was and what will be he saw in a vision of his sleep, as it will happen to the children of men throughout their generations until the day of judgment; he saw and understood everything, and wrote his testimony, and placed the testimony on earth for all the children of men and for their generations.[31]

Much of his namesake's book is dedicated to visions. He saw God's judgment of Watchers, the coming deluge of Noah's flood and judgment on mankind. And most intriguing of all was his "out of body" experience through the heavens, guided by the archangel Uriel.

An interesting footnote to Enoch's profile provides a clue that he may have been an honorary Watcher (one of the "sons of God"). One time, Lamech went to his father Methuselah, to ask him to seek an answer from his father Enoch because he knew many things. It further states that "..[Enoch] was beloved, and he shared the lot [of the angels], who taught him all things."[32] Later, we shall see precisely how Enoch may have been a Watcher.

True to his life and traditions, Enoch's death is also wrapped in mystery; later in life he simply disappears. Traditional scripture contends that he was "transformed" by God into the spiritual.[33] It could be the case, as an honorary Watcher, that he chose to live the final days with the people he tried to help.

Reality Unsuspended

This bizarre story of the Watchers, these "sons of God" whose giant offspring spread such evil, appears as fantasy except for those who suspend reality. But it is not so far-fetched, ignoring the assignment of evil and the mysterious heavenly origin, seeing them for what they truly are, the tale is clear in its historical context. It is the story of a clash between two cultures. As the tradition was handed down from generation to generation, its true meaning became clouded. Over many generations, the story faded into the obscurity of fable and myth.

The biblical account of Noah and associated legends, especially the *Book of Enoch*, simply suggest there were other people living before biblical times, which has been proven as fact by archeological evidence. And most mysteriously, it was these people who were credited with teaching mankind the methods of civilization, and with it, all the evils.

Although we have unveiled the identity of these "sons of God," exactly who they were and where they came from is still a mystery. In an Enochian parable, we discover the author tying the account of the Watchers to the biblical tale of Paradise. One of these "sons of God," named *Gadreel*, not only showed the children of men weapons and the blows of death, but he also led Eve astray in the Garden of Eden.[34] It is a compelling connection.

A key to understanding this story is in the realization that the characters mentioned are Sumerian or Akkadian, and that they are not spiritual entities, but men. Furthermore, the events surrounding the story of the Watchers occurred over a long period of time, before and while, Enoch was alive. It culminated with his great-grandson Noah and the deluge, which itself is problematic – five times the amount of existing water would be required to cover the earth's landmasses to the highest peak, an impossibility. According to the *Book of Jubilees*, these stories occurred during the third millennium BC, during the peak of Sumerian civilization.

Chapter 5
Roots of Genesis

According to the author of Genesis, Hebrew origins are Mesopotamian from "beyond the Euphrates River."[1] The direct ascendants of Abraham (founder of Hebrew faith) lived during the third Dynasty of Ur in the Kingdom of Sumer. According to the *Book of Jubilees*, Abraham was born in 1884 BC to Terah and Edna. We also know from *Genesis* that his parents had two other sons, Nahor and Haran, and served "other gods." Abraham, his father, his nephew Lot, and their wives left Ur for the land of Canaan, but settled in the city of Haran (in northwestern Mesopotamia, now a part of southeast Turkey).[2] When Abraham was seventy-five years old, he set out again for Canaan with his family. This time they completed the journey[3] but later moved to Egypt because of famine.

When Abraham was born, Sumerian civilization was already over 1,000 years old. All biblical history before his departure from Ur is obviously part of Sumerian history. As we already know, Sumer was the first culture identified as modern, where cities housed a large population who in turn farmed surrounding fields. It is also the first civilization where a uniform code of law existed and documents, written in cuneiform on clay tablets, recorded everything from business transactions to popular literary works of the day.

From a historical perspective, Sumerian culture appears from nowhere because of an absence of written documents before 3300 BC. Coupled with Sumerian mythology and cosmology, it has provided fodder for wild theories of extraterrestrials and global altruists of a maritime persuasion. The isolate Sumerian language (which has no known relatives) has added to the mystery. However, it is obvious from archeological evidence that the ascendants of the Sumerian people existed on the Mesopotamian Plain many thousands of years before its blossoming as the first society of modern civilization.

Abraham came from this civilization and we must strongly suspect the traditions he handed down were based on the kings and heroes of ancient Sumer. Abraham surely had a particular viewpoint specific to his own experiences and affected by his personal opinions. Nevertheless, the earliest traditions described in *Genesis* are actually Sumerian stories originally told by a man from Ur.

Prehistoric Mesopotamia

Mesopotamia is a region of southwest Asia between the Tigris and Euphrates Rivers in modern-day Iraq. The name "Mesopotamia" is of Greek origin (taken from an earlier Semitic name, possibly *Naharin*) for the river-country that stretches eastward from the Zagros Mountains to the northern Syria. Earliest evidence of its use comes from Egypt in the sixth century BC and simply means "water country." Over the course of its 5,000 year history, several kingdoms have governed its lands including Sumer, Akkad, Assyria, and Babylon.

Its earliest known settlements in the central plains are from the Hassuna culture that lasted from 6500 to 6000 BC. Hassuna villages were small and comprised of clay built houses. The inhabitants engaged in a mixed, dry farming (non-irrigated) economy, and created the first permanent kilns used to fire distinctive painted ceramics. They also used copper, and stamp seals to prove ownership.

According to archeologist James Mellaart, Hassuna pottery (with its western shapes) originates from the hill country halfway between Mosul and Aleppo in "Turkish Mesopotamia," in the regions of Mardin and Diyarbekir.[4] After its initial phases with monochrome pottery, its full development saw small rectangular planned houses that contained several rooms each. They were neatly built in pise (walls made of stiff earth or clay rammed between molds) with reed mats covering the floors. Hearths, ovens, and storage pits lined with bitumen were also common. This culture developed directly into the Samarran and Halafian traditions.

The Samarran culture lasted from 6000 to 5500 BC and was characterized by a distinctive painted pottery style with animal and human figures. Its geographic location marks the southern most extension of agricultural societies. Their communities consisted of large villages and fields with full-scale irrigation systems. This increased their crop yields and allowed for the settlement of the Mesopotamian Plain.

Named after the site of "Tell Halaf," the Halafian culture (6000-5400 BC) of central and north Mesopotamia was characterized by burnished and painted pottery, small villages of clay built houses, and a mixed dry farming economy. There is also evidence that they engaged in weaving. Halafians used stone tools, imported obsidian, and increased the use of copper and bronze.[5]

In southern Mesopotamia, Eridu culture and pottery was similar to Samarra, but with a distinctly indigenous character. A more significant local culture, the Hajji Muhammad, provided the foundations of Ubaid culture, which became fully developed by 4350 BC and occupied most of southern Mesopotamia. According to Mellaart, cultural evidence (mainly ceramic) suggests the Hajji Muhammad descended from the Zagros Mountains of Iran onto the plain.[6]

The Ubaid culture lasted until the beginning of the Uruk period, 4000 BC. Their pottery was a greenish color and decorated with brown or black geometric designs. They also used tools made of hard fired clay, metal, or stone and were responsible for the first temples in large settlements. During the fifth millennium BC, they expanded into northern Mesopotamia and replaced the Halaf culture.

For reasons still not fully understood, during the fourth millennium BC southern Mesopotamia underwent sudden growth. At the heart of the growth were the cities of Ur and Uruk. People moved closer together into larger villages and diversified into various professions for a more robust economy. Individuals became specialized in pottery, metalworking, and weaving. As trade increased, the need for accountability spurred the beginnings of writing and arithmetic. One theory for this sudden growth suggests that climatic changes had rendered older methods of agriculture less effective.

The Birth of Civilization

By 3000 BC, Sumerian culture was firmly established in southern Mesopotamia. The name Sumer is derived from the Babylonian name for southern Mesopotamia, "Mat Umeri," the meaning of which remains unknown. Its citizens referred to their country as *Kengi* which means "civilized land." Their language was *Emegir* and they were the *Saggiga* (which means "black-headed ones").

Sumerians compiled a list of all the kings who ruled Sumer from the time of Creation to the final Semitic conquest. This "Kings List" covers both mythical and historical times. The first kings reigned in prehistoric times, lived for unbelievably long periods of time, and ruled successively from the five original pre-flood cities: Eridu, Badtibira, Larak, Sippar, and Shuruppak.

A few scholars believe the unrealistically long reigns of the kings were a result of inaccurate translations from Semitic records. They believe a proper understanding of Sumerian numeric systems confirms how the error was made. Sumerians and Babylonians employed a sexagesimal number system (base 60). Not knowing that an older document listing the kings was Semitic (and therefore decimal) a Sumerian scribe would have naturally assumed it was sexagesimal. According to the theory, translating the symbols from base 10 into base 60 would have produced very large numbers.

The City of Eridu

According to Sumerian history, Eridu was the first city built by man and the home of Adapa, the Sumerian Adam. Eridu was dedicated to Enki (Lord of the Earth) and was a part of the city-state of Ur in historical times. King Alulim reigned in Eridu for 28,800 years and then Alialgar for the next 36,000 years. Eridu was abandoned and its kingship taken to Badtibira.

The City of Badtibira

Badtibira was located on the Sumerian Plain between Ur and Lagash and was unimportant in historical times. King Enmenluanna reigned for 43,200 years, Enmengalanna for 28,800 years, and Dumuzi (the Shepard and patron deity) for 36,000 years. Badtibira was then abandoned and its kingship taken to Larak.

The City of Larak

Although not positively identified, Larak was believed to have been on the Tigris east of Kish, and was dedicated to Pabilsag, the god of trees. King Ensipazianna reigned for 28,800 years until its kingship was taken to Sippar.

The City of Sippar

Sippar was the most northern of Sumerian cities. Its patron deity was Utu (Semitic Shamash), the god of justice and the sun. King Enmeduranna reigned for 21,000 years. After Sippar was abandoned, its kingship was taken to Shuruppak.

The City of Shuruppak

Shuruppak was dedicated to Ansud, the goddess of grain. This was home for Ziusudra, the Sumerian Noah, a prince of the town and the son of Ubartutu. Ubartutu reigned for 18,600 years, then the flood swept over the land. Afterwards, Kish, with its warrior deity Zababa, became the seat of Sumerian government.

The Sumerian Kingdom (3000 – 2334 BC)

When the Sumerian city-states were developing, life was complex and unpredictable in an often hostile environment. Yet they strove for order and organization. Some scholars believe that Sumerian cities were, at first, simple democracies with all citizens having the ability to vote. However, other evidence suggests a citizen's council elected a king only in time of war.

Sumerian kingdoms were not a family based monarchy, but a succession of kings ruling one city. Various titles for rulers were used: Ensi (Governor), Lugal (King), or En (Lord). As time passed, Lugal became a common title for rulers who controlled more than one city-state, and Ensi for those who ruled a single city. En became a common title for high priest.

Also during this period appears the first Sumerian literature, *The Epic of Gilgamesh*, which includes a Sumerian version of Noah's flood and *Enmerkar and the Lord of Aratta*. Enmerkar's envoy tells the story of a journey he made on behalf of the King of Uruk, through seven passes in the Zagros Mountains to the kingdom of Aratta, the biblical Eden. Enmerkar needed the precious stones, metals, and craftsmen available only in Aratta to build his shrines.

According to historian David Rohl, Enmerkar is the Nimrod we read of in *Genesis*, chapter ten. Kar is "hunter" in Sumerian. So he was Enmer the hunter. And we know from scripture that Nimrod was a great hunter in the eyes of the Lord. Enmer was transcribed into Hebrew as "nmr" (early Hebrew has no vowels) and by adding a "d" a description is attached to the name, specifically that of "rebel," which agrees well with someone building a tower to defy God. Finally, by adding vowels, "nmrd" is translated into Nimrod.[8]

The City of Kish

After the flood, the predominantly Semitic Kish arose as the premiere city uniting all of Sumer. Other cities, however, preserved their independence, yet accepted a loose federation with Kish. Some scholars believe that an archaic democracy was created, with Nippur as the governmental and religious capital. Here, delegates from all the cities would assemble to elect a king in times of war.

In the early third millennium, Etana, who ruled all of Sumer and surrounding lands, created the first Dynasty of Kish. According to legend, he was a pious, god-fearing man who stabilized the land. The Kings List refers to him as "the shepherd" and states that he reigned for 1,560 years. After him came a line of successive sons: Balih, Enmenunna, Melam-Kish, Barsainunna, Meszamug, Tizkar, Ilku, and Iltasadum.

The oldest historically proven king, Enmebareggesi (2700 BC), is believed to have rebuilt the house of Enlil in Nippur. The Kings List refers to him as "he who smote the weapons of the land of Elam." His son, Agga (2680 BC), unsuccessfully laid siege to Gilgamesh's Uruk and as a result ended Kish's Dynasty.

The City of Uruk

Uruk (originally named Eanna) succeeded Kish as the leading city of Sumer. It had two patron deities, An (the heaven god), and the goddess Inanna (Semitic Ishtar). From its ruins the oldest known writings have been found, which date to 3300 BC.

Meskiaggasher (2800 BC), son of Utu, founded the first Dynasty of Uruk. Meskiaggasher and his successors held the title of "En," which implies they were secular as well as religious leaders. The Kings List states that he "entered the seas and ascended the mountains," meaning he attempted to conquer foreign lands and explore sea lanes for trade routes (but may also depict his ascension into heaven as a god). Enmerkar, son of Meskiaggasher, built Uruk into a great city. And according to legend, he conquered the land of Aratta near the Caspian Sea.

Lugalbanda, a companion of Enmerkar (referred to as "the Shepherd") succeeded him. Dumuzi, "the fisherman, whose city was Kua," followed Lugalbanda and was associated with the "dying god" myth. Gilgamesh (circa 2680 BC), the mythical and greatest hero of antiquity, followed Dumuzi and conquered Nippur in his old age. Legend claims he was the son of the goddess Ninsun and a high priest of Kullaba.

Urnunga, son of Gilgamesh, conquered Kish. After that, the remaining Uruk kings were referred to as "Kings of Kish." Lugalkidul (2560 BC) was the final king of the first Dynasty, overthrown by Mesilim of Kish. Kish experienced a short, second dynasty under Mesilim (2550 BC), but was defeated by Mesannapadda of Ur.

The City of Ur

The City of Ur is the most well-known of Sumerian cities because of Hebrew Scripture. Its patron deity was the moon god, Nanna. Two cylinder seals from a royal cemetery were found bearing the inscription "Meskalamdug-King" and "Akalamdug-King of Ur." Neither name, however, is found in the Sumerian Kings List. As a result, it has been labeled Dynasty "0".

Excavations of Ur's royal cemetery produced seventeen tombs, fifteen of which contained the remains of numerous attendants of which most were female. Although some think human sacrifice may have been practiced, no tablets or seals describing such events have ever been found. It is likely that the early citizens of Ur practiced a religion where a king was seen as a deity and had his servants buried with him.

Mesannapadda (2560-2525 BC) founded the first Dynasty of Ur by defeating Mesilim of Kish. According to a bead inscription found at Mari, he was the son of Meskalamdug. Mesannapadda's son, Aannepadda (2525-2485 BC), succeeded him; and his son, Meskiagnunna (2485-2450 BC), succeeded him. A royal dedication tablet for his wife is the oldest Akkadian (Semitic) inscription found in Sumer. Elulu (2445 BC) followed Meskiagnunna and Balulu (2,440 BC) followed him.

Struggles between Kish, Ur, Uruk, and Lagash for control of Sumer undermined regional stability. Ur's dominance ended with an invasion from Awan, an Elamite city-state near Sousa.

The City of Lagash

Ur-Nanshe (2494-2465 BC) founded the first dynasty of Lagash thereby ending Sumerian domination by Ur. His origins are unknown, but inscriptions found regarding his reign state "the ships of Dilmun brought him wood as tribute from foreign lands." If this were true, then his power may have extended into Iran. Ur-Nanshe's son, Akurgal (2465-2455 BC), succeeded him and was likely killed in a war with Ensi Ush of Umma.

Eannatum (2455-2425 BC), son of Akurgal, who called himself "he who subjects the lands," defeated Enakalle of Umma. To commemorate this victory, he ordered a Stele of the Vultures to be made. It was one of the oldest historical documents ever found. Later, he conquered Uruk and Ur, as well as part of Elam, then marched north to take Kish, Nippur, and Akshak.

Zuzu, King of Akshak, led a northern coalition against Lagash but was defeated. As a result, Eannatum was recognized as the supreme king and crowned "King of Kish." His tributaries extended as far west as Mari. During his reign, he fought off the Elamites, and put down a Kisk and Akshak rebellion. His brother, Enannatum (2425-2405 BC) succeeded him. Ur-Lumma, Ensi of Umma along with foreign allies, invaded Lagash from the north.

Although Enannatum was successful in his defense, his armies were decimated, leaving the city vulnerable. Taking advantage of the situation was Il, En of Hallab, whose armies overran Umma. He proclaimed himself Ensi and later failed in an attempt to take Lagash.

Entemena (2405-2375 BC), son of Enannatum, finally overcame Il of Umma with the help of Lugal-Kinishe-Dudu, King of Uruk and Ur. Often fighting the influence of the priests, Entemena was the last great Ensi of Lagash and his reign ended in peace and prosperity. His son, Enannatum II (2375-2,365 BC), succeeded him. The next three kings, Enetarzi (2365-2,359 BC), Lugalanda (2359-2352 BC), and Urukagina (2352-2342 BC) were installed by priests. They oppressed the people through excessive taxation on such events as weddings, funerals, and profitable land sales for state officials.

Urukagina (2352-2342 BC), who claimed to have been chosen by the god Ningirsu to end the oppression of the poor, destroyed much of the old bureaucracy. His documents proclaiming reforms are the oldest in history to speak of freedom.

Urukagina reduced the priesthood's income, ending their unfair influence, and created a nearly ideal state. But this weakened Lagash so it could no longer defend itself. Lugalzaggessi of Umma sacked Lagash and burned all of its holy temples.

The Akkadian Empire (2334 – 2193 BC)

The Akkadians were a Semitic people who occupied central Mesopotamia, an area later known as Babylon. Akkad was the first Semitic empire to attain power. Sargon the Great (2334-2279 BC) established its capital at Agade, the biblical city of Akkad, with Ishtar as its patron deity. He was the first great empire builder and ushered in a new spirit of calligraphy. Such was his fame that two Assyrian Kings were later named in his honor.

Sargon the Great

According to a legend, Sargon was a self-made man of humble origins. A gardener found him, the story goes, as a baby floating in a basket on the river and raised him in his own calling. His mother is said to have been a priestess in a town on the middle Euphrates. He achieved the post of royal cupbearer to the ruler of the city of Kish. Defeating Lugalzaggisi of Uruk, who had previously united all city-states, he claimed to rule lands as far west as the Mediterranean. Thus, Sargon became king over all of southern Mesopotamia, the first great ruler of the Akkadian language.

His victory was ensured by each city's hope of regaining its independence from Lugalzaggisi without submitting to a new overlord. It was before these exploits (while mustering an army) that Sargon named himself Sharru-kin or "Rightful King."

With a desire to secure trade throughout the world, Sargon conquered cities from the middle Euphrates to northern Syria and the mountains of southern Anatolia. He also controlled Susa, the capital of Elam. Commercial connections flourished with the Indus Valley, the coast of Oman, the islands and shores of the Persian Gulf, the mines of Badakhshan, the silver-rich Taurus Mountains, Lebanon, Cappadocia,

Crete, and perhaps even Greece. Such was his fame that merchants in an Anatolian city begged him to intervene in a local quarrel. According to the legend, Sargon and a band of his warriors made an amazing journey to the city of Burushanda to settle the dispute.

Sargon's Legacy

The latter part of Sargon's reign was troubled with rebellions because of the logistics involved in governing the vast area his regime controlled. Sargon's son, Rimush (2279-2270 BC) succeeded him and quelled rebellions in Ur, Umma, Adab, Der, Lagash, Kazallu, Elam and Barakhshi (in Iran). Palace intrigue led to his assassination, possibly by supporters of his brother. An assailant, armed with a clay tablet, clubbed him to death.

Rimush's older brother Manishtushu (2270-2255 BC) succeeded him and founded the temple of Ishtar in Nineveh. Rebellions continued and the strength of the empire continued to wane. Manishtushu managed to keep control of Assyria and Sumer while expanding into the Oman region.

Manishtushu's son, Naram-Sin (2255-2218 BC), self-titled as the "King of the Four Quarters" and "God of Agade," succeeded him. A natural leader and warrior, he re-established Akkadian power by defeating another rebel coalition, retaking Syria and Lebanon, and pushing the control of the empire east to the Zagros Mountains. During the twilight years of Naram-Sin's reign, Gutians began their conquest of Sumer. According to legend, it was divine judgment for Naram-Sin's destruction of Enlil's temple at Nippur. He was the last great Akkadian King.

Shar-Kali-Sharri (2218-2193 BC), son of Naram-Sin, was the final King of the Akkadian empire. He tried to regain the prestige lost by his father, but internal revolts weakened his power. The governor of Elam declared independence, renounced the Akkadian language, and declared himself the "King of the Universe."

Battles with the Lullubi, Amorites, and Gutians intensified, further weakening his reign. Eventually his empire crumbled leaving only the city of Agade under his control.

Gutian Period (2193 – 2123 BC)

With the end of the Akkadian empire, anarchy followed, with city-states struggling for independence while fighting the Gutians. Lagash fell, and became the dominant Gutian city. At times the Gutians also controlled Ur, Umma, and Uruk. However, most of the their kings reigned for only a year or so (with the longest being seven). Utuhengal of Uruk (2123-2113 BC) led a successful rebellion against the Gutians and brought their ruling king before him to "put his foot upon his neck." Utuhengal restored stability, which prepared the way for a resurgence of Sumerian civilization.

Third Dynasty of Ur (2113 – 2004 BC)

Under the kings Ur-Nammu and Shulgi, Sumerian culture and civilization experienced a remarkable renaissance. Peace and prosperity existed throughout the land. The legal system was strengthened, calendar revised, and towns and temples rebuilt (the most notable being the ziggurat at Ur which still exists to this day). A conscious effort was made to re-establish Sumerian as the official language and to promote Sumerian culture.

After the death of Ur-Nammu (2113-2095 BC), a military governor seized Uruk and declared himself King of Ur, creating its third dynasty. He ruled all of Sumer, most of Assyria, Elam, Elba and Syria and promoted defense projects to help fortify the cities against the continuing wars with the Gutians.

Shulgi (2095-2047 BC) completed his father's defense projects and reorganized the government to lessen the likelihood of revolt. To achieve this, local garrisons were placed under the control of king-appointed commanders. After twenty years of war, he was successful in subduing the Hurrian, Subartian, and Assyrian territories. For their failure to pay taxes, punitive campaigns were launched against the Amorites and Palestine in 2055 BC. He also occupied Susa and installed a Sumerian governor. Scholars believe he published the oldest known code of law.

Shulgi titled himself "King of the Four Quarters," proclaimed deity, and continued to promote Sumerian culture. He married a Semite, Abisimti, and fathered more than fifty children. His wife remained a dowager (a widow who retains her husbands title and property) under his sons. His daughters wed the rulers of Warshe and Anshan.

Shulgi's son, Amar-Sim (2047-2038 BC), another self-proclaimed deity, succeeded him and called himself the "God who gives life to the Country" and the "Sun-God" or "Judge of the Land." He continued wars with the Amorites and Hurrians, but lost control of Syria and Elam. He died of an infection, which was a sign of displeasure from the gods according to Sumerian belief.

Shu-Sin (2038-2029 BC), brother of Amar-Sin and another self-deified ruler, continued fighting the Amorites. He built a 270 kilometer wall between the Tigris and the Euphrates rivers in an attempt to contain hostilities. He also campaigned in the Zagros Mountains against Iranian tribes, and cultivated trade relations with the peoples of Indus Valley.

Ibbi-Sin (2029-2004 BC), son of Shu-Sin, was the last king of Ur. As Elamites and Amorites encroached on Ur and Nippur, new city walls were erected to increase their defenses. However, Sumerian unity dissolved as cities concentrated their own efforts on defense. Famine and economic hardship further weakened their lines, enabling the Elamites to take the city.

Isin & Larsa Period (2004 – 1763 BC)

Nomadic Amorites conquered Ur at the beginning of the second millennium BC, ending the Sumerian civilization forever. Their language, although kept as a tongue of the elite, gradually faded into obscurity and was replaced by Akkadian. With the fall of Ur, the cities of Isin and Larsa gained prominence in Mesopotamia, but a unified kingdom was never achieved. During this unstable period is when Abraham left the city of Ur to begin the traditions of the Hebrew people.

During the next two hundred years, the cities of Isin and Larsa competed for supremacy in the south, while Mari and Assur grew to prominence in the north. Assur was the principal city of the Assyrians, and in the south was the famous biblical city of Babylon. Nippur gradually lost its importance and Enlil, his royal privilege enabling the Babylonian god Marduk to achieve prominence in the pantheon.

Mesopotamian Stories of Creation

Jewish tradition believes the *Pentateuch*, the first five books of the *Bible*, were written by Moses sometime around 1260 BC. Scholars, however, point to internal inconsistencies[8] and the existence of "doublets"[9] (two versions of the same story) as proof that several authors had a hand in its writing. Either way, as we have seen in the long history of Sumerian civilization, the early stories of *Genesis* existed before Moses or any other biblical authors. Ziusudra, the Sumerian Noah, and Enmerkar, the biblical Nimrod (who built the Tower of Babel) were all known stories well before the birth of Abraham and the creation of Hebrew culture. Professor of Theology, Gordon Wenham, explains:

> The stories themselves were well-known in the ancient world, long before the Israelites heard them. And really what we find in Genesis is a retelling of familiar stories that were well know in ancient Iran, Mesopotamia, with a completely new theological spin put on them. Instead of thinking of multiple gods, there's only one God. It's interesting when you come to the creation of man in the ancient stories, this was sort of afterthought, whereas Genesis sees the creation of man as the climax of God's activity.[12]

The Sumerians also had their creation stories. They believed paradise was a place called "Dilmun," as described in the myth of "Enki and Ninhursag." Although significantly different from the *Genesis* version of creation, Sumerian mythology contains certain parallels. Unlike *Genesis*, there is no single, unified "Eden" story. They are several.

Enki – Lord of the Earth

In Sumerian mythology, the world was formed out of the watery abyss, and the heavens and earth were separated from each other by a solid dome. Dilmun (or paradise) was a pure, bright, holy land, pristine and virgin. Enki, the Lord of Earth, and his wife laid down in this paradise at a time when man and animals lived in harmony. Enki blessed the land and filled it with lagoons and palm trees. He impregnated Ninhursag causing eight new plants to grow from the earth.

Nammu, queen of the abyss and Enki's mother, bid Enki to knead the "heart" of the clay that is over the Abzu and give it form. Abzu, meaning wise father, was the primal male god and the husband of Tiamat. At the request of the younger gods, Enki killed Abzu, his great-grandfather, and placed his temple over Abzu's body. In some stories, Abzu's dead body became the original foundation of the Earth which, before then, was covered by water. In this way Enki became the first tutelary god and Lord of the Earth.

Enki consumed the plants that were Ninhursag's children and so was cursed. For his actions, he received one wound for each plant consumed. Enlil, and a fox acting on Enki's behalf, called Ninhursag to make amends. She joined with him again and bore eight new children, each of which cured his wounds. The one who cured his rib was named Ninti, whose name means the "queen of months," the "lady of the rib," or "she who makes life."

The Serpent and the Tree of Life

There are other shades of biblical paradise in Sumerian literature. In Dilmun, there were no pains of childbirth. In particular, Ninhursag gave birth in nine days instead of nine months and her child passed "like good princely cream." The quarrels between herder and farmer deities, such as Lahar and Ashnan or Enten and Emesh, are similar to the famous quarrel of Cain and Abel. But in the Sumerian versions, death was avoided.

In the last chapter of the *Epic of Gilgamesh*, there is a curious reference to the heart of the biblical Eden story. Gilgamesh dies and the whole city mourns his death. At his funeral, the people make offerings to the gods. And for Ningizzida, the *god of the serpent and lord of the Tree of Life*, they offered bread.

The serpent was a common icon of ancient Sumer. In the cylinder seal of Gudaea (2100 BC), Ningizzida appears in Sumerian art as a human petitioner with serpent heads rising from his shoulders. He petitions a seated god who was holding a vase of flowing water and sitting on a throne also flowing with water. Besides appearing in human form as a god (represented by a horned headdress), Ningizzida also appears in animal form where he is portrayed as a winged, dual-horned serpent or dragon.

The Anunnaki and the Igigi

There is another creation myth in Sumerian tradition. The Anunnaki (also pronounced Annanage), were the children and followers of Anu, the God of heaven. Antu (meaning earth), was a colorless female being who was the first to consort with Anu. Together they produced the Anunnaki and the Igigi.

According to the myth of Atrahasis, there was a time when the gods were human. The ruling Anunnaki forced the weaker Igigi to perform the works of irrigation and drainage necessary for life in Mesopotamia. Tired of the work, they threatened the Anunnaki, but agreed on a compromise to settle their dispute. From a mixture of clay and blood, Ea and the mother goddess created the first humans to perform the work. Twelve hundred years later, man received forbidden wisdom and became too numerous and restless for the gods' comfort. Therefore, the decision was made to reduce mankind through pestilence and plagues. To hold the plagues in check, Ea advised mankind to withhold prayers and sacrifices from the other gods and worship one God. (Possibly the true origin of monotheism.)

Moses' Sumerian Secret

With the understanding that the Hebrews and Sumerians share a common history, it is likely the Hebrew version is based on older Sumerian versions. It is clear that proto-Hebrews (Akkadians) were a significant part of Mesopotamian culture during the late second millennium BC, but there is more. There's a hidden but striking religious connection between the ancient Hebrews and Sumerians within the story of Moses.

A daughter of the Pharaoh found Moses abandoned by his mother and set afloat in a papyrus basket, along the banks of the Nile. His rescuer raised him as a prince in the house of Pharaoh. His life must have been one of privilege as a son of Pharaoh, yet he knew he was akin to the

Hebrew slaves. He murdered an Egyptian taskmaster one day for whipping a Hebrew slave, then fled to Midian for fear of his life. There, Moses met Jethro and married his daughter, Zipporah.

Many years later, Moses was beckoned by God in the form of a burning bush and commissioned with the task of leading his people out of bondage.[10] Moses wanted proof to tell the Hebrews that his anointing was genuine so he asked God for his name. God's reply was, "I am who I am. This is what you are to say to the Israelites: 'I AM' has sent me to you." What Moses literally heard was 'eya asher eya' and this does mean "I am who I am," but it can also mean "I am the one who is called Eya."[11]

According to Sumerian literature, the god who warned Ziusudra (the Noah character) of the coming flood was Enki, whose temple was at Eridu. Enki's Semitic name, in the Akkadian language, was Ea (pronounced 'Eya'). Hittites simply referred to him as 'Ya'.[12] Using the proper name of an ancient god who was thousands of years old, and whom the Akkadian ancestors of the Hebrews worshipped, would surely get their attention. Moses had his proof in a very convincing way. He knew the ancient name of God, "Ea," which had been passed down through the generations from Abraham himself. Curiously, at that juncture in history, God changed his name to Yahweh "for all generations to come."[13]

By the time Moses recorded the first five books of the Bible, the oral traditions of the early *Genesis* stories were more than a thousand of years old. Their story, as almost everyone knows, begins in a land called Eden.

Four Sumerian stories[14] refer to a place called *Aratta*, also located in Eden (spelled Edin). To the Sumerians edin simply meant "fertile plain," referring to land just outside a settlement. To the Hebrews it meant "pleasure" and a place where life was lived voluptuously.[15] Most scholars believe the Hebrew "eden" derives from Sumerian "edin."

Aratta, tucked in a mountain valley, was an abundant land filled with trees and rich in precious stones and minerals. According to legend, Sumerian kings maintained diplomatic relations with this mysterious kingdom from earliest times. Their patron deity was the mother goddess Inanna, a deity of love, fertility, and war. Depicted as richly dressed or completely naked, she was considered fickle, attracting then rejecting men. Her name is also aligned with Uruk, one of the oldest Sumerian cities.

Aratta may have played a crucial role in the growth Sumerian religion, including the construction of temples and shrines as the tale of *Enmerkar and the Lord of Aratta* suggests. Political and trade relations between the two states was of such importance, the legend implies, writing was developed specifically for them.

The prophet Ezekiel described the Garden of Eden as a place where precious stones of all types were abundant and fashioned with extraordinary workmanship into "tabrets and pipes."[16] Could the biblical Garden of Eden and the Aratta be one and the same? Only by finding Eden can this question be answered. However, for those who have attempted to pinpoint its location, Eden has proved to be an elusive place.

-88-

Chapter 6
The Garden of Eden

- Locating Eden
- Dating the Garden of Eden
- Symbolism in the Garden
- Bridge to the Unknown Past
- The Kharsag Tablets

The *Matthew Henry Bible Commentary* suggests we should not concern ourselves with the location of the Garden of Eden. It proposes that the entire world was the legendary paradise, "Beautiful for situation, the joy and the glory of the whole earth, was this garden: doubtless it was earth in its highest perfection."[1] Until recently, this was the prevailing opinion among those who chose to ponder Eden's authenticity.

Twenty-five years ago, in his book *The Dragons of Eden*, the late Carl Sagan reduced the story of the Garden of Eden to a metaphor, explaining away its significance into biological events of evolution.[2] He suggests that this may account for the popularity of the creation story of *Genesis*.[3] Neither could be further from the truth.

Locating Eden

The *Book of Genesis* clearly describes the Garden of Eden as a physical place with a specific geographic location.[4] According to the text, the garden is in a land called Eden and contains the headwaters of the rivers

Pishon, Gihon, Hiddekel (Tigris), and Euphrates. The Pishon flows through a land called Havilah that is rich with gold, bdellium, and onyx. The Gihon flows through the land of Cush.

The two rivers Gihon and Pishon, as well as the land of Cush, have always been a mystery to modern man and have prevented a concise understanding of the Garden's geographic setting. No one has been able to pinpoint its location until now. In his book, *Legend: the Genesis of Civilization*, and television documentary, *In Search of Eden*, Egyptologist and Ancient Historian, David Rohl presents evidence for the historical (or at least geographical) truth of the Garden of Eden. Point for point he maps the description of the Garden to the Valley of Tabriz in Northwestern Iran.

The Hebrew words in *Genesis*, which have been translated into garden and Eden, are not quite how we think today of a garden and a country. Eden, we assume, is the name of a country like we refer to Canada, but that is not the case. The word "Eden" is rooted in the ancient Sumerian word "Edin" and describes an area of land outside a settlement. It means plain or uncultivated land. Garden (Hebrew gan) refers to an enclosed area, such as a "walled" garden.[5]

The *Genesis* author is really describing two locations. The greater location is a plain, and the garden (which is the second locale) is in the eastern part of the plain. We also know that the origins of the Gihon, Pishon, Tigris, and Euphrates Rivers are located in this plain. The Tigris and Euphrates rivers have always been known. And according to *Genesis*, the other two rivers should be in relative proximity. In the mountains between eastern Turkey and western Iran, there are two other rivers that flow into the Caspian Sea, the Aras and Kezzel Uizon. It is these two rivers that Rohl has traced back to be the Gihon and Pishon.[6] Here's how.

During the Islamic invasion of Persia in the seventh century, Arabic geographers referred to the Aras River as the *Gaihun*. The ancient name of this region through which the Gaihun flows is Cush. A certain mountain in this region, even today, is still called Kusheh Dagh, the mountain of Cush. The Gaihun, Rohl concludes, must be the Gihon.[7]

Another river, the *Kezzel Uizon*, is the fourth river of Eden. According to language experts, the Iranian letter U was translated into a Semitic P by the biblical author. Like the Minian city of Uishteri is known by the

Arabic name of Pishdeli, the Uizon translates into Hebrew as Pishon. Kezzel means gold. Even today, gold is still found in the Kezzel Uizon just as the biblical story describes.[8]

Geographic Location of Eden

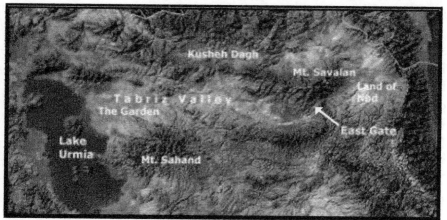

Satellite View of Eden

Therefore, the area of land called Eden is geographically defined as northwestern Iran and northeastern Iraq, between the Caspian Sea and the north plain of Mesopotamia. The garden itself is in the eastern part of this area between Lake Urmia and the Caspian Sea (known today as the Valley of Tabriz). The lake provides the western boundary of the Garden and the mountain ranges to the north and south provide the walls. At its eastern end is a gate (or pass) leading to a plain next to the Caspian Sea. *Genesis* refers to this area as "the land of Nod" and, according to Rohl, this land was referred to as Upper and Lower Nochdi, which means belonging to Nochd. He believes this was the land of Nod.

Everything else in the Eden story also fits. The mountain of God, Mount Sahand, overlooks the valley and the river of the garden. The red earth from which man was formed covers the foothills in the valley. (In Hebrew, Adam means "red earth.") The eastern gate, where God placed the Cherub with a flaming sword, is still known for its thunderstorms. It is an apt metaphor for the angel and his fiery weapon. At the entrance of the mountain pass is the village of Helabad, formerly known as "Kheruabad," which means "settlement of the Kheru people." Rohl believes that this may be a transformation of the Hebrew word *keruvim*, which is translated into "Cherubs."

The Kheru people were a clan of fierce warriors whose standard was a bird of prey, eagle or falcon. In ancient times, perhaps they were the true guardians of the pass.

The English word "paradise" means a perfect place to live and is synonymous with the Garden of Eden. Interestingly it is taken from the Persian word "Pare-da-sa," which means enclosed or walled parkland. The fourfold Persian garden called "paradise" is patterned after and symbolic of the Garden of Eden.[9]

Dating the Garden of Eden

The Archbishop of Armagh, James Usher (1581-1656), calculated the traditional date for the creation of the world at 4004 BC. Other scholars and commentators cite anything from 4026 to 3992 BC. In the nineteenth century, Hales arrived at 5411 BC using the age of the patriarchs given in the Septuagint.

The *Book of Jubilees*, a Midrash commentary on the *Book of Genesis*, places the creation of Adam in the year 3760 BC. Usher's, and other early biblical scholars', dating of the creation of the world (4000 BC) was due to historical lineage going back to Adam. They assumed, based on the prevailing church doctrine, that it occurred just before man's creation.

Absurd as a world creation date of 4000 BC is, the 3760 BC date for the Garden of Eden is reliable. Not only does it agree with biblical genealogy, but also historical evidence. Sumerian civilization, from which Abraham and the Hebrew people later emerged, started at that time. These were the first people we know of to create an oral tradition of history and transfer that tradition to written documentation as recording methods became available.

Symbolism in the Garden

David Rohl has satisfactorily proven the Garden of Eden physically existed, or at least that its description in *Genesis* accurately describes an existing geographic area. However, events of the story are still clouded in folktale and mystery. Rohl suggests that Adam was the first man to be remembered, a starting point for all future generations to look back to. This does make sense, but there are several other themes in the story that are more intriguing.

First we have Adam and Eve, beguiled by the serpent, and tricked into learning the difference between good and evil. As a result, Adam is forced to "till the land from which he came." Second, there is a rivalry between the shepherd and farmer sons (Abel and Cain), one that ends in jealousy and murder. Third, because of his crime, Cain is driven from paradise to build the first city, which he names Enoch after his son. Fourth, and quite intriguing, Adam and Eve bore another son after the death of Abel and named him Seth, who bears a son named Enosh. It was only after Enosh was born, that "men began to call on [or to proclaim] the name of the Lord."[10] All the elements of the story agree with the events of a cultural transformation. It also agrees with the evidence that, for some unknown reason, early Sumerian civilization underwent sudden growth.

Embedded in the symbolism of the story, we have the origins of agriculture (a sentence from God to till the land) and resulting economic competition as a result (shepherd versus farmer). We also have the origins of urban life (building the first city) and religion (calling on the name of the Lord). Everything symbolically mentioned in the Eden story *actually did happen* on the Mesopotamian Plain sometime during the early third Millennium BC.

Enoch expounds on the story in a less symbolic style. Introducing evil into the world is due, not necessarily to man's own weakness, but to the influence of another race of people known as "sons of God" – the Watchers. They taught the art of war, the use of metal and precious stones for adornment, antimony, coloring of the eyelids for beauty, enchantments, root cutting, astrology and constellations, knowledge of the clouds [weather], and the signs of the sun, earth, and moon. Above all, these sons of God are credited with teaching mankind the use of ink and paper[11] and because of this knowledge, evil flourishes. Civilization is the expression of knowledge, which can be used for creation as well as destruction. Could it be that man's expulsion from the garden is nothing more than a mythical way of saying knowledge leads to civilization?

The story of the Garden of Eden stands at the threshold of history, as does the story of the Watchers in the *Book of Enoch*. Sumerian mythology tells a similar story of learned civilization from a people called the Anunnaki. Their story too is shrouded in myth and mystery. However, through the science of archeology we can cross the threshold into prehistory and search for the true origins of civilization. In the cities of Jericho and Catalhoyuk, two historically unknown and unnamed cultures were living a city-based agrarian life thousands of years before the first cities of Sumer.

Bridge to the Unknown Past

Well known for its biblical tale of Israeli warfare in the *Book of Joshua*, the ruins of ancient Jericho lie in an oasis of the Jordan Valley, north of the Dead Sea. Excavation reveals almost continuous occupation from nearly 10,000 BC to 1580 BC. It is the oldest city ever found. At the base of the Jericho "tell" (an artificial mound that serves as a foundation) is the remains of a Natufian deposit, a rectangular platform surrounded by stonewalls believed to have been a shrine. Although the Natufian layer is twelve feet thick, it provides no further evidence of structural remains or subsistence economy. However, above it lays a more telling, pre-pottery Neolithic layer that displays the remnants of occupation between 8350 and 7370 BC. At this level, the settlement consists of circular brick houses surrounded by a perimeter wall and reinforced with at least one tower that included an internal stairway.

Named after the western Asian site of "Wadi Al Natuf," the Natufian culture represents the beginning phase of agriculture in the southern Levant region. (The Levant area covers the modern states of Israel, Lebanon, Syria, and Jordan.) A milder climate, associated with increased precipitation, replaced conditions of the Late Glacial Maximum about 10,500 BC. Natufians are also the original builders of Jericho.

This Mesolithic culture, characterized by chipped stone tools, bone ornaments, and a tendency toward permanent settlements, engaged in an extensive cereal-collecting and gazelle-hunting economy. Gradually, they favored a more settled lifestyle, living in permanent dwellings in small villages where they created religious shrines and performed formal burials.

According to James Mellaart in The Neolithic of the Near East, Natufians were descendents of Cro-Magnon. They were of rugged Euro-African descent from the Mediterranean area, Caucasians with dolichocephalic (oblong) skulls.[12] It is an odd cranial shape by today's standards; rarely found now, but typical of ice age peoples.

In later pre-pottery Neolithic levels (7220 to 5850 BC), the inhabitants of Jericho built rectangular houses with plaster floors and walls. Skulls, with facial features restored in plaster (and sometimes eyes set with cowry shells) have been found beneath floors and in open spaces, suggesting that ancestor worship may have been practiced. Evidence also suggests that they endeavored to domesticate sheep and increase their variety of cultivated plants. From the late fourth millennium BC until 1580 BC, Jericho remained an occupied and walled (fortified) city until its destruction by the Egyptians.

On the northern most boundaries of the Near East's Fertile Crescent is a rich plateau called Anatolia, in the central region of modern day Turkey. On that plateau, east of the Carsamba River, are the remnants of an ancient city called Çatalhöyük, which means, "forked mound." First discovered in 1951 by James Mellaart of the British Institute of

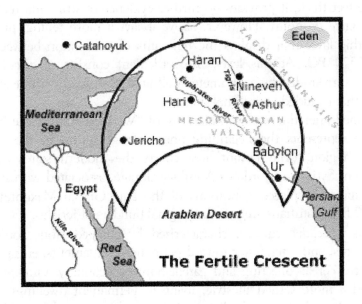

The Fertile Crescent

Archaeology at Ankara, Çatalhöyük was first excavated between 1961 and 1965. Since 1993, an international team of archaeologists led by Professor Ian Hodder has continued research and excavation.

During the early years of excavation, Mellaart uncovered a striking network of buildings and shrines erected by a pre-Neolithic people that lived more than 8,000 years ago. Çatalhöyük, it appears, housed a population of 5,000 to 10,000 people. The oldest layer has been dated to 6500 BC, although sterile soil has not yet been reached. Occupancy existed until 5600 BC and was then abandoned for unknown reasons. Catalhoyuk may very well be the first large city ever, twice the size of Jericho at its peak.

What Mellaart discovered is that the mound contained a large and closely packed street-less city. Continuing excavations have revealed a plan of rectangular houses, built in a labyrinth-like arrangement, and centered on small courtyards. Twelve layers of this style of construction exist, one on top of the other. Each house has its own separate walls but is built alongside its neighbor. New layers were built by partially demolishing an existing layer then building new houses atop of the ruins. This method of construction created the "mound" topography discovered by Mellaart. An interesting feature of the city is that no walls for defense were ever found, which suggests the city was never in need of fortification.

The houses consisted of mud brick, wooden beams, and plaster. Each unit was built according to a general plan; a main room, kitchen, storage room, and an area believed to be used as a shrine. Wooden columns between the houses supported horizontal beams, which provided the frame for flat roofs. Ceilings were made of clay pressed into reeds. Windows were placed in the topmost portion of the walls near the roof. Entry was provided by a hole in the roof accessible only by using a ladder.

Floors were created from lime-based plaster and covered with woven reed mats. Plaster walls were painted with designs in white, red, yellow, and black. Along the walls, benches and platforms accommodated the occupant's seating needs. Small niches carved into the walls served as beds. Kitchens used nearly one third of the available floor space with small, hearth style ovens set into the walls. Plaited baskets (for grains, tools, and other supplies) were found in the storage rooms near the kitchen.

One of the more bizarre aspects of Çatalhöyük's culture was their cemetery. When a family member died, the body was removed of all flesh (excarnated) and the bones placed beneath the sleeping quarters of the surviving generation. It seems that after the passing of a generation, the walls of the existing home were torn down and the area was filled in with soil in preparation for the next tenants. They literally lived on top of their cemeteries.

Like Jericho, early stages of farming and animal domestication existed in Catalhoyuk. Botanical remains of cereals (barley and wheat), pulses (peas, chickpeas, lentils, and wild legumes), and other seeds (pistachio, bulrush, pepperwort, and hackberry) have been found. Various fragments of other botanical remains are yet to be identified.[13] In the summit area of excavation a high percentage of sheep (goat) and cattle remains were found proportionally to pig (boar), horse, dog, fox, and hare.[14]

It appears their domestic life was fully developed. Obsidian from a nearby volcano was used for stone tools: blades, projectile points, and even knapped blades with serrated edges. Eighty percent of stone tools were made from obsidian, as were highly polished mirrors. The rest were made from flint and other stone. Wood was used to make boxes, bowls, platters, cups and spatulas. Animal bones were made into points for piercing, needles, plaster tools, cups, spoons, spatulas, jewelry, fishhooks, hammers, and handles for blades. Baskets, woven in spiral fashion, were made of straw or other coarse plant fibers. Mats for floors were of the same material. Clay was used for making pots. Numerous clay balls, both large and small, were unearthed. Although something of a mystery, they may have been used as heat transfer devices in cooking.

The people of Çatalhöyük made many different types of figurines out of clay and stone. Some were crudely made animals. Other, more refined figurines, include female statuettes (some holding animals) and seated male figures. The female figures are generally very plump. Some were giving birth to either humans or animals.

Articles of personal adornment and utility also suggest the people who lived here were modern. Some items found have been interpreted as bone toggles, belt buckles, bone rings, stone and clay beads, bone pendants, fishhooks, awls made of bone, beads from anklets, bracelets, and an exceptional flint dagger with a decorative bone handle.

There is also evidence of the manufacturing of textiles, possibly of wool or flax. With the presence of Anatolian trade goods found throughout the Middle East, the city must have been a hub for commerce, probably trading in obsidian, textiles, skins, food, and even technology. Stamp seals were found of various designs, possibly used to decorate fabric or walls, but may have also been used to stamp exported products ("made in Çatalhöyük").

The art of Catalhoyuk is striking and offers great insight into their belief system. Among the motifs used were geometric designs, flowers, stars, circles, and in some parts, the depictions of life. There were also human hands, deities, human figures, hunting scenes, bulls, birds, vultures, leopards, wild deer and pigs, lions, and bears. A mural depicting the eruption of a volcano (most likely nearby Mount Hasan) is the oldest known landscape art, probably painted around 6200 BC when the city had reached its zenith. This painting features the block-style settlement in the foreground and a twin-peaked red volcano in the background with smoke bellowing from its summit. Obsidian, the mainstay material of tools and other utilitarian items, may have been seen as a sacred material charged with the power from the gods, but the "Mother Goddess" seems a more likely candidate for a principal deity.

Figures of the "Mother Goddess" made of baked clay, as well as carved from stone, have been found consistently since 1961 throughout the continuing excavation. During the 1997 season, fifty-two figurines were found of various types (animals as well as humans) usually outside the living space.[15] The most common is the Mother Goddess.

"Queen" Figurine at Çatalhöyük

She is often seen as a woman with large breasts, with her hands resting on her protruding belly. The Mother Goddess is almost always depicted nude, lying down or crouching and possibly giving birth. One of the more symbolically, powerful figurines was found by Mellaart himself. It depicted a woman seated between two leopards, her hands resting on their necks. Mellaart believed that some structures were shrines to the goddess, but recent excavations have found that many of the religious ceremonies took place within individual homes.

Ian Hodder, current Director of the Çatalhöyük Archaeological Project, disagrees. He claims there is not enough evidence to suggest the

Mother Goddess was worshipped,[16] but admits it is clear that her figure was held in high esteem.

The bull was also held in high esteem in Çatalhöyük. Bullheads and horns were plastered into place and adorned interior rooms. There were murals (depicting the same) that were painted on shrine walls. Female breasts, suggesting the room itself became the body of a goddess, often accompany bullheads along interior walls. These bullheads were formed in high relief like statues. Some were genuine skulls covered with clay and baked into hardness. Several shrines were filled with horns. Benches, where worshippers would sit or lie, were cradled by the huge sweeping horns of the now extinct Aurochs bull.

The practice of excarnation is portrayed in eerie frescoes where the dead are placed in strange, open funeral houses. Griffin vultures strip away the soft tissue of the deceased. One painting displays a vulture with human legs, wings outspread over a small headless figure. Vulture skeletons have also been found in bull shrines, hidden in clay breasts, with the beak creating the tip of the nipple. Interestingly, one skeleton was found in excavation precisely as the vulture murals portray, headless and in his grave with his left hand over his genital area. Although thought to be the god of some funerary cult, the vulture and practices of excarnation are still a mystery. One possible explanation is that the practice involved the belief of "sky burial."

Links to Ice Age Europe

The Anatolia Plain and its culture at Catalhoyuk was the most advanced center of Neolithic culture in the Near East, predating Sumer by several thousand years. The civilization there shines brightly among the present-day peasant cultures.[17] What is strange is that they left no permanent mark on the cultural development of Anatolia or anywhere else after 5000 BC. Residual elements of their society can be detected in the Halaf culture of north Mesopotamia, but it too disappeared. According to Mellaart, its most lasting affect was in Europe. It was to this new continent that the Neolithic cultures of Anatolia introduced the first the concepts of agriculture, stockbreeding, and the religion of the Mother Goddess.

Professor K. Kokten and Dr. E. Bostanci have shown that, in the Antalya region, ice age art of the west European type existed in Anatolia. The culture that produced the Neolithic Revolution in the Near East is, to a great extent, of Upper Paleolithic stock. There are some anthropologists who believe the Eurafrican race, the earliest race found in Pre-Neolithic cemeteries, depict descendents of Upper Paleolithic man in Europe.[18] And it is this transition, from hunter-gather groups to farmer-shepherd societies, that is most likely responsible for the disappearance of the old animal art. The transition, of course, was gradual and by no means universal.

The Kharsag Tablets

In 1985, former exploration geologist, Christian O'Brien along with his wife Joy published a translation of the Kharsag tablets from the library at Nippur.[19] Nippur lays 100 miles south of Baghdad, Iraq and for thousands of years was the religious center of Mesopotamia. It is here that Enlil, the supreme god of the Sumerian pantheon, created mankind.

Written in cuneiform, these Sumerian-Akkadian texts tell the story of a thriving settlement of creator gods, the Anunnaki. Interestingly, the name of their settlement was "Edinu," the same root word used to describe Adam and Eve's homeland in *Genesis*. O'Brien connected this tale of living gods who were often described as having serpent eyes and shining faces (also referred to as the "shining ones") with the Enochian story of the Watchers. He concluded that they and the Anunnaki were one in the same.

O'Brien's book, *The Genius of the Few* received little notoriety. However, it was congratulated by a few scholars, including the British Museum Sumerian expert, Dr. Irving Finkel. In 1996, British author, Andrew Collins expounded on O'Brien's work with *From the Ashes of Angels*, an intriguing well-researched book examining the birth of civilization and Enoch's tale of the Watchers. According to Collins, the Anunnaki were the princely offspring of heaven and earth who had arrived in the mountains and set up camp in a fertile valley. They called their land Kharsag or Edin. It describes either a central fenced enclosure or a lofty fenced enclosure.[20]

These mythical sons of God developed a sophisticated agricultural community that included irrigation as well as plant and animal domestication. Their homes, as the story goes, were made from cedar. Larger projects included a reservoir, a granary, and other buildings. One structure was entitled the "Great House of the Lord Enlil," which stood in grand fashion above the settlement. In the surrounding valleys there were tree plantations, other cedar enclosures, and orchards planted with trees bearing a threefold fruit. According to O'Brien, the community thrived for a very long period of time. Harvests were plentiful, with excess grain stored in the granary. Apparently, they allowed outsiders into the community as partners or helpers to share the labor as well as the bounty. [21]

There were fifty founders of the community. The primary leader was Enil, the "Lord of Cultivation," and his wife Ninharsag, the "Lady of Kharsag," also known as Ninlil. She was the "the Shining Lady" as well as "the Serpent Lady." The latter led O'Brien to believe the snake goddess was worshipped at Nippur. Also among the leadership were Enki, "Lord of the Land," and Utu (or Ugmash) a sun god. The Anunnaki were said to have had a democratic leadership with a council of seven that came together for major decisions. Occasionally, the Supreme Being, Anu (meaning heaven or highlands), would join the council as an adviser. [22]

Could this settlement of "creator gods" be responsible for the mythical story of Adam and Eve in the Garden of Eden? The evidence is compelling. If it is, then where did these people obtain their knowledge of civilization? Where did they come from?

Archeologists Mellaart, Kokten, and Bostanci have already noted a continuing tradition of Upper Paleolithic man on the central plains of Turkey. As they have cited, these traditions lie within a very different world; the archaic cultures of the ice age, the people and culture known as Cro-Magnon.

Chapter 7
Cro-Magnon Civilizations

- The Discovery
- Life in the Ice Age
- Cro-Magnon Cultures of the Paleolithic

Since the invention of the motion picture camera, Hollywood films and television have dramatically influenced the general perception of 'caveman,' more suitably known as *Cro-Magnon* man. He was portrayed as muscular and large, a brute wearing animal skins, dragging his mate around by the hair. 'Ugh' he would say to his fellow caveman, as he held a thigh of meat to his face. In a childlike fashion, he painted the walls of his cave. This has been the general perception, but could not be further from the truth.

If you happened to meet one today, dressed in jeans and a sweatshirt, you would be unable to distinguish him from anyone else. Although he built no cities and wrote no literature that we know of, he was as behaviorally modern as anyone today, with the same affinity for symbolism, technology, art, and family.

Cro-Magnon man was tall, with an erect posture, well defined chin, small brow, prominent nose, and domed head that was curiously elongated. During his time, he wore garments made of softened leather that were sewn with needles of bone and thread from the dried gut of an animal butchered in the hunt. He adorned himself with necklaces, bracelets, and amulets created from shells, flowers, teeth, and bones. He also built permanent settlements that were designed to withstand the cold winters and lasted for years.

He lived in pit huts, similar to the teepees of the Great Plains Indians. A hallow served as a floor with poles erected as a frame for which a quilt of animal skins served as an insulating shell, and rocks placed along its bottom edge provided stability. During the summer months, he lived in portable, lightweight tents while following animal herds (which were a primary source of food) and dug shallow pits in the permafrost to serve as natural refrigerators. Lamps and hearths were used for lighting and baking.[1] Campsites were typically complex and displayed forethought of construction. They were typically facing east to catch the warmth of the morning sun.

The Discovery

Since the dawn of modern civilization and what we call history, no one knew this race of humans ever existed. The forces of nature buried the evidence of their life deep in the ground. Our history, as far as we knew, began some time around 4000 BC. However, discoveries in France and Spain during the nineteenth century changed everything.

In March of 1868, workmen laying a railway line near Les Eyzies in the Valley of Cro-Magnon, dug into deposits of an ancient rock shelter and exposed its layer-cake style stratum. Archeologists, Edward Lartet and Henry Christy, soon discovered the strata contained the skeletal remains of five individuals: three adult males, an adult female, and a child. Buried with them were stone tools, carved reindeer antlers, ivory pendants, and marine shells. An unknown people, they were obviously very old and the first find of their kind. Since then, all skeletal remains of like kind are assigned the name "Cro-Magnon;" and there were many more to follow. As years of work continued and many more sites were uncovered, it became clear that 40,000 years ago, a race of people settled in the western regions of Europe in the modern day countries of Spain and France.

Further discoveries provided evidence that Cro-Magnon settlements stretched from South Africa to modern day Israel and Western Europe to Siberia. But no other area was as densely populated as Western Europe. The finds were astonishing and provided much information about life many thousands of years ago.

As a nomadic hunter, Cro-Magnon thrived on plentiful herds of wild horse, deer, goat, bison, and mammoth, but supplemented his diet with nuts, berries, and fish. He hunted individually, as well as collectively, using various weapons that later included the bow and arrow and fishnets made from vine. His tools were intricate and specialized for hunting various types of prey. Harpoons for fishing were barbed to increase effectiveness. Cores of stone were used to mass produce long, thin blades further modified to create projectile points, knives, and scrapers. Spear-throwers were employed to extend the arm of the hunter and velocity of the spear. Bone and antler were expertly crafted into utensils, some artfully decorated. Needles of antler or bone were used to sew skins for clothing.[2] Although debatable, it is also believed that some clans built canoes to catch larger fish further from the shore. Intelligent and innovative, he was well equipped to survive, and thrived in his environment.

Life in The Ice Age

Forty thousand years ago, when Cro-Magnon first appeared on the Iberian Peninsula, conditions were extremely harsh. A vast ice sheet (several miles thick) extended out of the Arctic southward to the southern borders of Norway and Sweden. Just beyond the icy conditions lay an arid environment sparsely covered with hardy vegetation. Annual temperatures averaged 43° (6° Celsius), conditions similar to today's arctic high. Winters were very cold, averaging –6° (–24° Celsius).

Two thousand years later, milder conditions prevailed and lasted for the next 4,000 years. Forests spread across most of southern Europe with tundra and open woodland in the north. With much of the planet's water frozen in large glaciers, sea levels were nearly 200 feet below present levels.

Twenty-two thousand years ago, conditions grew worse as the northern hemisphere entered a period referred to as the Glacial Maximum that lasted another 8,000 years. As temperatures cooled, available moisture became increasingly locked into the polar ice cap dropping sea levels 400 feet below present levels. Large ice sheets spread throughout northern latitudes while ice caps donned the Alps and Pyrenees. Conditions were very cold and dry throughout Europe except for isolated pockets of vegetation in and around the mountains of southern Europe. Forested areas were almost non-existent. Southern Europe was reduced to desert-like conditions, with sparse grasslands covering the plains. Northern Europe consisted of dry, open tundra. Permafrost extended east to west across most of the continent and to the latitudes of central France. Summer temperatures averaged 52° (11° Celsius) at latitudes corresponding to central France. Winters averaged 2° (–19° Celsius), similar to present-day Siberia. Near the Mediterranean Sea, temperatures were warmer; 10° lower than present in both summer and winter.

A warming trend 14,000 years ago brought increased precipitation, and conditions to what we are familiar with today. It took another 2,000 years for open woodlands to cover the European countryside. By 9,000 BC, woodland began to replace steppe vegetation. Birch and willow prevailed in southern France, oak in Spain, coniferous woodlands in eastern Europe, and birch and pine in the northwest.

Cro-Magnon shared Europe with another race of humans called Neanderthals, for nearly 10,000 years. Although recognizably "human," they lacked the cognitive abilities to compete aggregately and, as a result, gradually succumbed to extinction. While it is almost certain that Cro-Magnon encountered Neanderthal, violent confrontation was the exception and not the rule. Fleeing territorial expansion of their new neighbors, Neanderthals simply ran out of prime territory to sustain themselves.

With Cro-Magnon man came the beginnings of communal hunting and fishing, the first artificial dwellings, and the first evidence of belief systems. Clothing was made first with tanned animal skins and later with woven cloth. Necklaces of beads and other personal items were created to adorn the body. A great variety of tools were created to perform the tasks of everyday life. Based on these types of tools, archeologists have subdivided the grand Cro-Magnon culture into five subcultures: Aurignacian, Gravettian, Solutrean, Magdalenian, and Azilian.

Cro-Magnon Cultures of the Paleolithic

Aurignacian

Named from the site of Aurignac in the Pyrenees where it was first discovered, the earliest society of Cro-Magnon is known as Aurignacian.

Their culture lasted from 40,000 to 28,000 years ago and was a geographically widespread phenomenon. It spanned lands from Spain (the Santander region) to South Wales with concentrations in the High-Danube region of Germany, Austria, and the Moravian region of Slovakia. In France, they occupied small valleys in the Dordogne region around Les Eyzies-de-Tayac and in the piedmonts of the Pyrenean mountains.

Other than the cave at Chauvet-Pont-d'Arc, the presence of the Aurignacian culture is sparse in the Ardèche of France. However in the gorges of the Ardèche River, a few Aurignacian flint artifacts have been found in the cave of Figuier, Saint-Martin-d'Ardèche and the small rock-shelter of Les Pêcheurs (Casteljau). In the Gard region, Aurignacian artifacts have been found at Ouilins and Esquicho-Crapaou (Sainte-Anastasie) dating to 32,000 BC.

Tools and tool types of the Aurignacian culture displayed standardization. Over time they included end-scrapers for preparing animal skins and burins for engraving. Flint tools were made from blades of stone rather than flakes. Projectile points (for hunting) were made from antler, bone, and ivory. Among their significant innovations was the development of body ornamentation including pierced shells, animal teeth, carved bone pendants, bracelets, and ivory beads. The sudden explosion of exquisite art found at the Chauvet-Pont-d'Arc cave was certainly among their most striking achievements.

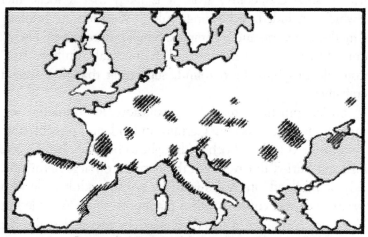

Geographic Extent of Aurignacian Cultures

Gravettian

Named after the cave at *La Gravette* in the Dordogne of Southwest France, the Gravettian culture existed between 28,000 to 22,000 years ago. Like their predecessors, their culture was also widespread. Settlements ranged from southwest France to Wales and Eastern Europe. Artifacts have also been found in mammoth hunters' campsites in Russia. Although regional differences exist, Gravettian lifestyles are remarkably similar wherever artifacts have been found. Speculatively, communication between settlements may account for such similarities.

When Gravettian culture appeared, a significant behavioral shift emerged. Large organized settlements, comprised mostly of simple tent structures, were founded in open lands. Animal remains suggest that some settlements were occupied for most of the year. Others settlements were quite elaborate, such as Dolni Vestonice in modern day Czechoslovakia. There, huts were made from mammoth bones and included storage pits for food preservation.

Excavation analyses also suggest function may have varied between huts. One hut, set apart from the main settlement, was likely used to produce small figurines of clay, then "fired" in a nearby hearth. The well-known small female figurines called "Venuses," usually stressing breasts and buttocks, were of Gravettian origin.

To live in such cooperative style, it is likely that a social hierarchy existed which included behavioral rules. Weapons technology and hunting methods became more complex. Small pointed stone blades, with one blunt edge, became their standard. Remarkably, uniform stone and bone projectile tips have been found, suggesting that they were highly skilled craftsmen.

Their burial practices mark a revolution in thinking and the beginnings of a belief system. Certain individuals, possibly the hunt leader, were covered with red ocher (thought to be symbolic of a return to the womb) and buried in caves with the remains of large herbivores. The "Red Lady of Paviland" in Wales (actually a young adult male who died 27,000 years ago) was covered with a mammoth skull. A triple burial at Dolni Vestonice contained a female flanked by two males; the hand of one was extended over her pelvic area. Two adolescents at Sungir, Russia were buried head-to-head wearing thousands of ivory beads made from mammoth tusks and a headdress comprised of arctic fox canines.

Solutrean

Solutrean culture, named after the site of Solutré and known for a unique style of tool making, flourished roughly 17,000 to 21,000 years ago in southwestern France. They were primarily known for beautifully made symmetrical, bifacial flakes of a laurel-leaf design with shouldered points. The origins of their industry are somewhat disputed, but some evidence suggests that it was an invention indigenous to the Dordogne region of France. Others assign its sudden appearance to the arrival of a new people.

The laurel-leaf and willow-leaf styles of point and blade construction, highly regarded because of detail and fine workmanship, distinguished the Solutrean as a great tool making culture. These techniques were to be used for thousands of years to come and marked the transition from unifacial points (points flaked on only one side) to bifacial (two-sided flaking).

Unifacial points were common early in the Solutrean period. Laurel-leaf blades and bifacial points gradually replaced them. Solutrean technology also marked the first use of the edge-to-edge percussion flaking technique called *outré passé*. Some items that were made this way were used for adornment. They were so fine in their craftsmanship that they preclude use as tools (suggesting purposes of luxury alone). Bone needles have also been found, pointing to the use of fitted clothing, quite useful in a near-glacial climate. Although bracelets, bead necklaces, pendants, bone pins, and colored pigments are evident for personal adornment, examples of Solutrean art are rare. They consist of sculpture in low relief and incised stone slabs.

Magdalenian

The Magdalenian culture, named after the rock shelter in Le Madeleine, France, existed between 17,000 and 13,000 years ago. It is perhaps the most impressive of the Paleolithic period. During this time, the bone industry reached its highest level. Elaborate harpoon points, tridents, and even needles were common. Bone tools were often engraved with animal images and included adzes (ax-like tool with a curved blade at right angles to the handle, used for shaping wood), hammers, spearheads, harpoons, and needles. Magdalenian stone tools include blades, burins, scrapers, borers, and projectile points. Some tools, which ranged from microliths to instruments of great length, display an advanced technique of fabrication. Weapons were highly refined and varied and the atlatl (spear-thrower) first came into use during this time. Along the southern edge of the ice sheet, small boats and harpoons were developed which reflected a society consisting of fishermen and hunters.

The most extraordinary achievement of Magdalenian culture was its spectacular cave paintings which reached a zenith in the latter part of their period. Early cave art is characterized by coarse black drawings. But later, it included beautifully made figures in polychrome (decorated in many or various colors). The famous artwork in the caves of *Altamira* and *Lascaux* belong to this period, the most intriguing stage of human development ever (or at least in the Franco-Cantabrian area). After visiting Lascaux, Picasso himself declared that, "nothing of its quality has been painted since."

Appearing in the subsoil of the chamber area were objects such as serrated harpoons, slender needles, scrapers, decorated spatulas, beaded necklaces, glass beads, engraved plaques, and small pierced bones. The most striking is a pendant carved in the shape of a goat's head that, since its discovery, has transformed itself into the symbol of the cave and of the prodigious Magdalenian culture.

Azilian

First recognized at Le Mas d'Azil (a cave in Arige, France) the Azilian culture was a declining remnant of scattered Magdalenian communities. It lasted from 11,500 to 11,000 years ago. Centered in the Pyrenees region, it spread to Switzerland, Belgium, and Scotland, and was one of the earliest representatives of Mesolithic culture in Europe. Bone and flint items were less refined, with a focus on small geometric shaped tools commonly used in composite tools called microliths. Bone work was limited to crude flat barbed points. Schematically painted pebbles have also been found at several Azilian sites. Some think that these were the beginnings of a simple alphabet. The Azilian, the last Paleolithic people, were followed by the Tardenoisian culture, which covered much of Europe during the Mesolithic.

Prehistoric Cultures Based On Tool Industry

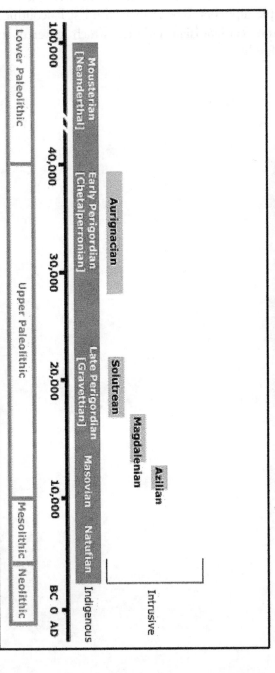

Chapter 8
Cro-Magnon Art & Technology

- Cave Art
- Paint Technology
- Portable Art
- Paleolithic Fashions
- A Behavioral Time Gap

The appearance of Cro-Magnon man in Western Europe was as explosive as the appearance of the Sumerian civilization in the Mesopotamian Valley 33,000 years later. Due to the natural preservative qualities of caves, the archeological evidence for their creativity, grasp of mental imagery, and artistic techniques are overwhelming. Hundreds of caves display thousands of images in France and Spain. According to Ian Tattersall, renowned anthropologist of the American Museum of Natural History in New York City, the evidence points to a revolution in evolution, a revelation within the mind of man and a new type of human being. Nowhere else in the archeological record appears this level of sophistication.[1] For the first time, mankind was making his presence known.

Most anthropologists agree. Randall White, Professor at NYU, believes they were complex (conceptually, symbolically, technically, and logistically) from the very beginning. And according to David Lewis-Williams, Professor Emeritus at the University of Witwatersrand,   South

Africa, their appearance was a quantum leap in thought processes of mankind.[2]

In Paleolithic encampments and caverns, art was expressed in almost everything they did. From cave paintings to figurines, man expressed himself creatively, especially his interest in hunting and the essence of womanhood. Some cave paintings, thought to be a later endeavor of the Magdalenian period, are now proven to be 30,000 years old. A newly discovered cave in Chauvet (1994) displays 300 or more animal images on its walls. "Venus" figurines (small, fire-hardened clay idols of nude women) although predominant in Gravettian culture, have been found all across Europe in all periods of Cro-Magnon culture.

Art was also depicted in respect for the deceased. Carved pendants, bracelets, and other grave goods accompany most skeletal remains. In a 28,000-year-old burial site in Russia, two youths and a sixty-year-old man were entombed and adorned with pendants, bracelets, and necklaces. Their burial clothes contained more than 3,000 ivory beads, of which each bead took an hour to craft. Perfectly straight mammoth tusks were laying next to the juveniles, their natural curves straightened by boiling in water. However, not all the deceased were buried in such a lavish way. Some bodies were disposed of modestly, indicating a class structure and social hierarchy.[3] Regardless of the scale, burial ceremony was a regular part of their culture.

Spectacular items of artistic merit suggest a depth of culture and multifarious thought. Bone and stone plaques have been found with complex markings. One in particular is thought to be a lunar calendar. Other plaques have been interpreted as tally marks of hunting expeditions. One of the lesser-known, but more impressive discoveries, was that Cro-Magnon played music. Bone flutes, percussion instruments, and even xylophones have been found in some of the oldest Aurignacian sites and have been dated up to 30,000 years old.[4]

Clearly any intellect that displays such art, especially when found in all facets of life, can by no means be primitive and must be regarded as highly intelligent. Artistic expression and intelligence go together; perhaps the former is a result of the latter. Whatever the reasons for their art, it was as much an important part of their society as it is in ours.

Today, possession of great works of art is a symbol of accomplishment and wealth. Although not everyone is an artist we all have the capacity.

Art is part of us. Finger painting is often one of the first acts of self-expression we teach our children. Some continue this tradition of expression throughout adolescence and into adulthood; others never stop. It is this concept of self-expression, the relationship of art and intellect, which is found so majestically painted in the Paleolithic cave.

Cave Art

Over 200 caves containing Paleolithic art have been discovered in Western Europe. Numerous caves elsewhere also depict occupation during the ice age. However, nowhere else is there such majestic works of art as in Spain and particularly France. Not all are easily accessible. An underwater cave in Cosquer, France can only be viewed with the aid of scuba gear. At the time the cave was occupied, sea levels were 200 to 400 feet lower than today's levels. Some cave paintings were created only after crawling on one's stomach through dark tunnels for hundreds of feet.

Paintings focused on the hunted animals such as bison, cattle, and reindeer. They were drawn using natural colors and animal fats, but there are others containing images of predatory animals (such as bears, woolly rhinos, and panthers). People, however, were usually portrayed as stick figures.

Their painting styles, known as Franco-Cantabrian, embraced various techniques including the use of fingers, sticks, pads of fur or moss for daubing and dotting, and blowing through a hollow bone or directly by mouth. Foreshortening and shadowing were also used and skillfully employed. Several pigments used were made from iron oxide, black manganese, or other minerals. Images were often crowded close together, sometimes with obvious respect for previously applied paintings. Irregular surfaces were often decorated in relief; separate styles, presumably from different eras, can be detected. There are thirteen styles at Lascaux Cave alone.

Michel Lorblanchet, Director of the National Center of Scientific Research in France, has spent most of his career studying cave art in France and Australia where today's aborigines still practice their traditional rock art. Learning techniques from these aborigines, he tried to reconstruct images from Paleolithic art in France, most notably the back-to-back horses of Pech Merle. As paint, he used powdered red ocher and black manganese dioxide mixed with water, the pigments most likely used by Paleolithic artists. By using his fingers, hands, and arms to mask off areas, then blowing paint from his mouth, he was able to re-create Paleolithic style paintings.[5]

Altamira

Bison at Altamira

Accidentally found in 1868 by Modesto Cubillas, Altamira has been referred to as "The Sistine Chapel of Quaternary art." Marcelino Sanz de Sautuola originally researched the cave and when his findings were published in 1880 (*Brief Notes on Some Prehistoric Objects of the Province of Santander*) many scoffed at his prehistoric deductions. It was not until 1902 that the prehistoric chronology of the paintings was recognized. Altamira was the first cave ever discovered to contain Paleolithic art. Thanks to a natural collapse at the end of the ice age (10,000 BC), the cave was preserved until its discovery in 1868.

Altamira Cave is found next to the Spanish village of Santillana del Mar on a gentle slope of Mount Vispieres. Its entrance faces north, with tunnels and chambers stretching 800 feet into the mountain. The entrance leads to a chamber called the *Ceiling of the Polychromes* where painted and graven images dance in the dim light. Twenty-one magnificently painted bison are outlined and shaded in black, while their red bodies are engraved in glistening limestone. They crouch, lie down, shake their manes, and seemingly charge across the ceiling. Mingled with the bison are a giant red deer (measuring more than eight feet from nose to tail), a wild boar, black goats, human bodies with animal-like heads, and abstract designs of undetermined meaning.

Nine other galleries form the rest of the cave that winds into a very narrow tunnel known as the *Horse's Tail*. In the central galleries are more engraved and painted animals: bison, auroch bulls, goats, horses, and deer. Mysterious geometric shapes (rectangular, conical, and stair-shaped), with negative handprints and "macaroni," adorn these galleries. (Macaroni is a series of parallel lines created by dragging fingers along the soft clay wall, possibly the most ancient decoration in the cave.) The terminal gallery, called the *Horse's Tail*, is a narrow passageway 100 feet long at the deepest part of the cave. It has many images which are mostly engravings. Most interesting are the "masks," bulges from the walls which have been marked with paint so they appear as an animal's face.

Excavation at Altamira revealed the existence of two archaeological levels. The oldest belonged to the Solutrean culture, 18,500 years ago. Stone tools found at this level consisted of a wide variety of flint points with a concave base or notch, and a projecting lip on one side which made it easier to affix on a wooden shaft. The smallest points can be associated with arrowheads and the use of bows. Pendants, burins, scrapers, bone awls, gravers, and percussion tools (for removing flakes from a core) were also found.

Above the Solutrean level is another layer of occupation dating from the Magdalenian Culture (15,000 years ago). Flint points are nonexistent, having been replaced by those made from antler and bone. Needles, spatulas, instruments for smoothing leather, and wedges are also common. The most striking feature is the abundance of harpoons and their variety of decoration.

An article entitled *Documentation of the Rock Art in the Central Sector of the Cantabrian Coast-An Evaluation of Work Techniques*, written by A. Moure Romanillo from the University of Cantabria, catalogues an analysis of Paleolithic pigments between 1993 and 1996. Accelerator mass spectrometry (14C-AMS) dating techniques were applied to colors for two of the polychromatic bison figures. The resulting dates were between 14,330 for "Bison #33" and 13,570 years old for "Right Bison #44", suggesting the art in the cave was created over a long period of time.

Lascaux

Discovered on September 12, 1940 by four boys looking for their lost dog, Lascaux Cave has one of the largest examples of Paleolithic art. Comprised of two large rooms and several other broad, decorated galleries, the cave contains nearly 1500 engravings and 600 drawings

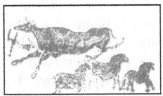

Bison & Horses At Lascaux

painted in yellow, red, and black. Represented in the art are bulls, bears, horses, stags, ibexes, reindeer, and rhinoceros all accompanied by dots and undetermined geometric symbols. Entrance to the cave, originally no larger than a foxhole, slopes steeply into the main hallway called *The Great Hall of Bulls*, where a vast fresco is comprised of three groups of animals: horses, bulls, and stags.

A continuation of this hallway leads to the *Painted Gallery* that beholds a magnificent series of flowing images. It is the height of Paleolithic art, according to the French Ministry of Culture. Figures of ibex, bulls, bison, horses, and cows cover the entire upper reaches of the walls, as well as the surface of the vault.[6]

Also connected to the Great Hall of Bulls is a lateral passageway that leads to the *Chamber of Engravings*. This chamber is a smaller rotunda than the Great Hall of the Bulls, but stands out due to the large number of painted and engraved figures. There are more than 600 in all. Three tiered sections cover the walls and ceiling, each with its own specific theme: aurochs in the lower frieze, then deer, and covering the entire dome, horses. A maximum overlapping of subjects exist in this chamber. There are superimpositions, scrapings, and obliterations that make it difficult to interpret the figures. At its rear the floor falls away, allowing access to the *Shaft of the Dead Man*.[7]

This mural's meaning is a mystery, yet the principal themes expressed are obviously man, bison, and rhinoceros. This three-piece painting centers on an anthropomorphic image and portrays the confrontation between man and bison, with a fleeing rhinoceros on the left. Below the man is a painted "stick crowned with a bird's head." It is nearly identical with the human silhouette (a strange comparison). There are several other secondary elements. In particular is the hook sign, which perhaps represents a spear-thrower, as well as a long Assegai – a slender spear with a simple shaft with a pointed tip. It is drawn diagonally, and level with the entrails of the disemboweled bison. The lowered head and stiff tail portrays the animal's aggression as if it were ready to gore its enemy.[8]

Next to the Chamber of Engravings, consisting of a series of adjoining chambers that gradually become smaller, is the *Main Gallery*. Five panels, each with its own characteristics, exist on both sides of the symmetrical chamber.

At the far end of the Main Gallery is a long, straight corridor that opens into the *Chamber of Felines*, the furthest recess of the cave. Images of this mural are modestly proportioned. Because of the extreme frailty of the rock face, the figures have been poorly preserved. The animals here are different from all others in the cave. Horses are the dominant feature, but there are also six felines figures. Aurochs are notably absent. As in the Chamber of Engravings and Main Gallery, engraving has been used extensively. The decorative work ends in a double line consisting of three sets of two red dots. This is perhaps, the graphic analogy of a topographical boundary marking the extremities of the sanctuary, similar to that found in the Shaft of the Dead Man.[9]

Chauvet

Jean Marie Chauvet, Eliette Brunel Deschamps, and Christian Hillaire were searching for Upper Paleolithic art near Ardeche in Southwestern France on December 18, 1994. In an unexplored cave, they found precisely what they were looking for. After clearing debris from around a hole, Eliette squeezed through and scooted down a tunnel that emptied onto a ledge overlooking a large echoing chamber. With the aid of a

Horses at Chauvet

rope ladder, they entered the chamber and realized their discovery: paintings of animals, handprints, sequential dots, mammoth, and rhinoceros.[10]

Located on the steep side of a cliff in the gorges of the Ardeche (a tributary of the Rhone River), the cave is named after Jean Marie Chauvet. It displays more than 400 engravings and paintings.

Chauvet is in a remarkable state of preservation and contains the oldest known paintings in the world. The nature of the animals represented, in general, are not those that were hunted (for example rhinoceros, bears, lions). Shading techniques and perspective, used to enhance the images, are also unique. Perhaps this is to suggest that they were a living part of the cave. Samples, taken from the charcoal drawings of two rhinoceroses and one bison, yielded dates between 30,340 and 32,410 years old. A torch mark from a calcite layer yielded a date of roughly 26,000 years old. The difference in dates, between the images and the torch marks, indicate that the cave was used by consecutive generations over a long period of time. Another possibility is that Solutrean cultures collected Aurignacian-age charcoal from the cave floor to create new images of their own.[11]

Pech Merle

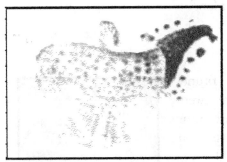
Spotted Horse at Pech Merle

Discovered by André David and Henri Dutertre in 1922, Pech Merle (Hill of the Blackbird) is referred to as the *Sistine Chapel of the Quercy* (The pre- Napoleonic name of the province, still in popular use). Abbé Lemozi explored and excavated the cave for the next seven years. The upper network of the cavern, which has been known since 1900, shows no signs of prehistoric use but the lower level is a magnificent labyrinth of Paleolithic art.

Within the walls of first chamber is the *Black Frieze*. It beholds a horse, four bison, eleven mammoths, and four aurochs painted in manganese oxide (or possibly charcoal). On a ledge are spotted horses, two bison, and a mammoth, also in black. Below the ledge are more mammoths and bison, with another mammoth creativity displayed within the natural relief of the wall. On the ceiling is the outline of a bison as well as finger-drawings portraying mammoths in an open circle. Oddly, the figure of a woman stands next to the mammoth.

Further into the cave are paintings entitled the *Wounded Man*, the *Bison Woman*, and more "Dotted Horses" dated at 25,000 years old. Pigment from a bison image has been dated to be 20,000 years old, suggesting that this cave was also in service over successive generations.[12]

The quantity of animal bones excavated within the cave testify to significant human activity in the cave during prehistory. (A rare occurrence despite the popular stereotype they always lived in caves.) The footprints of a teenager frozen in time 10,000 years ago when he or she walked across the soft cave floor, are even more captivating.

The entire region must have been a center of human activity. Within eight miles of Pech Merle, usually along the river, are twelve other caves depicting Paleolithic art:

- Brasconies (Symbols and punctuations red or black, a red horse)
- Carriot (Paintings and engravings, deer, bovine, horse, bison)
- Christian (Engraved horse, painted and engraved bison, punctuations, and symbols)
- Counterfeiters (Symbols and punctuations)
- Cantal (Symbols, rubbed hand, punctuations, and ibex)
- Melanie (A bison)
- Marcenac (Deer, horses, bison and symbols)
- Holy Eulalie (deer, capridés, horses, wild boar, bear and symbols)
- Paper maker (1 bovine, and three symbols)
- Mill (black bison)
- Bigourdane (Engravings of reindeer)
- Pergouset (Engravings: horses, bison, capridés, strange animals, vulvas, human silhouette) [13]

Cussac

At Cussac (near Bordeaux, France) over a hundred images of mammoth, rhinoceros, deer, bison, and horses are engraved into a cave wall. Unusual in Paleolithic art, Cussac also contains the iconography of birds (most likely geese) and strange figures with long muzzles and open mouths whose precise identification remains unknown. Female

Engraved Horse at Cussac

silhouettes and sexual representations, including several isolated female sexual organs, are also visible along with numerous finger tracings. One wall (twenty-five yards long) is covered with forty figures including a twelve foot-long bison. Claw marks beneath it suggest habitation by bears before human occupation.

The antiquated nature of these images suggests that they were created during the early phase of the Upper Paleolithic, most likely Gravettian (28,000 to 22,000 years ago) or possibly Aurignacian (35,000 to 28,000 years ago). Paw extremities traced by an "X," and the absence of perspective on limb attachments, support the notion that these are some of the earliest examples of art.

Seven graves were also found. The bodies were placed within a depression of the floor (probably bear hollows previously dug into the clay). One of these graves contained a nearly complete human skeleton with several bones still in anatomical connection. It was an unprecedented find.

Rouffignac

Mammoth at Rouffignac

Sometimes called *Cave of the Hundred Mammoths*, the dominant artistic theme at Rouffignac is (as the name suggests) the mammoth. One hundred and fifty-four images of these animals cover the cave walls and ceilings. The choice of mammoth as the focus is a mystery, since Paleolithic artists typically chose horse and bison to paint in caves. Of over two hundred decorated caves throughout Europe, Rouffignac contains half of all the mammoths portrayed. (Mammoth bones are rare in the southeast of Europe.) On *The Great Ceiling*, a throng of sixty-five various animals, including the standard horse and bison, are located above a pit from which the ceiling extends. This surrounds the most complete mammoth image in the cave.

Because of the uniqueness of the animals represented, scholars (mostly non-French) are still debating the authenticity and dating of some of the Rouffignac images. Concerns focus on a frieze depicting three rhinoceros figures and a part of the ceiling featuring ibex figures.

Paint Technology

A chemical analysis of pigments has shown that Paleolithic artists went to great lengths to create certain colors. Naturally occurring colors, such as yellow goethite, red hematite, iron oxides, black charcoal, and manganese dioxide, were typically used. A team of scientists from the French National Museum has determined that some colors were heated to produce different shades of yellow and red. The process of heating pigments has been used throughout history beginning, as far as we know, with the Romans.[14]

An analysis of unused pigments, found in a chamber at Troubat Cave in southeast France, revealed that twenty-five percent of the samples tested were heated directly in a fire. Maghemite, an iron oxide that forms when exposed to organic matter, was found in some of the samples. This indicates that the pigment was in close proximity to charcoal. Baking the pigment in a protective container would create the desired shades, but without the maghemite. Since the unused pigments were concentrated in a single chamber, that part of the cave was most likely used solely for paint preparation.[15]

In 1990, Clottes, Menu, and Walter published a detailed analysis of pigments to identify exactly what Paleolithic paint consisted of. Using Scanning Electron Microscope technology, they determined that pigments from the Niaux Cave in the Pyrenees were from two different "recipes." Both recipes included what paint specialists refer to as "binders" and "extenders," suggesting the artists were familiar with fairly sophisticated technology. According to the study, the paint recipes were detailed enough that they could tell if two different paintings were from the same palette. They were also able to determine that those same paints were prepared at a different site at La Vache because of the paint residue found on tools.

Portable Art

Cave painting was not the only art Paleolithic man engaged in. Figurines of men, women, and various animals (carved in stone, ivory, and bone) have been found across Europe's prehistoric sites. Most prominent are the little statues of women called "Venuses." They usually portray the woman with exaggerated breasts, buttocks, and stomachs. The oldest has been dated to the Aurignacian culture (30,000 years old), but the majority were carved between 22,000 to 28,000 years ago and credited to the Gravettian culture. Some figurines were hardened by being baked (fired) in an oven. One particular site, in the modern day Czech Republic, reveals clay statuettes that were baked in a kiln producing heat up to 800 degrees Fahrenheit.[16] They were as intricately carved as the colorful cave murals were painstakingly painted.

The Galgenberg Venus

Galgenberg
Venus

The Galenberg Venus was recovered from the Galgenberg site in southern Austria in September 1988. This carved portrait of a faceless woman is the oldest in the world. Since charcoal and stone tools were unearthed at Galgenberg, it is believed to have been a campsite often used by Paleolithic hunters. The layer from which it was excavated was dated to 30,000 BC. Originally found in several pieces, this small statue (after reconstruction) stands 7.2 centimeters high and weighs only 10 grams. The artist who carved it used amphibolite slate taken from the local area.

Although the front is three-dimensional, the reverse is flat. The figure gives an impression of movement with her upper body turned to the side, one breast jutting to the left, the other forward, left arm raised, and the right hand resting on the thigh. Because of its "dancing" appearance, it was christened "Fanny" after the famous Viennese dancer Fanny Elssler. The Galgenberg Venus is displayed in the Weinstadt Museum in Krems an der Donau.

The Venus of Willendorf

Venus of
Willendorf

Discovered in 1908 by Josef Szombathy, near the town of Willendorf, Austria, the Venus of Willendorf was originally thought to be between 12,000 and 17,000 years old. Most recent dating procedures, used during the 1990s, have assigned an earlier date of 24,000 to 26,000 years old. The statuette was carved from oolitic limestone, a calcite compound formed into small pearl-like spheres from warm marine water (not found in the region). Detail of the statue is remarkable, but like all other Venus figurines, it lacks a face. Most notably, the pubic region was detailed with a vulva. According to Abramova (1960), the circular decoration about her head is thought to be a cap of seashells, pierced teeth, and ivory pendants (as depicted in twenty-one Gravettian-age graves in Italy).[17]

Her great age and exaggerated female features have established her as an icon of prehistoric art and can be found in various texts on art history as the ideal example of Paleolithic art. The Venus of Willendorf, more renown than all other Paleolithic figurines, is on exhibit in the Museum of Natural History in Vienna, Austria.

The Lady of Brassempouy

Archeologists Edouard Piette and Joseph de Laporterie, excavating near Brassempouy, France in 1894, discovered the Lady of Brassempouy with five other figurines. Also known as the "Lady with the Hood," she was carved from ivory (possibly a mammoth tusk) and is very small; one and a half inches tall. Dated to be 22,000 to 24,000 years old, she is on display at the Museum of Nationals Antiquities in St. Germain en Laye, France.

The Lady of Brassempouy

Unlike all other Venuses, this sculpture has a face. No other statue from the Paleolithic depicts such realistic facial features. The checkerboard styled engraving about the Lady's head and neck has always been thought to be an elaborate hairdo similar to today's 'cornrow' style. However, Professor of Anthropology, Olga Soffer of the University of Illinois, has uncovered compelling evidence suggesting a hairdo may not be the case.

Soffer's interest focuses on ancestral ways of life in the Pleistocene, reconstructing what they were and why they changed through time (including hunter-gatherer cultural practices during the late Upper Paleolithic). In the Czech Republic, she found evidence for the use of textiles. Clay fragments between 22,000 and 29,000 years old, exhibit the impressions of woven fiber. According to Soffer, some of the impressions were left by accident; others were deliberate (such as lining a basket with clay to make it watertight). A detailed examination revealed several styles: open and closed winds, plain weaves and nets, some of which required a loom.[18]

Headdress patterns on the 'Lady' looked familiar, so Soffer and her team analyzed a group of figurines with exciting results. The checkerboard pattern was representative of a woven hat called a snood (a small netlike cap worn by women to keep the hair in place). Soffer's team also found that a significant number of the figurines were depicted to be wearing belts, bandeaux (brassiere), and bracelets.[19]

The Venus of Laussel

Venus of Laussel

Laussel, in the Dordogne region of France, is a terrace 300 yards long with a strategic view of the valley below. A ledge of rock above it provides shelter. Originally thought to have been a domestic site, Laussel is now believed to have been a ceremonial center.

Discovered within the shelter in 1911 by J.G. Lalanne, was the "Venus of Laussel." It was carved into a block of limestone using flint chisels. The engraving had been highly polished except for the head. Originally painted red, the engraver used the natural curvature of the rock to provide realistic quality to the image. She holds a bison horn in her right hand. The horn is notched with thirteen marks, possibly representing the thirteen days of the waxing moon and months of the lunar year. While obviously a frontal portrait, the lady is actually looking away towards the horn, her hair draped over a shoulder. This 17-inch tall carving is believed to be between 20,000 and 22,000 years old. The Venus of Laussel, also known as "The Lady of the Horn," is on display at the Museum of St. Germain in Spades, France.

The Venus of Abri Pataud

Excavated from 1958 to 1964, Abri Pataud (shelter of Pataud) is a large rock shelter at Les Eyzies in the Perigord region of southwestern France. The shelter was a domestic site located between the cliff and blocks of fallen rock. Recovered artifacts include hearths, animal remains, flint tools, jewelry, several art objects, and even debris from the painted decorations of the rock-shelter.

Venus of Abri Pataud

Discovered by Hallam Movius, this engraved image is similar to the Venus of Laussel. It is a faceless representation of a woman etched into a block of stone 58 millimeters long, but lacking arms. According to Movius, it came from level three (Perigordian VQ), which dates to 21,000 years ago, one of the coldest periods during the Wurm glaciation.

The Kostenki Venus

Found at the Russian site of Kostenki in 1988, the "Kostenki Venus" is one of the most well-known objects from the ice age. The height of the surviving fragment is 13.5 cm (5.5 inches). It is unique not only for her massive size and prominent navel, but for bracelets engraved on her wrists which are joined at the front like a pair of handcuffs.

Kostenski Venus

Venus de Lespugue

Discovered in 1922 by Saint Perrier in the cave of Les Rideaux, the "Venus of Lespugue" is carved from ivory, stands 5.75 inches tall, and is between 18,000 and 25,000 years old. Part of Soffer's study, the Venus de Lespugue shows remarkable attention to detail by the artist. According to Soffer, she was originally wearing a skirt made from plant fiber and comprised of eleven cord piles.

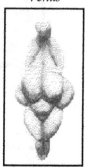

Venus de Lespugue

Some of the cords reveal as many as forty twists suggesting that great care was taken in creating the material. The general design of the skirt is tapered (not unlike a tail) with a long central cord with bordering pieces and increasingly shorter cords toward the lateral margins of the skirt.[20]

The Lion Lady - Die Lowenfrau

The Lion Lady was found in Hohlenstein-Stadel cave in the Valley of Lone, Baden-Wurttemberg, Germany, 1931. Fragments had to be fit together from more than 200 tiny pieces. Although called a lady, it is an anthropomorphic image with the head of a lion. In its arms are several carved striations. Standing twenty-eight centimeters high, six in diameter, and made of ivory, the lion (about 32,000 years old) is one of the oldest figurines ever found from the Aurignacian culture.

Lion Lady

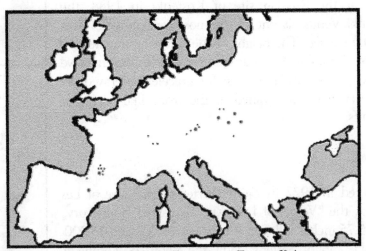

Distribution of Venus Figurines in Europe & Asia

Paleolithic Fashion

Several theories have been offered over the years that try to explain the widespread occurrence of these figurines. The most recent theory is that they represented the "Mother Goddess" from which all life comes, her swollen belly depicting pregnancy. Others believe they symbolize fertility. But it is unclear why hunter-gathers would need aid in fertility, unless they were already domesticating animals and growing crops. According to scholars, there simply isn't enough evidence concerning Paleolithic societies to develop a solid theory. Some believe the figurines were cult based. Tattersall believes they were not, but agrees that they were a traditional part of culture. Others disagree and none agree on any one theory.

Olga Soffer, a fashion expert turned anthropologist, has taken a new approach in studying Venus figurines. After discovering impressions of woven fibers in clay fragments from Central Europe, she believed one might find evidence of textile accessories. Professor Soffer and her team completed and published a study of 200 Venus figurines from the Gravettian age. Although her interpretations of the significance of figurines are debated among her peers, the body of evidence she amassed was groundbreaking. It is noteworthy to mention that Soffer and her team studied the originals; an important approach, since some of the more intricate designs on the surface of figurines are too shallow to project a similar cast image.

She discovered that caps, belts, bandeaux, and skirts (originally made of woven fiber) were found intricately carved into the figurines. Some of the items bore realistic depictions of fiber-based construction. Others consisted of horizontal lines encircling the body, as in the Venus of Dolni Vestonice I.[21]

Previously thought to be a Paleolithic hairstyle, the patterns about the head of some figurines portray a net or snood (as was mentioned about the Lady of Brassempouy). According to Soffer, the Venus of Willendorf is the best example of headgear that portrays a fiber-based cap or hat. A close examination shows a spiral, hand-woven item that may begin with a knotted center, in the style of some types of coiled baskets.[22] Although far removed from ice age Europe, netted headgear has been found on female bodies in Danish bogs.

She also discovered regional differences between West, Central, and East European figurines. Bandeaux are present in almost all the East European figurines wearing headgear. Bracelets and necklaces are found in East and Central European Venuses, but are nonexistent in Western Europe. String skirts are portrayed in West Europe with an occasional attached belt. Basket hats are often found with a woven bandeaux, belt, necklaces, and bracelets in central and east Europe.

All this points to differences in cultures, and compliments Soviet archaeologist Maria Gvozdover's earlier analysis of the figurines. Gvozdover's figurine study concluded that western Europeans favored accenting the hips and thighs while easterners chose breasts and bellies, with a mixture of both in central areas.

One of the more intriguing pieces of evidence is that male figurines are rare, and only female statuettes of the Upper Paleolithic depict garments. Soffer believes that each figurine had its own role in a society based on body type. In conjunction with two previous studies (Gvozdover 1989 and Kloma 1991), she believes that women of the Upper Paleolithic engaged in fashion. Her set of data (and that from Leisure in 1997) suggests that between the eighteenth and twenty-eighth millennium BC, Upper Paleolithic women in Europe were talking about what was important to them; woven and plaited clothing, headwear, and other accessories made from plant material.[23]

Evidence of the clothing they actually wore, however, is found only in burials. It is sparse, since biodegradable material, over time, does not survive the corrosive forces of nature. Three complete burials in Sungir (near Vladimir, 150 kilometers east of Moscow) from 25,000 years ago, clearly contain a placement of beads on the individuals. The unique placements of these beads, and deformations of the strands, are evidence of hooded shirts, pants with attached footwear, also hats, caps, and capes. The three individuals buried were an elderly male, adolescent female and a boy between seven and nine years old. They wore many bracelets, amulets, necklaces, and rings.[24]

In conclusion, Soffer suggests that female labors, in producing woven baskets and textile goods, were symbols of achievement and part of a highly regarded economy in Paleolithic societies. Therefore, they wore woven garments to depict the female of the time correctly and woven accessories were carved into the figurines. Some of her colleagues suggest that her approach may be too female-centric, but it must be remembered that differences between the sexes throughout history have always been depicted in opposing social roles. Why would Paleolithic society be any different? Soffer's insights into Paleolithic life are as brilliant as they are basic.

A Behavioral Time Gap

The durability of stone and bone, and circumstances unique to preserving cave paintings, has privileged some objects over others in ways not necessarily intended by their creators. We really have only a small portion of their culture that we can try to understand. Other indicators of human behavior, such as music, myths, rituals, body painting, and woodcarving, all symbolically suggest social and cultural information in modern cultures but were not saved within the archeological stratum. One can suspect, however, that Paleolithic man indulged in these as well.

The earliest fossils of anatomically modern man were discovered in Africa and the Middle East, yet they did not have an accompaniment of art in any form. Other African excavations do contain art, but cases of these are sparse. So why did anatomically modern humans exist for 60,000 years before they decided to create images? What happened 40,000 years ago to bring images into such widespread existence in Europe? Despite these mysteries, one point is clear: creating images is not a universal experience of human activity. It wasn't then and it isn't today. Nevertheless, it is a clear sign of modern human behavior, one that often accompanies systems of belief and religion.

Chapter 9
Prehistoric Beliefs & Religion

- Patterns in Paintings
- Shamanistic Beliefs
- The Mind in the Cave

The study of Paleolithic sites during the twentieth century has revealed perceptible patterns of artistic expression in content, location, and quality. The decoration of disposable objects – a projectile point for example – has been found to be less intricate than a pendant, which would be of personal value and used for a lifetime. Logically (and quite obviously), the more disposable the object, the less one is inclined to decorate its surface. Portable art, figurines, and other carvings were thought to be a part of everyday life, never to be found deep in a cave. Yet in 1985, several hundred stone plaques were found deep in *Enlene*, a cave in the Pyrenees.

Animal representations have systems associated with them in specific contexts. Bison are often found on stone plaques and cave walls, but never on tools and ornaments. Horses are common on antler engravings, combinations also exist. Phallus-fish and horse-reindeer are the most common for antler carvings, yet the horse-bison combination never exists, despite being a common combination on cave walls. Although the reindeer was a primary prey of the hunter and is commonly engraved on limestone slabs, it was rarely painted.

Patterns of Paintings

Several studies during the 1960s determined that the distribution of paintings in various caves was not random, most notably by Andre Leroi-Gourhan (66 caves were in his sample) and Annette Laming-Emperaire. Certain animals and symbols were consistently associated with other animals and symbols. In central areas of the cave, the horse was found to be associated with the bison, whereas carnivores and humans were usually found in the depths of the cave. Although disagreements exist concerning interpretation and explanation of these statistical studies, it is accepted that caves were painted in some predetermined fashion. Andre Leroi-Gourhan inferred that the pattern must reflect a body of knowledge working within the context of an existing, well developed oral tradition. Put more simply, their culture contained a belief system of some kind. Explaining exactly what this belief system was, however, has been an evolving matter.

During the nineteenth century when cave art was first discovered, it was originally thought to be purely for aesthetics, art for the sake of beauty. As scientists continued their research, it was clear there was more to Paleolithic art than first thought. A theory, describing a mystical relationship between man and animal, soon developed. Early twentieth century scientists believed that prehistoric societies were based on the "totem" concept. In other words, a clan would affiliate themselves with a certain animal and may have referred to themselves as such (for example the bear people or elk people). The objective of the totem was often the founder or guardian of their culture. Through totemism, they would seek to increase their success during the hunt.

Abbé Henri Breuil (1877-1961), a pioneer in the study of cave art, proposed a theory about the cave being used in a ritual fashion to prepare for a hunt. The hunting party involved would descend into the depths of the cave and ritualistically kill their prey by drawing a spear or wound on the sides of animals. Esoteric symbols around the animals were thought to be representative of traps or nets. However, little evidence supports this notion. Fewer than twenty percent of animal representations show marks of injury. Breuil also believed "rites of passage" were performed in the cave to celebrate entry into adulthood.

Interpreting esoteric symbols on cave walls has always been a debatable subject and continues to be so today. Leroi-Gourhan applied sexual significance to these esoteric signs, suggesting Paleolithic man divided the world into items presenting the male and female, similar to a 'yin and yang' principle. Male symbols and animals were always paired with female symbols and animals in complimentary opposition.

In his 1983 book, *The Creative Explosion: An Inquiry Into The Origins Of Art And Religion*, John E. Pfeiffer proposed another way of understanding deep cave art. He contended that cave art was a device used by Paleolithic priests to impress potential followers, thus perpetuating their leadership role. In the dark of the cave, with only a handheld torch, flickering light would produce an effect in which painted images would appear to move. After some time in the darkness, sensory deprivation would make the initiate "suggestible." This was a perfect context for passing on cultural knowledge from one generation to another. Pfeiffer proposes "twilight-state" thinking as being the driving force behind efforts to see everything whole. He suggests that if the pressures of life demanded passionate belief and the following of leaders for survival's sake, then individuals gifted with such qualities (the ability to fall readily into trances) would out-produce more unwilling individuals.[1] Although this idea runs contrary to more modern scientific ways of thinking, there is notable merit to it. Even today, the followers of religious cult leaders and political zealots accept their leadership's doctrines almost without question, thus in effect making it their own.

Shamanistic Beliefs

Most recently, David Lewis-Williams in *The Mind in the Cave* (Thames & Hudson, 2002), has proposed a more suitable theory in explaining cave art including esoteric symbols (wavy lines, zigzags, dots, etc.). By studying the South African San people specifically, and other primitive cultures (as well as research into brain function), Lewis-Williams believes these esoteric symbols originated with trances that led to altered states of consciousness. The cave was special and entered for the express purpose of entering the spirit world. It was a conduit to gain information important to the continuing life of the community. Through sensory deprivation (possibly from consuming hallucinogens), Paleolithic man experienced a dream-like state of which the first effects are seeing esoteric symbols. As a record of his visions, or perhaps for creating ambience, he painted that which he saw on the walls of the cave. David Lewis-Williams argues that the evidence of the images themselves, as well as their contexts, suggests some Franco-Cantabrian cave art was, at least in part, intimately associated with various ritual practices.

Called shamanism, this belief system has always been common among primitive cultures and is still found today in regions of Siberia, Africa, South America, and with Native American Indians. Mircea Eliade's *Shamanism: Archaic Techniques of Ecstasy* (Princeton University Press, 1972), a near encyclopedia-level work, explores shamanic traditions of the Americas, Australia, Indonesia, Oceania, Tibet, and China. Even shamanic traditions of ancient Europe, such as the Greek myth of Orpheus, Persian views of the afterworld, and the Germanic God Odin, are addressed. According to Eliade, shamanism has a very long and near universal history in mankind.

Typically, shamans are those who act as a medium between the visible world and an invisible spiritual world. Aided by animal helpers and other supernatural beings, they contact spirits, heal the sick, control the movements and lives of animals, and change the weather. The word itself (shaman) is drawn from the Tungus language of central Asia.

The Mind in the Cave

So why did Paleolithic man paint what he painted? It has to do with the very nature of the human brain. Lewis- Williams builds a model of consciousness shaped like a horizontal 'Y,' the forked part to the right. The alert, awake mind is the left half of the horizontal 'Y,' whereas the forked area represents two possible states of altered consciousness. The lower section of the fork represents the hypnagogic state (falling asleep) which farther to the right becomes sleep then unconsciousness. Everything about this state of altered consciousness is normal. The upper section of the fork represents an abnormal or induced (more intense) state of altered consciousness. It begins with an entopic state and progresses down a path through construal, ending in hallucination.

Whether induced by pathology (mental illness), pain, or pharmacology, this intensified path is a result of sensory deprivation.

In the first stage of this more intensified altered state of consciousness, people will experience visions of dots, grids, zigzags, nested catenary curves (a hyperbolic cosine), and meandering lines. Regardless of culture, the available light, and state of the eyes (open or shut), scientific studies have shown that all people experience generally the same geometric symbols. Although scientifically referred to as geometric percepts phosphenes, Lewis-Williams calls this an entopic phenomenon (from the Greek meaning "within"), since its source is within the eyeball itself. (Pressing a finger onto a closed eye can create a simple form of an entopic image.)

More elaborate entopic visions, called "form constants," originate from the optic system. Patterns of connections between the retina and striate cortex, as well as neural circuits within the cortex, determine geographic form. There are spatial relationships between retina and the visual cortex. It is simply how the eye and associated nerves are physically arranged so we can see. When psychotropic substances are ingested, the process of seeing is reversed, and the neural structure of the optic cortex is seen as a visual perception. The hallucinogenic substance interferes with the normal firing of nerve connections and, in effect, causes the optic nerve to "backfire." People experiencing this condition are actually seeing the structure of their own brains.[2] The Tukano people of Columbia, for example, take the psychotropic vine Yeja and experience grids, zigzags, concentric circles, and endless chains of brilliant dots, which they depict on their houses and the bark of trees.[3]

In the second stage of the intensified path, the subject tries to make sense of the entopic impressions by elaborating mentally on the images and turning them into iconic form. For example, a round shape will be seen as an apple, breast, bomb, etc., depending on the individual's current state of mind. If the individual is hungry it will be an apple, or a breast if sexually excited, or a bomb if afraid.

There is a significant change in imagery during the third stage. Most people experience a swirling vortex or a rotating tunnel, marked by a pattern of squares analogous to television screens. It draws its subject into its depths. Images on these 'screens' are the first produced iconic hallucinations. Eventually, they overlay the entire vortex of entopic phenomena and give way to iconic hallucinations. Western peoples describe these as funnels, alleys, cones, vessels, corridors, and pits; items familiar to western culture. People of other cultures, however, often describe it as being a hole in the ground. According to Lewis-Williams, shamans typically speak of reaching the spirit world through a hole in the ground.

Images of this third stage are full hallucinations that may include all the senses. Drawn from memory, they are often associated with powerful emotional experiences. Items change into one another and are vivid. A background of entopic imagery may continue, resulting in bizarre effects. For example, a man may have zigzags as legs. Hallucinations, however, have no basis in the structure of the eye or brain and are therefore culturally based. The world they lived in and the animals of the land and the hunt would naturally be the focus of visions for a hunter-gatherer.

Lewis-Williams also draws a general model of the Paleolithic caves in association with his model of consciousness, and provides the caves of Gabillou and Lascaux as examples. The first chamber in the cave is rather large and adorned with vast murals of animals (like Lascaux's "Great Hall of the Bulls") where a group or several groups would meet, possibly for rituals or to integrate experiences. Deeper into the cave, a "vortex" area, and representative of the transition from stage two to stage three, leads into an even deeper area where the "vision quest" (or full hallucination) takes place.

The Motive for Art

In seeking to understand motives for Upper Paleolithic art, it must be considered that they, like us, were a diverse people with various knowledge and skills divided among individuals who all worked together for the good of the community. It is likely there is no single cause for cave art. David Lewis-Williams sees, in the geometric and visual forms of art, the various stages of universal and neurologically produced altered states of consciousness. While it is true that man is biologically wired for hallucination, it seems doubtful that *all* Paleolithic artists were shamans whose trances, experienced deep in caves, were vision quests. Even among Native American Indians, images resulting from consumption of hallucinogens rarely represent an all encompassing explanation of graphic art. Yet Lewis-Williams builds a strong case for the shaman as an important part of the Cro-Magnon culture. The shaman was, possibly, the first priest ever, and perhaps man's first attempt to communicate with God.

Although we can never know the precise dynamics, the models composed by Lewis-Williams explain much about Cro-Magnon culture given the available evidence. Since long periods of time in total cave darkness can produce hallucinations (sensory deprivation studies have proven this), it remains speculative whether hallucinogenic plants were used to induce these visions.

Chapter 10
Mysteries of Cro-Magnon

- Last of the Cro-Magnons
- The Basque Culture of the Pyrenees
- Mysterious Origins

Ten thousand five hundred years ago, a global warming trend brought vast changes into the European climate. Precipitation increased enabling expanding woodlands to slowly replace open grasslands and tundra. Animal life was forced to adapt or perish. Although the direct cause is debatable, these changes must have played a large role in the disappearance of such large animals as the mammoth, mastodon, and other ice age fauna. It also brought new sources of food, such as fruit bearing trees, and allowed human populations to expand into areas previously uninhabitable.

This climatic change along with the accompanying cultural change marks the beginning of what scientists call the Mesolithic period, or Middle Stone Age. It lasted for the next 5,000 years and is perhaps the least studied period of human history.

Mankind, en mass, endeavored to farm. The first known area to use agricultural techniques was the Fertile Crescent on the eastern shores of the Mediterranean in about 8,500 BC. By 6,000 BC farming was practiced from northwest India to Greece. By 3,000 BC it encompassed all of Europe, North Africa, and southern Asia.

Last of the Cro-Magnons

The last Cro-Magnon culture lived during the earliest phase of the Mesolithic. Centered in the Pyrenees, the Azilian culture reached north into Switzerland, Belgium, and Scotland. Settlements were usually located on dunes or sandy areas. Most likely man adapted to the changing environment by forming permanent communities along rivers and lakeshores where fish and mollusks were plentiful. Composite tools became smaller, more delicate. Art became more schematic, less colorful, and often limited to red. By 7000 BC, other cultures – such as the Tardenoisian, Maglemosian, Ertebolle, and Asturian – grew to prominence. At this point, archeological evidence of traditional Cro-Magnon culture simply disappears.

So what happened to the art-loving culture that existed in Europe for so long? There is no distinct trace that would lead one to believe that they became Romans, Greeks, Phoenicians, or any other known ancient cultures. Most likely they dispersed, adapted new ways of life to cope with the changing environment, and assimilated into other local cultures, or perhaps advanced their own in ways not understood.

Archeologist Janusz Kozlowski of the Institute of Archeology in Krakow, Poland, observed that Gravettian Venus figurines display more characteristics in common with the figurines of the early Neolithic of the Near East than with the late Magdalenian or Epigravettian Venuses. As an example, he cites figurines from Kostenki and Catalhoyuk.[1]

In 1977, it was suggested by the late Dr. Carl Sagan that Cro-Magnon may not be our ancestor, but physical anthropology provides more factual evidence. Cro-Magnon's physical traits can be found today in certain parts of Europe, north Africa and some Atlantic Islands. According to studies performed by Howells and Lundman (1967), the Berber and Tuareg peoples of northern Africa, the Guanches of the Canary Isles, the Basques of northern Spain, and people of the Dordogne Valley and Brittany in France all have skull characteristics similar to Cro-Magnon.

There is some linguistic evidence as well. Professor Henry Fairfield Osborn, Curator of the American Museum of Natural History, believed that Cro-Magnon left two cultural relics that have survived into modern times: the Berber speaking Guanches of the Canary Islands and the unique Basque language of the Pyrenees Mountains in northern Spain and southern France. Early studies in European ethnology suggest the Basque people speak a language possibly inherited directly from Cro-Magnon man.[2] In support of their theory, they cite some Basque words. Most notably, the word for knife is *stone that cuts*, and ceiling, *top of the cavern*.[3]

The Basque Culture of the Pyrenees

The Basque people have traditionally called their country *Euskal Herria*, which means the Basque Country. There are about 600,000 Basques in the Spanish provinces of Vizcaya, Guipúzcoa, Alava, and Navarra. The three French provinces of Labourd, Basse-Navarre, and Soule, now merged into a single province, contain less than 80,000 people.

The Basque language (Euskara) is one of the most ancient languages of Europe in the sense that it existed in the area before any others. It is distinctively different and has no known relatives. Scholars believe that Basque was once spoken over a much larger area of Europe than it is now. Today it stands isolated as two small linguistic islands surrounded by languages alien in vocabulary, syntax, and grammatical structure. According to Michael Harrison (who has done much work on the subject), the Carthaginians and Romans recorded this fact: the Basque culture was widespread in ancient times.[4]

University of Iowa Professor, Roslyn Frank, suggests the ancient Basque people were extraordinary in their technical achievements and exceptionally skilled seafarers. She believes that they are remnants of the megalith builders who left behind dolmens, standing stones, and other rock structures across Europe and possibly the east coast of North America. Some evidence suggests that they made regular expeditions to North America to fish and trade for beaver skins. Recently discovered British customs records show large Basque imports of beaver pelts between 1380 and 1433.[5]

There is other evidence to suggest that they may have visited America. During the 1940s, Dr. W.W. Strong interpreted 400 inscribed stones from Pennsylvania's Susquehanna Valley near Mechanicsburg to be of Phoenician character. More recently, others (such as Barry Fell in his book *America BC*) support the idea and claim the Mechanicsburg Stones were the work of Basque settlers around 600 BC.[6] Fell believes the Basque language is related to the Cree Indians of North America. Although interesting, his theories have gained very little (if any) academic acceptance.

However, the Basque culture is unique and, in its history and cosmology, quite different from Western traditions. It deserves a close assessment. For thousands of years, they have remained isolated from the influence of expanding empires of earlier times. As a result, their culture and language have remained fairly intact. Dr. Frank has studied the Basque culture at length over the past twenty-five years, and has provided some interesting comparisons to the principles of Western thought.

Her interests in the Basque culture began as a Spanish Professor teaching the literary works of Miguel de Cervantes Saavedra, the author of *Don Quixote*. Spanish literature led to the study of the Beguine movement of the twelfth century, which in turn led to an investigation of traditions, beliefs, legends, and myths of the Basque people. She gathered a host of clues, including stone monuments and archaic systems of measurement, which suggest the Basque culture was far more sophisticated and less remote than was previously thought.[7]

Frank discovered that during the Middle Ages, bands of performers who roamed from village to village reinforced a widely held belief that bears were very special animals. Apart from bears having extraordinary powers, mankind (it was believed) descended from them, and there was a time, long ago, when humans and animals lived together in harmony. According to Frank, these European bear legends go as far back in time as 12,000 BC.[8] They are the surviving traditions of a once hunter-gatherer culture, now agrarian.

Bear stories throughout Europe are remarkably similar and sometimes nearly identical. Frank believes the folktales go back to a time when the stories were a part of the night sky. This explains why Europeans view the Big and Little Bear constellations as circling the North Star. It is no wonder that so many European folktales describe a being who is half-bear and half-man. According to Frank, it is as if their social values were written on the sky.

She supports this sky-watching theory with some current data. Throughout the ages, the Basque people have erected stone octagons in near perfect circles in the hills of the Pyrenees. Each stone is aligned with great accuracy to the cardinal and inter-cardinal points of the compass. Most likely, they were a coordinate system for navigation, with the center stone serving as the North Star. As recently as ten years ago, Basque shepherds still used these stone octagons to map the territory to be used for grazing.

In a more recent study with Mikel Susperregi, Frank has mapped out their cultural identity and compared it to traditional Western culture. The Basque mind-set, she discovered, is quite different. The basic structure of Basque mental imagery (based on their cosmology) draws its meaning from a radically different worldview. For example, there is simply no word or phrase in the Euskera language that would express the Western polarity of mind-to-body and reason-to-instinct. Their word *gogo* is the nearest representation and it loosely refers to one's consciousness.[9]

In Western thought, we are willing to view events and people in polarity, such as black-or-white, where white is good and black is bad. Basque culture does not embrace this rationale. Their understanding of the world rests in a more complimentary fashion. Black and red, for example, are heterarchical equals and represent two oscillating poles of being and reality. White is not the opposite of black. Red is its complement. For example, to them black is good and having a black sheep in the flock is good thing. Black is actually a positive color with foundations grounded in the ideas of fertility, fruitfulness, and wholeness. Black animals in general are therefore helpful.[10] In historical times, black animals were sacrificed for this very reason. The same reason the ancient Hebrews would sacrifice an unblemished white lamb.

Of great interest is the black he-goat. Contrary to the authorities of the Spanish Inquisition, the much-maligned black he-goat was not, according to the Basques, the embodiment of evil or Satan. It is viewed as the keeper, guardian, and healer of all domestic animals. He is the *Aker Beltz* (he-goat black in Euskara), the Spirit Animal Guardian.[11] In Basque tradition, the male goat (particularly one that is black) represents great curative powers and exercises a beneficial power over animals entrusted to its care and protection. To ensure the health of domestic animals, the recommendation was to have one black he-goat on each farm.[12] Until the 1950s, many farms still kept a black he-goat to 'ward off' death and disease and to foster fertility among their animals.

According to the Greek geographer Strabo (64 BC-24 AD), in ancient times the people of the Pyrenees were known to the Greeks as *Ouaskonous* (the people of the he-goat) because of their habit of sacrificing goats to their gods. It is difficult not to speculate and infer a connection with the Watcher, Azazel, and his connection to the Hebrew practice of sacrificing a goat on the Day of Atonement. This of course, would mean the ancient Basques had a much broader range of influence.

Frank believes they did have a wide range of influence and that its origins predate current Western thought, which has been in place for at least 5,000 years. The question must be asked then, if the Basque culture is a surviving remnant of a once-prevailing European culture, then what happened to its prevalence?

A new culture emerged with naturally appealing traits that grew into a new European identity. It was not a sudden change, but a gradual conquering of thought. Frank cites from the work of George Lakeoff and Mark Turner, *More than Cool Reason: a Field Guide to Poetic Metaphor* (1989), and their concept of the "Great Chain." This "Great Chain" is a description not only of what hierarchies exist in the world, but what people believe they should be. For example, the hierarchy of life is God, man, woman, then the animals. This is the natural order of dominance,[13] with its roots reaching into the cultures where myths declared man's origin was in the sky-god. This patriarchal view of culture is not merely a historical matter, but it also dominates much of modern social and political behavior.

Since the older culture held its origin in the ancestry of bears, they would have no place in a world where God or gods were considered the creators of life. Western thought views black as bad and any black animal as an omen of bad luck. This may very well have it roots in an emotional reaction to a previously prevalent culture.[14] It is also likely, that a new and dominant culture viewed any other worldview as evil; just as abolishing witchcraft has a long and vile history within Christianity.

Roslyn Frank and Mikel Susperregi's comparative study is really a part of a much larger project (under the patronage of the *Institute of Basque*

Studies) which is focused on recovering the metaphysics associated with an earlier pan-European cosmology.[15] The Basque language, as it exists today (relatively unchanged for thousands of years), provides them with a means for recovering the thought processes intrinsic to this earlier cosmology.

Does this mean the Basques are direct descendants of Paleolithic peoples? No one really knows for sure. It is possible and even likely. There is no evidence for any sudden change in the population of the area for thousands of years before the arrival of the Celts, and later the Romans, during the first millennium BC.

Is this absence of evidence, evidence of absence? Not hardly. The historical and ethnological evidence seems substantial.

Mysterious Origins

More mysterious than Cro-Magnon's fate is their origin. Where Cro-Magnon arrived from is unknown and, according to some scholars, they were not indigenous to Europe.[16] Sudden changes in Cro-Magnon culture (most noticeable in their tool kits) suggest they were migrating over a long period of time and appearing as sequential waves over a 30,000-year period. Based on the presence of innovative tools in Eastern Europe, the orthodox theory of Cro-Magnon origin is in the East, following the general theory that man originated in Africa, moved north and east, then west. However, recent finds from the Aurignacian age in the Spanish peninsula predate the earliest eastern sites and suggest that an eastern origin may not be the case.[17] Obviously a northern origin is not possible due to the Scandinavian ice sheet which made northern Europe virtually uninhabitable. This leaves only the south or west as possible sources.

Cro-Magnon settlements existed in Africa, and clearly tool technology existed there well before 40,000 years ago. Blade tool technology is obvious up to 80,000 years ago. Barbed bone points found in Zaire have been dated from 60,000 to 80,000 years old. There is also evidence for flint mining and long-distance transport of raw materials. Modern African cranial structure, being more similar to Cro-Magnon than Europeans, also suggests they migrated from the South. However, supporting archeological evidence of advanced culture is sparse. African Cro-Magnon sites contain little of the symbolic and behavioral evidence so distinctive in European sites, which is a requirement for being the host culture for such a massive migration.[18]

If such a culturally well-defined people were to migrate from a particular geographic area, one would expect to find substantial roots of their ethnicity, technically as well as behaviorally. Yet in Africa, this does not seem to be the case.

David Lewis-Williams disagrees, and argues that although there was a comparatively sudden burst of symbolic activity, the explosion was not universal nor was it an indivisible 'package deal.' The idea that all the different kinds of art and fully developed symbolic behavior suddenly appeared in western Europe, he believes, is a creative illusion. He insists that events need to be placed in a wider perspective. If the modern mind and modern behavior evolved sporadically in Africa, it follows that the potential for all the symbolic activities that we see in Upper Paleolithic Western Europe was in existence before Homo Sapien communities reached France and the Iberian Peninsula.[19]

There is, however, one other direction to look in. Maybe they arrived from the west, but how far west? Just off the west coast of Africa are the Canary Islands. The *Museo Canario*, the Museum of the Canaries, rests in the heart of Las Palmas on the island of Gran Canarie. The primary focus of the island's museum is the pre-conquest history of the Canary Islands. However, it also boasts the largest collection of Cro-Magnon skulls in the world. Another interesting feature of the Canaries is that they contain agricultural terraces built from rounded boulders. These are found throughout the islands. On the island of Tenerife lays an even more mysterious structure, a pyramid complex made of black volcanic stone. The architectural and engineering techniques used to build these six "step" style pyramids are similar to those found in Mexico, Peru, and ancient Mesopotamia.

The main pyramid complex, including its plazas, was found to be astronomically oriented to sunset at the summer solstice (a common feature of other sacred structures in different parts of the world). Skeptics believed they were a random pile of stones, but archaeologists from the University of La Laguna and Dr. Thor Heyerdahl (of "Ra Expedition" fame), proved the structures to be of human construction. Excavation revealed that they were built systematically with blocks of stone, gravel, and earth. Carefully erected stairways on the west side of each pyramid

Geographic Location of the Canary Islands

lead up to the summit, to create a perfectly flat platform covered with gravel.

Who built them is a mystery. The earliest known inhabitants of Tenerife Island are the Guanches, now extinct as a separate race of people. They are thought to be the descendants of North African Berbers. However, based on the historical evidence concerning their culture, they did not possess the technology for that kind of construction. Following Heyerdahl's express wishes, no theory is forced on the visitors to Guimar. A sign with a simple question mark labels the exhibit.

The Canary Islands are intriguing and obviously played a role in the movement of Paleolithic peoples. As does Africa, it lacks the evidence of a base culture from which migration took place. Pushing the model further west requires a migration from the Americas, which is nonsense. Or is it? The Americas have their own mysterious and controversial past.

Chapter 11
Ancient Engineers of the Amazon

- The Roads of Bolivia
- Ancient Fisheries

Four hundred years ago, when settlers from Europe began to colonize the New World, they found a vast pristine land of jungles, forests, and rivers. The lands were savage, unexplored, and sparsely populated. The aboriginals, both tribal and totem, were without civilization. Yet amazingly, they displayed cultural, linguistic, and genetic diversity. During that time, the Bible was the primary, if not the only, source to explain the regional and ethnic differences of the world's cultures. It made no reference to the populations of the Western Hemisphere.

In 1604, a Spanish missionary named Jose de Acosta, suggested a natural land bridge had joined North America and Asia. Migrations took place, he thought, just 2,000 years before his time. Edward Brerewood, an English scholar, observed similarities between Asian Mongols and Native Americans. In 1614, he promoted a theory suggesting migration by way of the Pacific Ocean.

History has assumed the Americas have always been in a state of primeval flora until conquered by the Europeans and their mechanical innovations. This has been the favored view since Jose de Acosta proposed his theory. William Denevan, however, has an entirely different view. In 1962, he was a college student aboard a commercial flight, 700 miles east of the Andes Mountains. He noticed something peculiar in the landscape where the jungle breaks into grasslands:

I went berserk, jumping around the airplane going from window to window, leaning over passengers, trying to get some photographs of these fantastic features I've never heard about before. The whole landscape suddenly turned into platforms and ridges and long features, either canals or causeways. This was quite spectacular, and the biggest moment of my life, I knew these were not natural features.[1]

What he saw were circular fields, raised mounds of earth, square lakes, straight lines extending for hundreds of miles, and a patchwork of raised beds and canals. Denevan was convinced that what he viewed from the airliner was an ancient system of agriculture, an important discovery, and a "lost and unknown prehistoric system of farming in the Amazon that doesn't exist today."[2] With local archaeologists he explored hundreds of miles of canals and gathered relics from local farmers. This was just a fraction of the 200,000 miles of canals from Venezuela to Brazil. One relic collected was dated at 7,000 years old. These agricultural fields number in the hundreds of thousands. There's over a thousand miles of causeways and probably thousands of artificial mounds. Some of the canals connect different river systems, enabling people to move from one system to another. According to Denevan, this landscape had been massively rearranged in prehistoric times.[3]

Since then, William Denevan has gone on to make ancient agriculture of South America his life's work and is now Professor Emeritus at the University of Wisconsin in Madison. His 1992 paper, *The Pristine Myth: Landscape of the Americas in 1492*, describes the vastness of ancient earthworks in the Americas.

According to Denevan, the numbers are staggering. Five hundred thousand hectares of abandoned, raised fields survive in the San Jorge Basin of northern Colombia. At least 600,000 hectares of terracing, mostly of prehistoric origin, occur in the Peruvian Andes. Nineteen thousand hectares of visibly raised fields have been found around Tiahuanaco at Lake Titicaca. Twelve thousand hectares of raised fields existed around the Aztec capital of Tenochtitlan. With a hectare being 100 acres, these above figures total an astounding 113 million acres.[4]

Evidence of ancient agriculture is also found in North America. A complex canal system, in the Salt River Valley of Arizona, was formed to irrigate prehistoric farmland. Nearly 175 sites of Indian garden beds, up to several hundred acres each, have also been reported in Wisconsin. An eerie fact: combine this with the irrigation systems on the north coast of Peru and more land in prehistory was cultivated than today.[5]

Denevan believes that what has been documented is only a small portion, a lasting fragment of a once cultivated continent. He believes the remaining fields are less than twenty-five percent of what actually existed. Most fields were destroyed by erosion, buried under sediments, or removed in the face of urban progress.

Aboriginal Americans, like their counterparts in Europe, endured by manipulating the land. Unlike Europeans, who domesticated animals for meat, they brilliantly engineered entire ecosystems to produce an environment conducive to elk, deer, and bison. In South America, it seems they planted part of the Amazon rain forest to grow a diverse assortment of fruit, nut, and palm trees.[6]

The vastness of these earthworks encouraged Denevan to believe a great population once existed in South America (at least fifty to one hundred million) by the time Columbus reached America. There may have been more people living in the New World than the Old. When Spain and Portugal launched their invasions and made their claims, European disease brought to America by the first explorers and colonists spread throughout the continent killing ninety percent of the population.[7]

The Roads of Bolivia

Clark Erickson, Associate Professor of Anthropology at the University of Pennsylvania and Associate Curator of University Museum of Archaeology and Anthropology, has been studying the pre-Columbian earthworks of the Bolivian Amazon since 1990, mainly in the Baures region. Baures (the name of a region, a district, a town, a language, and a native ethnic group) is located along the Amazon drainage basin near Brazil in northeast Bolivia. Its ecosystem is an assorted mix of forests, savannas, vast open grasslands, extensive wetlands, several navigable rivers, and large shallow lakes. Excessive flooding occurs in this area three to five months of the year during the rainy season.[8]

Unlike many cultures of South America, the Baures did not suffer demographic collapse. So the roots of their culture reach far in to the distant past. Early Jesuit missionaries discovered the Baures were successful farmers of cacao and cotton. They lived in numerous, large villages protected by moats and palisades. Fourteen separate "moated" villages on forested islands were mapped in 1995 and 1996 near Baures and Bella Vista, although they probably did not hold water except during the monsoons. The missionaries considered them more civilized than any of the other peoples they met.[9]

Primary interests of Erickson's research are the roadways stretching across the land in an almost perfectly linear fashion. These roads are easily seen from the air, and larger primary routes can be seen from orbit 470 miles above earth. They appear as dark straight lines covered by small trees against the pastel-green grasses of the savanna.

The roads, which are raised causeways of earth, connected settlements on forest islands in the savannas to larger forested villages next to rivers. Typically, a raised road exists between two canals and is made of the excavated earth that produced the canals,[10] thus creating a two-lane water-street with a sidewalk in the middle. East of the town of Baures, between the San Joaquin and the San Martin Rivers, is the densest concentration of earthworks. Called the *Baures Hydraulic Complex*, it contains thousands of linear kilometers of causeways and canals.[11]

Erickson's method of research is unique and combines old techniques, like the use of aerial photographs, with more sophisticated techniques, such as remote sensing. They include ground survey, surface collections, topographic mapping, posthole coring transects across sites and earthworks, small-scale excavations of features, and recording artifacts from private collections in the region. He uses the term "landscape archeology" to describe his work.

Radiocarbon dating, from samples throughout the Amazon, suggests that these roads were pre-Hispanic and that they were built and used between 400 and 2,000 years ago. Although excited and confident of his early analysis, Erickson had more questions than answers. In his 2001 article in *Expedition* Magazine, *Pre-Columbian Roads of the Amazon*, Erickson asks: Who built these roads and when? Why were they built? What did they connect? And why are there so many roads? [12]

Ancient Fisheries

In his continuing efforts of landscape archeology, Erickson has determined that ancient Bolivians were highly advanced in their efforts to tame the environment. He has discovered zigzag structures; sections of raised earth four feet wide and two feet tall, that change direction every 30 to 90 feet and reach across the savanna from one forested island to another. Where these zigzag structures form a sharp angle, funnel-like openings are associated with small, circular ponds. A number of these structures put together form enclosures called *weirs*. [13]

In 1989, forty-eight linear kilometers of weirs were found in a sample area of savanna. According to Erickson they did not function as check dams or berms for flood-recessional farming, nor is there evidence of crop furrows or field platforms between the structures. It appears that these structures have no other purpose than to serve as fisheries, which also produced snails as a secondary source of food. Large numbers of *Pomacea gigas* snails have been found beside the zigzag structures. [14] Trees, shrubs, and other plant life that grew around these weirs attracted game and other wildlife. The palm *Mauritia flexuosa*, grew voraciously and produced up to 5,000 pieces of fruit a year. Other plants served as raw materials for basketry, mats, hammocks, bowstrings, and thatch.

According to Erickson, the complex of the fish weirs and ponds was a form of intensive aquaculture. They used simple, but elegant, technology to transform the landscape into aquatic farms covering 500 square kilometers. In other words, the Baure people domesticated the landscape instead of domesticating animals. It was sufficiently productive to support a large population in a marginal environment. [15]

Historical ecologists believe the current South American environment is not a product of undisturbed nature, but of man's intervention and ingenuity. Researchers Erickson, Stahl, Piperno, Roosevelt, and Denevan all believe that aboriginal Americans have been manipulating the natural environment to serve their needs for as long ago as 12,000 years [16] corresponding to the end of the ice age. Of course this implies that their ascendants were living there well before then. Such complicated endeavors from primitive people, so long ago, appears contrary to the accepted beliefs of American prehistory. The Americas are perhaps more mysterious than any other continent.

Chapter 12
American Paleolithic

- Discovering the Folsom Culture
- Developing the Clovis Paradigm
- The Sandia Culture
- Sandia Cave Confusion

A catastrophic event occurred 12,500 years ago to cause the extinction of nearly all the large animals in northern latitudes. During this mass extinction, natural waterways on the floodplains of North America experienced a vast reduction in size. Springs dried up, regional water tables shrunk, and many older streams in the Southwest disappeared altogether. A wetter climate resumed 1,000 years later, but rivers and their associated tributaries retained a narrower girth. As a result, sand and gravel deposits from the previous climatic era were buried under an accumulation of new sediments. This created conditions ideal for the preservation of evidence for this mass extinction and a convincing chronological record of events. There was, and is, a clear division within the layers of soil between two epochs; the ice age and post ice age (Pleistocene and Holocene).

The bones of common large mammals (especially horses, camels, and mammoths) do not occur above this abrupt stratigraphic separator. The evidence of man becomes more distinct, perhaps resulting because of fewer water holes; a hunter's advantage.

During this new and warmer climatic era, human populations expanded rapidly. Science generally accepts three prehistoric migrations into the New World across the Bering Straits; over land, glacier, or by sea. The first group of people, the *Amerinds*, migrated 11,500 years ago; the second group, the *Nadenes*, 1,000 years later and the final migration, between 3,000 to 5,000 years ago by the *Aleut-Eskimos* of Alaska.

In 1935, Nels Nelson, of the American Museum of Natural History, discovered evidence of small blade technology during the ice age in both Alaska and Siberia. For him and the scientific community this proved without a doubt that large populations crossed Beringia into the Alaskan territory.

Through the influence of textbooks and television documentaries, especially over the past thirty years, it has become generally accepted that mankind first arrived in the Americas 12,000 years ago through an ice-free corridor in what is now Canada (between the Cordilleran and Laurentide glaciers). He descended into the heart of the North American continent, east to the Atlantic coast and south to the tip of South America. Their descendents, it is believed, became the American Indians of the Western Hemisphere.

Discovering the Folsom Culture

The foundation for this Siberia-to-Alaska model began in 1926, when fluted projectile points (dating to 8,000 BC) were found near Folsom, New Mexico. On a spring afternoon, George McJunkin was riding in Dead Horse Gulch, eight miles west of Folsom, when he noticed something white glistening in the sun. On further inspection, he discovered gleaming white bones protruding from the sandy soil. McJunkin told his friend, Carl Schwachheim (a collector), who in turn contacted the curator of Denver's Museum of Natural History, J.D. Figgins. He determined the bones were from extinct animals, a giant bison and deer.

Embedded next to a bison rib was a projectile point of superior quality. Nothing had ever before been found like it. This unique style became known was as *Folsom*.[1] Barnum Brown, archeologist for the American Museum of Natural History, began a three-year excavation at Folsom that produced the remains of fifty extinct bison and sixteen arrowheads of this distinctive type.

In 1927, nationally known experts were invited to visit Dr. Figgins at Folsom. Archeologists Frank Roberts Jr., Barnum Brown, and Alfred Kidder viewed, *in situ* (lying exactly where they had been found), more fluted spear points next to the bones of an extinct species of bison. They reported the discovery at the annual meeting of the American Anthropological Association.

A consensus regarding the authenticity of the Folsom site was reached and the beginning of New World prehistory was pushed back many thousands of years. The scientific community had corroborated the existence of a Paleo-Indian culture which produced a fluted, projectile-point. Human occupation in the New World was determined to be 10,000 years old. A landslide of archaeological investigations and discoveries spanned the next decade.

In 1929, at a Geological Society meeting, Barnum Brown's spear-points were verified as Folsom points.[2] Soon after this, Folsom spear-points were identified across the continent (including those that were previously excavated and unidentified). Five years earlier, on land owned by William Lindenmeier near Fort Collins, Colorado, years of erosion revealed the remnants of an ice age campsite. Judge Coffin and his son (a geologist from Colorado State College) collected 83 points now known to be of Folsom origin.

On June 9, 1934, *Literary Digest* reprinted a Smithsonian announcement from the U.S. National Museum. These newly identified and distinctive Folsom points had also been found in two collections gathered from Virginian sites the previous May. This provoked a flood of letters, and spurred the editors to seek clarification from the Bureau of Ethnology. Archaeologist Frank Roberts, who directed follow-up excavation at Folsom, printed his clarification on July 28. He continued to work at the Lindenmeier site in Colorado through 1940.

Meanwhile, excavation at Folsom, New Mexico grew to more than 19,300 square feet (including 23 test pits) and at places to a depth of 17 feet. Although no mammoth remains were found, nearly 20,000 bones were recovered, mostly bison. The number of projectile points discovered totaled 645. Fifty-nine were whole and fluted (a few fluted on only one side), 79 whole or fragmentary non-fluted, and 323 unfinished (preforms). Twenty fluted points were found on the surface as well.

Roberts issued a report explaining his realization of Folsom ancestry in the Old World.[3] He tried to link Folsom pressure-flaking techniques to European (Solutrean) origin. He believed migrations, originating in Central Asia, reached America as soon, if not sooner, than the more western areas of Europe.[4] However, Roberts died in February of 1966 before finishing his final report. The Smithsonian reassigned it to a doctoral student named Edwin Wilmsen.[5]

Picking up on Roberts' hunch of Solutrean origin, Wilmsen measured 111 unmodified flakes from Aurignacian and Solutrean levels at Laugerie-Haute. His measurements confirmed negligible differences from points found at the Lindenmeier site, inferring that identical methods of production were used. Yet he concluded that classic European types in America were best considered accidents.[6] Unfortunately, during their excavations, Roberts and Cotter overlooked fire spots, hearths, and charcoal, whose future value was then not realized. Most of the carbon samples taken from upper levels revealed dates that were inconsistent with ice age plant and animals. In the final analysis, Wilmsen supported 9,250 BC as the soundest date.[7]

Developing the Clovis Paradigm

Six years after the discovery of Folsom points, a different style of point was found among the skeletal remains of a mammoth near Clovis, New Mexico. These Clovis points were fluted, larger, longer, and clearly designed to hunt mammoth and mastodon. They were evidence of a hunting lifestyle distinct from the bison-hunting Folsom people. Their characteristics included finely worked edges and a central groove along both faces (called a flute) that allowed easy attachment to a wooden shaft. The typical blade measures ten inches long by four inches in width and was produced by a combination of percussion and pressure flaking. Smaller and fluted from base to tip, Folsom points were clearly an improvement of Clovis point technology.

More discoveries at Dent, Colorado in 1932, and Blackwater Draw, New Mexico in 1933 confirmed the existence of this Folsom forerunner.

As is the tradition, this culture and blade technology became known as "Clovis" for the first find of its kind.

At Sanders' Gravel Pit, the remnants of a butchering station was unearthed next to a water hole. Evidence indicates that it was used as an ambush site for ice age hunters. The site was used intermittently for thousands of years, beginning with people of the Clovis culture and lasting well into historical times.

Folsom points made from bluish stone were found on the surface. Mammoth bones were later unearthed three feet down, with a Clovis point beneath one of the animal's vertebra. Another mammoth was found alongside flakes from crafting tools. An un-grooved point and two cylindrical bones, beveled at both ends were also found. Although referred to as Folsom-like, they were clearly from Clovis technology. Miners found four more Folsom points, probably used for bison hunting, closer to the surface. A "Yuma" point, like those from the Clovis Lake bed laid on a surface 'dump site'. Bones, all within a five-foot radius of the early Clovis find, included mammoth, extinct bison, deer and rodent, as well as turtle (carapace) fragments. Various sizes of horse bones were also found, but only in the deeper layers. Numerous blades, with an absence of stone flakes or chips, and animal debris, from butchering and skinning, confirm it was a site for field dressing animals. The area was so productive, excavation continued from the 1930s until 1966 under various auspices.

In 1932, three Clovis points, along side mammoth bones were also discovered on the northeast plains of Colorado near the town of Dent. A railroad foreman, Frank Garner spotted large bones exposed by a recent flood in an area near the South Plate River. The geology of the formation suggests the animal carcasses were deposited there before the Wisconsin glacial maximum (16,000-13,000 BC). An excavated mammoth jawbone was carbon-dated to 9,250 BC.[9]

By 1935, Clovis points were identified across the continent from Nova Scotia to South America. In 1938, Junius Bird excavated points with a fishtail-like base at Fell's Cave, Argentina. They were found with extinct species of horse and sloth. Similar

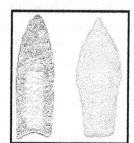

Fluted (left) and Non-Fluted Spear Points

points were also found in Canada, Ecuador, and Central America, indicating a widespread early presence in the Americas. Over following decades, the idea that Clovis culture represented the first peoples of America began to gain general acceptance.

In February of 1962, gravel quarrying resumed at Blackwater Draw in New Mexico. A cache of seventeen punched blades, some unfinished, were soon discovered. Later, archaeologist F.E. Green of Texas Tech University discovered mammoth bones eroding out of gray sand near the original excavation. He collected nine Clovis artifacts dating to the end of the ice age (between 11,000 and 9000 BC). According to Green, they were flaked by indirect percussion to curve in a prismatic cross section, just like Clovis points. Green found more mammoth bones in the gray sand above the gravel bedrock and more Folsom points with miscellaneous artifacts, but no more Clovis points. Of all points found at Blackwater Draw, only two were true Clovis points.[10]

Green also directed the El Llano excavation at Portales, New Mexico. There he recovered four mammoth skeletons and part of a fifth, as well as 166 Clovis artifacts that included thirty-nine scrapers and eight projectile points. James Warnica reported the results as a possible connection with cultures in Europe or Asia. He referenced Aleksei Okladnikov's volumes (1955, 1961) on Siberia,[11] and envisioned an Asian migration.

C. Vance Haynes dated charcoal from the El Llano bone-bed to 9220 BC. Clovis artifacts found *in situ*, at six other high-plains sites averaged 9400 BC. These were confirmed by overlying sediments dating to 8460 BC and earlier underlying sediments at 9650 BC.[12] He announced in *Science* magazine that no Clovis points could predate 10,050 BC. But from the Aubrey site near Lewisville, Texas, Clovis dates registered older than expected at 11,450 BC.[13]

Haynes claimed that Blackwater sand and clay predated Clovis artifacts and concluded they were intrusive.[14] With help from Jeffrey Sanders, Dennis Stanford, and George Agogino, he later elaborated on the intrusion with the example of a mammoth tusk Green had discovered in November of 1963 in the north bank of the stream. It was dated as contemporary with Clovis artifacts. Carbonized plant remains, that Haynes collected during August of 1963 (from the upper and lower level of Unit C in the north bank), dated to 9680 and 9040 BC.

Unit C sand somehow intruded on Unit B pre-Clovis clay. Lumates from decayed plants suggested the same and were dated to 10,380, 10,840, and 9450 BC, from the bottom up. He took great pains to prove that the blue layer of clay was earlier than the sand and, with conservative colleagues, kept trying to keep Clovis from exceeding 9,550 BC. Interestingly, peck patterns made from a tool to reduce the tusk were formed using the same techniques as those from ice age cultures of eastern Europe.[15]

The Sandia Culture

In 1927 during a treasure hunt, Boy Scouts from Albuquerque Troop 13 cleared stones blocking the entrance to Sandia Cave. However, once inside caliche concretion prevented access to the larger areas of the cave. Eight years later, cave explorer Kenneth Davis managed to break through and recovered the claw from an extinct giant ground sloth, and other remains from ice age animals. Davis forwarded the artifacts to Wesley Bliss, a University of New Mexico graduate assistant in anthropology. This spurred Frank Cummins Hibben, University Museum Curator, to excavate Sandia Cave. Wesley Bliss excavated the neighboring Davis Cave. By 1936, the Davis cave proved to be sterile, so Bliss and his team joined the Sandia project.

Hibben directed the Sandia Cave excavation from February to June of 1936.[16] Hampered by concretions, caliche, and silicon dust from quartz-based ocher, the work proved difficult. From June to October they were rained out. On February 1, 1937, Bliss and Hibben completed a joint report. Oddly that summer, Bliss apparently moved to Canada and left no forwarding address.[17] Proofs he had sent to Albuquerque, reporting the work from his solo months never reached their destination. However, his manuscript was published in *American Antiquity*, taking both Bliss (then at the University of Pennsylvania) and Hibben by surprise. The editor of *American Antiquity* explained that Bliss' manuscript lay for more than a year in his files before publication.[18]

Hibben and Brand, enraged at being pre-empted by a subordinate no longer associated with UNM, attacked him and his article. Bliss focused on proving that rodents had disturbed the soil below the stalagmite layer through a natural cleft in the cave's front portion. He assured Hibben he would not argue his corrective findings.[19] Hibben's preliminary report stated that the tunnel-like cave did not allow abreast diggers.[20] Bliss said the diameter averaged sixteen feet, Hibben said ten. Nonetheless, excavation advanced from both ends.[21] They managed seven meters in front and five in back during the first season.

Upon reaching the lowest level they found four, two-and-a-half inch diameter limestone river pebbles arranged evenly around a hearth of native limestone. Next to one of the pebbles was a projectile point made from gray chert (which does not occur naturally in the Sandia Mountains). They were "practically on the virgin floor," reported Bliss, during whose watch the hearth and point were discovered.[22]

The hearth lay thirteen meters from the cave's front, measuring almost eighteen inches in diameter and nearly a foot deep. It was littered with charcoal lenses and fine ash from oak and other wood. The jawbone of a camel was found beside it, but was not mentioned in his 1941 final report. Next to another fireplace (at meter 15), Hibben found a second point that was side-notched at the base and similar to the Solutrean style found in Europe.[23] Hibben unconventionally, though correctly, referred to these projectiles as javelin points. The points, which were triangular in shape with a convex base, were entirely napped. They were to become known as 'Sandia points.' Hibben claimed to have identified a Clovis precursor and direct ancestor.

With a volunteer workforce, he resumed excavation in 1938. A grant from the American Philosophical Society in 1940 enabled the purchase of a motorized blower, which greatly improved the speed of excavation. By screening loads at the mouth of the cave during daylight hours, numerous artifacts were discovered. Looser soil of the Sandia layer made meter locations of Sandia finds more definite. Residents of that layer were the cave's first, and were found on bedrock below basal clay two inches thick.

Sandia Cave Confusion

Sandia Cave is the largest of many caves in the Sandia Mountains, twenty miles northeast of Albuquerque. It is located on the slope of a mountain nearly 200 feet above the Las Huertas Canyon floor. Situated on a steep incline, it is accessible only by using a ladder from a ledge eleven feet below its entrance. Inside the cave, human occupation existed intermittently at all depths though primarily toward the entrance. The Sandia people used only the first forty-five feet of the cave, but the succeeding Folsom people used over 300 feet. The top layer of soil consisted of dust, bat guano, rat dung, and Pueblo Indian debris. Below the topsoil is a layer of caliche crust eleven inches thick that sealed a 20-inch Folsom layer, which was littered with stone and bone fragments. Two complete Folsom points, three broken, three non-fluted, a spatula carved from ivory, gravers, scrapers, and knives were found in the Folsom layer. All of these items suggest a very long period of occupation for the Folsom culture. Three Clovis-like points were also found.[24]

The Sandia Layer

Beneath the Folsom layer was a finely laminated, sterile layer of yellow ocher averaging nine inches thick. Below it was a thirteen-inch Sandia layer. Herbert Krieger called Sandia Cave "an enigma since the first reports." He questioned Hibben's separate Sandia layer and failure to distinguish the strata of artifact recovery.[25] Hibben claims he clearly delineated the yellow-ochre layer that sealed the Sandia from the Folsom layer. It yielded nineteen whole and broken Sandia points.

The earlier Type-1 Sandia points were larger and less finely crafted than the later and longer Type-2 points. They also displayed typical Solutrean shouldered asymmetry (pointed at both ends) rather than having a Clovis-like concave base. Of all the points that were found, only one was fluted and thinned at the base. Type-2 points were recovered from the higher (later) Sandia level and were very long, willow-leaf shaped, and side-notched. A white Type-2 specimen with fluting was discovered at the *Lucy Site,* south of Lucy, New Mexico in the Estancia Valley (central New Mexico), where Hibben excavated during the summer of 1954.

Some of the points from Sandia Cave proved hard to classify as one or the other and were a mixture from two different Sandia occupations. Two unique Sandia points were chipped from andesite, others from various flints, chalcedonies, and chert, including a brown variety not known to exist in the immediate region. Still others were identified from the Texas Panhandle. Obsidian was identified from the Jemez Mountains forty-five miles north of Albuquerque. Chalcedony, typically translucent and multicolored, was from the Pedernal Mountains area, sixty-five miles southeast of Albuquerque. Specimens from the Folsom layer were typically quite different; made from chert concretions jutting from the cave wall.

Three snub-nosed scrapers, made from Pedernal chalcedony, matched those from early levels of the Tierra del Fuego caves in South America. Junius and Margaret Bird excavated two caves in the Rio Chico Valley south of the Argentine border. They discovered three grooved limestone balls weighing two ounces each, similar to those found at Sandia Cave. In the Rio Chico caves, these balls were discovered just above the earliest level when residents used large stem-less triangular points before the arrowhead stage.[26] Balls, such as these, were also discovered at the mastodon butchering site of Monte Verde in Southern Chile, as well as Archaic Poverty Point, in Louisiana.

Animal Bones

Sandia-level bones included mammoth, mastodon (a rare instance of both elephant genera in the same location), horse, bison, and camel. The Folsom-layer horse was a different species (possibly *occidentalis*). The bison was a species slightly smaller than was found with Folsom points. Ground sloth, wolf, and other unidentifiable remains were also found. Two bones in Sandia Cave were worked to resemble a stone Sandia point; the better preserved one was carved from a camel's long bone. Hibben also found a projectile shaft made from ivory.

The caliche layer above the Sandia level contained bones of wood rat, bat, mountain sheep, elk, mule deer, porcupine, bear, and sloth (surprising in the post-ice age era). Charles Hunt decided the sloth bones belonged in the stalagmite layer below, which man or rodents had transferred up.[27] The poor preservation of bone fragments led Dominique Stevens and George Agogino of Eastern New Mexico University to question Hibben's identification of other genera and species, particularly a mammoth in the Folsom layer.[28] In the stratum, Hibben recognized a series of wet-dry layers referring to different geologic ages from which he used to date artifacts. (Carbon dating was not discovered until 1946 by chemist Willard F. Libby.)

Geologic Dating

Kirk Bryan of Harvard University correlated the yellow ocher layer with the rain-soaked age of the Wisconsin glacial maximum, which during that time made the cave untenable. Therefore, the Sandia stratum was either early or pre-Wisconsin (earlier than 23,000 BC), with Folsom following much later during the ice age.[29] A return of heavy rains again flooded the cave, forced Folsom people out, and created the caliche layer over their living-floor.

Hugo Gross of Bamberg, Germany approved Bryan's geology of Sandia Cave. The yellow ocher layer matched European cave loam, collected up to twenty-two feet thick and intercalated between frost-formed lower breccia (rock composed of sharp-angled fragments embedded in a fine-grained pattern). It also contained Mousterian (Neanderthal) artifacts and Upper Paleolithic breccia, similar to the Göttweig loam. Both were formed during the long Würm I and II temperate periods dating to 40,000 and 26,000 BC. The 16,000-year old American equivalent separated the early Wisconsin from main Wisconsin ice age periods, which were contemporary with the European Altwürm and Hauptwürm periods.[30]

Carbon-Dating Confusion

In 1948, Hibben sent two charcoal-hearth specimens, that Bryan had collected (the only ones saved), to Libby at the University of Chicago for carbon dating. Even though the samples were inadequate for solid-carbon measurement of the time, Libby tested them and allegedly produced dates of 15,000 and 18,000 BC. According to Hibben, the samples geologically correlated a much higher date range. Fearing a carbon-dating error, he emphatically discouraged publication. (Frederick Johnson of the Peabody Foundation in Andover, Massachusetts found no record of such dating at Chicago or any other lab.)[31] Hibben replied he had no idea where or how Bryan (who died August 22, 1950) had acquired the dates.[32] Hibben further stated the dates he had were given in his lecture *Early Man in North America* on July 17, 1951 at Erlangen University, where he used 17,000 BC for the Sandia and 9000 BC for the Folsom layer. Both were taken from Bryan's geological analysis.[33] Bryan, however, dated the Sandia level before, and the Folsom just after, 23,000 BC.[34]

Meanwhile in 1952, H.R. Crane from the University of Michigan's Randall Lab carbon-dated two ivory samples that Hibben had taken from two separate tusks found in the Sandia level. Both exceeded 20,000 years old.[35] In 1954, Hibben supplied him with a third ivory sample. Bowing to convention, however, Crane decided that all three ivory samples were dated to 9000 BC, safely 500 years within the Clovis boundary (although he admitted 18,000 BC was more appropriate). Hibben believed they were at least 5,000 years older.[36] Caliche located *above* (and therefore younger) the hard gray Sandia layer at Lucy dated 12,350 BC.[37]

Sandia Points Everywhere

Both 1 and 2 Type Sandia points, fluted and non-fluted, occurred at the Lucy site with bone artifacts like those Hibben had found in Sandia Cave. William Roosa thought that both Sandia types and the single Clovis point at Lucy were used in killing and cutting a single Proboscidean (mammal of the elephant family). Two other Type-1 Sandia points were hafted as knives.[38]

Once Sandia points were identifiable they turned up over an alarmingly wide area in existing collections. In 1941, Hibben believed that Type-1 points occurred sporadically throughout the Mississippi Valley to the east coast, while Type-2 was restricted to southeast New Mexico and bordering portions of Texas.[39] By the end of 1945, he could count only thirty-eight reasonably certain Sandia points from southeast New Mexico and bordering West Texas, central Oklahoma, southwest Missouri, southern Iowa, and eastern Colorado.

Marie Wormington noted three Sandia points that she regarded as genuine, and felt they should be added to Hibben's collection of thirty-eight. One was from eastern Alberta, found by Russell Johnston. The other was from northeast Alabama, found by Harold Klein in 1953. The third Sandia point was found on the surface by Keith Dixon (reported in 1953) at Long Valley, Mono County, California near the shore of an ancient lake.[40] There were also three Type-1 points that New York State archaeologist, William Ritchie found at the Reagan Site in Vermont (in association with fluted blades), and four from Roosa found in 1960 at

Gowanla Creek in northwest New York, with ailerons like those from the Parpallo Cave in Southeast Spain.[41] It appeared that Hibben's 1941 estimate of Type-1 point distribution might be correct after all.

According to Hibben, Dr. L.S. Cressman found a large Type-1 point in Oregon under very suggestive circumstances. Exactly what Hibben meant by this is unclear. He discounted it, claiming it was not authentic because of uncertain origin. Fourteen of his specimens were found with the bones of extinct animals. Others were found at great depths suggesting great antiquity. He referred to the known distribution of Sandia points as scanty, spotty, and unconcentrated,[42] which, of course, would be expected of a less numerous pre-Clovis culture.

Making Connections

Since 5,000 years separated European Solutrean from American Clovis, Lawrence Guy Straus insisted that a Solutrean connection was weak. He was reacting to a remark of Dennis Stanford of the Smithsonian that Solutrean and Clovis were not so far apart. Frédéric Sellet estimated a 6,000 to 7,000 year difference from Straus' 1990 carbon dates.[43] Whatever the interval, Bruce Bradley of Cortez, Colorado found a perfect match of a Laugerie-Haute Solutrean flake with a Clovis flake from Blackwater Draw.[44]

Jack Hoffman from the University of Kansas viewed Clovis weapons as 'too good' and their makers 'too numerous.' They spread too quickly over too much of the hemisphere to have been pioneers. Surely they had learned their point crafting techniques from existing people.[45] Because Clovis points show aesthetic care beyond utility, Stuart Fiedel inferred their culture was rather flamboyant.[46]

Hibben believed that Sandia projectile points were a transitional stage between Solutrean and Clovis, thereby identifying the Clovis ancestral homeland as Iberia and European. Under academic review, however, Hibben's Sandia points failed to convince the scientific community.

Confusing? Yes, but it illustrates the various aspects and difficulties of the scientists and their theories as the evidence was first discovered and debated. It would not be the last controversial site displaying evidence of ice age occupation in the Americas. Events surrounding the discovery and investigation of a Clovis forerunner referred to as "Sandia Cave Confusion," would set a tone of high skepticism of Pre-Clovis claims, a skepticism that has lasted throughout the twentieth century. The idea that Clovis culture represented the first peoples of America emerged into a paradigm known as "Clovis First." Academic practices that upheld this theory, in association with all levels of education, developed it into the consistency of a brick wall.

Chapter 13
Breaking the Clovis Barrier

- Kennewick Man
- Monte Verde, Chile
- Cactus Hill, Virginia
- Allendale County, South Carolina
- Other Pre-Clovis Sites

The first crack in the "Clovis First" wall appeared in the Yukon Territory of Canada in 1976. A fishing expedition discovered triplet caves in the foothills of the Ogilvie Mountains, fifty miles southwest of the Vuntut Gwichin village of Old Crow. All three caves, known as the Bluefish Caves, were more suitably described as cavities. They contained a vast amount of well-preserved animal remains from horse, caribou, sheep, bison, moose, elk, mammoth, saiga, muskox, bear, wolf, and lion. Cultural remains in the first two caves consisted of bone tools, micro-flakes from crafting tools, and small cobbles which were found near the bedrock. Tools and other 'shaped' objects were found at the entrance and interior: cores, micro-blades, angle burins, burin balls, and notches. High quality chert (usually blue, occasionally speckled, and rarely black) was used to create these tools were considered exotic to the region. Their source is still unknown.

Animal remains, found in all three caves, provided undeniable evidence of human habitation; cut marks, scrape marks, chopping marks, and striations on bones from the butchering of the animals. Carbon dating of a horse femur from cave #1 revealed a date of 12,900 years old, a saiga

from cave #3 to 13,400, and a mammoth shoulder in cave #2 to 15,500.[1] Found just outside cave #2, in the lower level of the excavation, was a bone tool (presumably a flesher) dated to 24,820 years old. It was split lengthwise from a caribou tibia, exhibited a planed facet, and was highly polished along the edge of the distal break, probably due to use. It was an extraordinary find. A bone flake and its parent core from a mammoth bone, also produced similar results.[2] The results of the Bluefish discoveries, as Jacques Cinq-Mars explains, were far-reaching into the knowledge of prehistoric migrations:

> This evident relationship between the in situ Bluefish data and that from the secondary deposits of the Old Crow Basin clearly indicates that our region, namely the Porcupine River Basin and the adjacent uplands, was the scene of a long series of cultural manifestations, the earliest of which, according to data from the Old Crow basin, seems to have occurred around 40,000 BP [before present]

(Morlan, et al. 1990). In other words, even though examples have not yet been uncovered in Alaska and Siberia, it appears that the first detectable signs of a human presence in Beringia date back to the Wisconsinan interstadial.[3]

Undeniably, at least in the Alaskan-Yukon area, man had been living in America for a very long time, as long ago as 40,000 years and well before the appearance of Clovis culture.

Kennewick Man

A second blow to the Clovis paradigm came on July 28, 1996, when two men found a human skull in the Columbia River at Kennewick, Washington. Police were called to investigate the alleged crime scene, but upon viewing the skull, the county coroner decided to call archeologist James C. Chatters, a forensic archeologist from the University of Washington and the founder of *Applied Paleoscience*. During the next month, Chatters recovered many of the wave-scattered bones to assemble a nearly complete skeleton, missing only the sternum and a few small bones of the hands and feet.

Kennewick Man, as the skeleton became known, was initially believed by Chatters to be of recent origin because of Caucasian traits of the skull, possibly a European settler from the nineteenth century. The skull was curiously oblong (dolichocranic) rather than round (brachycranic). It had a narrow face, prognathous rather than broad and flat. The cheekbones receded slightly and lacked an inferior zygomatic projection. Kennewick Man's eye sockets were long, broad and round orbits, and his mandible was v-shaped with a pronounced deep chin.[4]

Later, Chatters questioned recent origin when he detected a gray object within the partially healed right hip of the skeleton. CT scans revealed the base of a leaf-shaped, serrated projectile point, typical of Southern Plateau assemblages common during an age lasting from 8,500 to 4,500 years ago.[5] Tests were quickly performed in an attempt to date the skeleton:

A fragment of the fifth left metacarpal analyzed by AMS has an isotopically corrected age of 8410 +/- 60 B.P. (UCR

3476) (ca 7300 to 7600 B.C.). Amino acids and stable isotopes indicate heavy dependence on anadromous fish. DNA was intact, but two partially completed extractions were inconclusive.[6]

What was a white man doing in northwest America almost 9,000 years ago? Several Columbia River Tribes[7] of the area claimed he was Indian and requested joint custody of the remains. The Army Core of Engineers, owners of the land Kennewick Man was discovered on, requested that the National Park Service study the situation in light of the Native American Graves Protection and Repatriation Act and make a recommendation. After their analysis, they ordered release of the remains to the tribes. Eight prominent archeologists[8] filed suit claiming the skeleton was too old to be an ancestor of any modern day Native American Indian, but to no avail. Before reburial, several religious groups were allowed to hold memorial services in the bones' presence. Among them were representatives of the Columbia River Tribes and members from a California group known as the Asatru Folk Assembly, a European pagan religion.

Other sites have produced similar results: Browns Valley, Minnesota 9,300 years old; Spirit Cave, Nevada 9,200; Gordon Creek, Colorado 9,700; and Wilson-Leonard, Texas, 9,500-10,000 years old.[9] This handful of human skeletons show some regional variation. But as a group, their skulls are quite different from the broad faces, prominent cheekbones, and round cranial vaults characterized by modern Native American Indians. These people had long and narrow cranial vaults with short, relatively gracile faces. According to the Smithsonian Institution, "Physical anthropologists see a greater similarity in these crania to certain Old World populations such as Polynesians, Europeans, and the Ainu of Japan."[10]

Chatters believes the Kennewick discovery, and others of like kind, may require an altering of theories about how the Americas were peopled. Kennewick Man, he believes, must have belonged to a different human strain than present-day Native American Indians. His book, Ancient Encounters – Kennewick Man and the First Americans, published by Simon and Schuster in 2001, relates his experiences.

Monte Verde, Chile

Between 1977 and 1985, Tom Dillehay of the University of Kentucky excavated the remains of an ancient campsite at Monte Verde, thirty-one miles inland from the Pacific Ocean off the southern coast of Chile. In 1997, a team of researchers led by University of Arizona geochronologist, C. Vance Haynes, confirmed that as far as they are concerned, it was the oldest site in the New World. This forged a new pattern in American archaeology. Michael Waters and Stuart Fiedel, however, were claimed there were control problems in the excavation. Nevertheless, Monte Verde has been accepted as Pre-Clovis, officially 14,500 years old.

In 1997, Dillehay discovered another site[11] several miles upstream from the original Monte Verde excavation (called Monte Verde II). It promises even older remains. Preliminary excavations deep in a sand layer, exposed primitive stone tools, bits of charcoal, and lenses of clay; possibly the remains of a hearth. They were vestiges of life from an unknown ice age peoples. Geologist Dr. Mario Pino from the Southern University of Chile in Valdivia, is confident that sediment layers where the artifacts were found are 33,000 years old. He claims there is no doubt about it[12] because of the geological position of the soil stratum itself.[13] So far, carbon-14 dating has corroborated his beliefs. A piece of charcoal within the stratum produced a date of 33,370 years old.

Southern Methodist University archeologist, David Meltzer supports Dillehay's view; "But now we realize we don't really know when the human entry time was [in America]," Meltzer said in a New York Times interview. The older layer is "really intriguing," he said, "but we can't conclude anything about it until we have a better sense of what's there."[14] The work on Monte Verde II is just beginning.

Cactus Hill, Virginia

Forty-five miles south of Richmond, Virginia, along the banks of the Nottoway River, archeologists Joseph and Lynn McAvoy identified remnants of human occupation in two sediment layers in a windblown dune called *Cactus Hill*. Excavation of the hill during 1993 produced Clovis spear points found in the upper layer of sediment, with stone points and other artifacts in the lower layer. Carbon-14 dating revealed ages of 10,920 and 15,070 years old for the upper and lower layers. Charcoal from the deepest part of the lower layer revealed a date of 19,700 years old, but has yet to be proven it is of human origin.[15]

American archeologists are always skeptical when artifacts this old are found, but McAvoy seems confident. A procedure for estimating last exposure to sunlight (called optically stimulated luminescence) confirms the radiocarbon dates. According to tests performed at the Virginia Polytechnic Institute and State University in Blacksburg, the soil from which the artifacts were recovered is undisturbed, evident by high concentrations of microscopic plant remains.[16]

After years of work, in April of 2000, the Director of the site, Joseph McAvoy presented a series of papers to fellow scientists at the annual Society for American Archaeology conference in Philadelphia. Three pre-Clovis dates were among the presentation: 15,070, 16,670, and 16,940 years old.[17] Interestingly, the pre-Clovis stone points were said to be similar to western European specimens of the same period. Dennis Stanford of the Smithsonian Institute believes it is possible ancient Europeans may be responsible.[18]

Allendale County, South Carolina

In the early 1980s, David Topper led Al Goodyear to a chert quarry in the central Savannah River Valley of Allendale County, South Carolina. For many years, Goodyear had excavated the area but stopped at the 12,000 year-old Clovis layer under the assumption of finding little else. However, with the news of the Monte Verde finds in South America, Goodyear decided to dig a little deeper. In May of 1998, his volunteer force excavated a small square past the Clovis layer. Twelve inches in, they found what are presumed to be small stone flakes and flaked tools, as well as several rocks apparently piled together by human hands. In somewhat disbelief, they excavated two more small areas and found similar evidence.[19]

Most items recovered were small burin-like tools of a simpler technology and lacked bifacial evidence, a common characteristic of Clovis tools. Several stone hammers were also found as were weathered cobbles from a nearby hillside, much different from the quartz and chert used by the Clovis culture. Debris from local cobbles in varying sizes was also discovered, apparently smashed for the chert inside. Even the hammer-stones they used were not of the large size found today in the Savannah River. It seems they used whatever they found on the hillside, and what was found did not look like Clovis tools.

Since acidic sands within the soil destroyed most of the organic material, Goodyear sent samples to be dated by optically stimulated luminescence. Results from the archaic level revealed dates of 7,700 years old and toward the bottom, 13,000 to 14,000 years old, just as they were supposed to. Carbon-14 testing, in two sediment samples taken from under the terrace produced results of 23,000 years old. Although research is not complete at Topper, it seems clear to Goodyear that the site is very old, with artifacts existing below the 16,000-year-old layer.[20]

Other Pre-Clovis Sites

Over the years, other Pre-Clovis sites have been proposed and discounted. In 1950, George Carter claimed to have discovered evidence of a hearth eroding from the sea cliffs near San Diego, California. In Tuli Springs, Nevada in 1955, dates as early as 27,000 years old were suggested only to crumble under further inspection. Scott McNeish, in Pikimachay, Peru produced dates of 70,000 years old and more recently in Pindejo Cave, New Mexico with dates of 27,000 years old. During the 1970s, Louis Leakey and Dee Simpson's simple stone tools found at Calico Hills, California were claimed to be 200,000 years old, but could not gain academic approval. Leakey suggested he uncovered a tool complex similar to early human industries discovered in Africa. The Laguna Beach skull and Santa Rosa Island site have also been denied as Pre-Clovis. Although many of these sites could be Pre-Clovis, they share drawbacks that make them inappropriate for scientific acceptance. The list goes on.

During the dynasty of the 'Clovis First' paradigm it was at least unacceptable, if not outright heretical, to suggest evidence of human habitation before 10,000 BC in the Americas. But in the ruins of the "Clovis Wall," the intriguing stories of Hueyatlaco, Mexico and Pedra Furada in Brazil (ahead of their time and now more acceptable) reveal a deepening mystery in the story of mankind in the Western Hemisphere.

Niede Guidon, Fabio Parenti, Cynthia Irwin-Williams, and Virginia Steen-McIntyre, scientists we will meet in the next chapter, dared to speak the facts long before the finds at Monte Verde, Cactus Hill, and Allendale. To some, their stories may be more disturbing than they are enlightening. Yet these stories are not about the fanciful pet theories of a journalist-run-amok, nor are they the stories of scientists protecting a particular ideal. They are about archeologists who carefully excavated, examined, tested, and retested the evidence they discovered. Their work and research tell the tale of humans existing in America long before the first cultures of Cro-Magnon in Europe.

Chapter 14
Digging Deeper

- The Hueyatlaco Anomaly
- Pedra Furada
- Meadowcroft

In June of 1933, paleontologist Juan Armenta Camacho discovered a large mammoth bone protruding from an eroding bank of a stream in the Aleseca Arroyo, two miles south of Puebla, Mexico. The bone contained an embedded spear-point knapped from flint. During the next 30 years, he discovered more than a hundred partial skeletons of mastodons and mammoths and bones as well as extinct camel, horse, and antelope. Many of the bones had been sharpened for use as tools, broken for marrow, or engraved. One mastodon bone was engraved in Magdalenian (European) style representing a large feline leaping on a mastodon.[1]

Despite government confiscation of his fossil collection, Camacho and anthropologist, Cynthia Irwin-Williams discovered four more sites in the region that produced fossil bones and stone artifacts. This led to excavations during the 1960s at Hueyatlaco where sediment consisting of volcanic ash and pumice (nearly twenty-five feet deep) lay atop a gravel formation in the Tetela Peninsula. The excavation and the resulting data it produced fostered serious controversy and dispute among the archeological academia.

The Hueyatlaco Anomaly

Published in the online magazine, *Disputatio* in May 1999, is an article entitled *Anatomy of an Anomaly* by Professor of Philosophy, Mark Owen Webb and Suzanne Clark of Texas Tech University. The article, although about archeology, chiefly addresses philosophy and the human reaction to anomalous events. It is a reasonably detailed report describing the events regarding the controversial Hueyatlaco excavations.

At Hueyatlaco (a few miles south of Valsequillo in the Mexican Province of Puebla), excavation began in 1962 and lasted eleven years. Cynthia Irwin-Williams, the principal investigator, characterized the location as a prehistoric "kill site" that produced artifacts of non-local origin. It was an ideal campsite with small streams nearby to aid in butchering animals. Crude projectile points, made by a less sophisticated culture, were discovered, but so were tools of a more advanced nature.

Controversy began in 1967 when Jose L. Lorenzo, Director of Prehistory at Mexico's National Institute of History and Anthropology, alleged that site laborers planted artifacts and had commingled them with other artifacts in a way that made it impossible to separate. Cynthia Irwin-Williams retorted that the allegations were utterly without any basis in truth. She added that Lorenzo was motivated by distorted personal hostility and the irrational inability to change an opinion. In 1969, she further challenged the allegations with written statements from reputable professionals of both anthropology and archaeology.

By June of 1969, the dating of the artifacts was complete. It was an event that would prevent the site from being added to the archeologists' portfolio of late Asian migration. Radiocarbon dating on shellfish produced an age at least 35,000 years old. The uranium method delivered a more unbelievable result of 260,000 ± 60,000 years. Another uranium method test of a mastodon tooth from El Horno was dated to be older than 280,000 years. Again using the uranium method, a camel pelvis was dated to be 180,000 years old and a horse leg bone, 260,000 years old.

In an attempt to explain these extremely old dates, it was suggested that they were located in an erosion prone area such as a stream channel, which would suggest the layer bearing the artifacts was of a younger age. It was not to be. Drs. Steen-McIntyre and Harold Malde, both from the U.S.

Geological Survey, and Roald Fryxel of Washington State University, returned to Hueyatlaco in 1973 to map the bed's stratigraphic sequence. They found that the artifacts did not lay within a stream channel, and therefore were not younger than the ash deposits covering them. In another effort to explain the incredibly old age, volcanic ash layers were sampled and studied.

Under a petrographic microscope the samples looked "shaggy" with a "picket fence" appearance. (Relatively young samples are different, and have freshlooking, crystal surfaces.) Some vesicles (openings) contained puddles of water indicating that they were of considerable age. Dr. Steen-McIntyre had performed these same procedures on ash layers from Yellowstone National Park, which were dated to be 251,000 years old. Indeed, according to Steen-McIntyre, samples from Hueyatlaco bore a striking resemblance to those from Yellowstone.

Geochemist from the U.S. Geological Survey, C.W. Naeser, also tested zircon crystals from the ash and mud layers using the zircon fission-track method. Similar dates were returned; 600,000 ± 340,000 years old for the mud, and the Hueyatlaco ash 370,000 ± 200,000 years old. Conservative dates would be 260,000 and 170,000 years old for both the mud and ash.

Both sets of dates agreed with Dr. Steen-McIntyre's observations of 251,000 years. Three separate methods, calculated by three separate geologists, yielded similar results, yet the results were met with skepticism and hostility. Irwin-Williams refused to believe them. Nevertheless, Various team members published their work to her dissatisfaction. "Anatomy of an Anomaly" authors, Webb and Clark, wrote that:

> Irwin-Williams was clearly distressed that date estimates place human presence at Valsequillo long before 30,000 BP, the earliest date she could accept. It is not improbable that Irwin-Williams feared her career was in jeopardy in light of such dates. She certainly feared (or at least was wary of) what might happen if she was associated with fringe elements.[2]

Harold Malde and Roald Fryxell announced their early dates for the Valsequillo site in a meeting of the Geological Society of America, which was reported on the UPI wire on November 14, 1973. Irwin-Williams reacted with anger. (Webb and Clark apparently obtained a copy of Irwin-William's letter to a colleague in Alberta.) Her reaction:

> My capsule comment on the situation [expletives deleted] is that this is one of the most irresponsible public announcements with which it has ever been my misfortune to become involved. Of the three dating methods used by Malde on the materials, two are so new that we have essentially no information on their validity. The third (fission-track dating) gave an anomalous result of about 300,000 [in other words, no date at all]. [3]

In the years since, the experimental methods of Tephrahydration and Uranium have been found to be reasonably reliable, but the debate among the scholars continues. Malde and Steen-McIntyre encourage an early date (200,000 years old) while Irwin-Williams a more conservative, but still controversial, early date of 20,000 years old. Virginia Steen-McIntyre's opinions were published in *Quaternary Research* (16:1), 1981, in an article titled *Geologic Evidence for Age of Deposits at Hueyatlaco Archeological Site, Valsequillo, Mexico*. *Science Frontiers* Magazine also published it in their May-Jun 1982 issue:

> The evidence outlined here consistently indicates that the Hueyatlaco site is about 250,000 yr old. We who have worked on geological aspects of the Valsequillo area are painfully aware that so great an age poses an archeological dilemma. If the geological dating is correct, sophisticated stone tools were used at Valsequillo long before analogous tools are thought to have been developed in Europe and Asia. Thus, our colleague, Cynthia Irwin-Williams, has criticized the dating methods we have used, and she wishes us to emphasize that an age of 250,000 yr is essentially impossible. [4]

Michael Waters of Tucson, Arizona voiced dismissal of Hueyatlaco because of conflicting and confusing fission-track and uranium-thorium dates, even though artifacts lay in association with extinct fauna. He claims it is unknown when those types of animals became extinct in Mexico.[5] Such misgivings have excused rejection. Only two conclusions from Hueyatlaco are possible: either modern man lived in America 250,000 years ago or there is a systematic error in the primary methods of geological dating. Dr. Virginia Steen-McIntyre believes the former is the case. Hueyatlaco, Mexico is not the only prehistoric anomaly in America. There are, in fact, several but the story of Pedra Furada in Brazil utters similar theory-breaking evidence produced by qualified scientists.

Pedra Furada

On a rare visit to São Paulo in 1963, the Mayor of the remote, drought-stricken São Raimundo Nonato informed the Paulista Museum staff that pre-Portuguese cliff paintings were discovered near his town. (São Raimundo Nonato is in southeast area of the Piauí Province, in northeast Brazil.) Archaeologist Nième Guidon, made an initial survey by mule in 1970 and reported that 275 rock shelters existed in towering cliffs for 120 miles along the Rio Piauí. Of the cliffs, 186 were bearing murals in red, yellow, black, gray, and white. The representations were typically on ceilings and walls. Engravings, or peckings, were more common than paint. She tabulated 15,000 motifs: animals, including armadillos, *caybara* (world's largest rodent), ostrich-like rheas, trees, people, crabs, and abstract symbols.

In 1973, she discovered *Toca do Boquierão do Sítio da Pedra Furada*, commonly referred to as Pedra Furada. It was a sandstone shelter, tucked away behind several waterfalls (Pedra Furada means perforated rock). At the entrance to the canyon, the shelter stood 60 feet above the canyon floor in the towering cliffs of Serra Talhada.

Niede Guidon and her team began excavation in 1978, and was joined by Fabio Parenti in 1984. Although rudimentary in form, the Pleistocene layer revealed many flaked stones as well as stone structures, plainly not of natural origin. Some of the stones, burned and accompanied by charcoal, were believed to have been the remnants of hearths.[6]

Hearths were found in all layers, usually circled with rock from the nearby cliffs. In October 1986, carbon-dates of the charcoal ranged from 3000 BC to 30,200 BC (at Level 14) in consistent sequence. Projectile points were plentifully from 31,000 BC, with scrapers and other flaked tools by 23,000 BC. The earliest murals occurred between 30,000 and 25,000 BC. Five deeper levels (15 through 19) yielded a large and varied assortment of primitive tools flaked from small quartz and quartzite pebbles, in association with hearths. By July 1991, they had reached bedrock that dated to 48,500 BC. AMS redating of samples yielded even higher dates.

Anthropologists paid little attention to this site until *Nature* magazine published Guidon and Parenti's results in 1993, issue 362:114. The oldest occupied layer, according to Guidon and Parenti, was 50,000 years old.[7]

Stuart Fiedel found the absence of Pleistocene animal remains troubling, as if he was unaware that mammoths, mastodons, bison, and horses never reached Brazil. He also noticed a four-foot gap of no occupation between 15,000 and 6400 BC that was not reflected in the natural geologic strata.

David Meltzer, James Adovasio, and Tom Dillehay, among other hasty visitors to the awesome cliffs in December of 1994, reacted as other anthropologists had with their own pre-Clovis sites. In defiance of overwhelming evidence, they rejected an ice age date and announced the Clovis primacy of American settlement unshaken (which they themselves had shaken at Monte Verde). Some scholars suggest competitive motives for their rejection since they raised none of their objections at the site, which were subject to immediate test.[8]

They assaulted Guidon and Parenti's results a year later in *Antiquity* magazine (issue 68:695, 1994), arguing that the crude stones alleged to be human artifacts were actually 'geofacts.' These are artifacts produced by natural events such as rocks falling on one another from nearby cliffs. Guidon countered by explaining that their facts were wrong and that they were not objective because of their support of the 12,000-year-old Asian migration theory. According to Guidon, the flake-scars on the stones in question have equal technical characteristics, many of which have more that one scar on the same edge. Two of them, in fact, have five successive parallel scars on the same edge, which are very unlikely to have occurred in nature.[9]

They also placed Pedra Furada on the valley floor instead of sixty-five feet above it, as it really is, and suggested natural fires of caetinga (a plant) to explain charcoal remnants. Notably, they were unaware that this vegetation grows nowhere but Piauí and does *not* burn, yet they claimed natural fires occurred only in hearths. Exasperated, Guidon and four major specialists exposed the false allegations one by one. In defiance of her defamers, she managed to get access roads built and to memorialize the entire rock shelter as a national park.[10]

Ruth Gruhn, Professor Emeritus at the University of Alberta, Edmonton, Canada, takes a balanced approach in understanding the events surrounding the Hueyatlaco excavations. She believes the truth of Pedra Furada was buried in a critique published by several North American researchers who attended a field conference at the site in 1993. Gruhn urges that it cannot be so easily discounted. The essential issue at Pedra Furada is whether any real stone artifacts came from the ice age deposits within the shelter. Detractors of Pedra Furada have suggested the specimens classified as artifacts could have been flaked naturally in a high-energy depositional environment. Yet no such environment existed within the sheltered area where the specimens were found. Sediments that created the shelter floor arose from the slow weathering of the sandstone overhang. This process, in itself, suggests the validity of the site.[11]

The subsequent change of Meltzer and Dillehay's pre-Clovis ideas is perhaps a testament to the evidence (at least at Monte Verde and perhaps Pedra Furada). True scientists will always base their theories on fact and, in the face of contradictory evidence, will eventually embrace ideas that better explain the available data.

Meadowcroft

The continent of North America is not without its controversial sites. During the 1970s, Mercyhurst College professor, James Adovasio excavated a rock shelter in the cliffs overlooking Cross Creek, thirty miles southwest of Pittsburgh, Pennsylvania. Carbon-dates from charcoal samples reveal the site was occupied as long ago as 30,000 years. Adovasio discovered a non-fluted (pre-Clovis) point from a lower layer of soil 220 feet thick, the earliest evidence of human habitation within the shelter. Although he maintained good stratigraphic control, according to other scientists, there were still issues surrounding his data, specifically radiocarbon dates and projectile point diagnostics. Additional excavations were performed during the 1990s to repair slumps and check data.

Meadowcroft is divided into eleven well-defined, natural levels of soil. All levels, except the lowest, contain evidence of intermittent human occupation with 104 charcoal samples yielding 52 dates. Processed by four different labs, (except for four samples) all were internally consistent in absolute stratigraphic sequence from 33,000 BC to 1265 AD.

The variety of evidence suggests that it was a processing station of hunter-gatherers. Large burned areas, consisting of ash and charcoal lenses, point to the use of fire pits and fire floors. Refuge pits, non-fluted points, knives, and scrapers were found with animal bones, edible-plant remains, and hackberry seeds.[12]

Prismatic blade technology found at Meadowcroft and the related Cross Creek sites resembles that from the Clovis culture.[13] Michael Collins detected two overshot flake scars on one face of a lower level (2a) blade which he dated between 10,850 and 10,350 BC. He also noted that the blade technology was generally smaller than, but similar to, the Upper Paleolithic of Western Europe.[14] Michael Waters, dubious of dates crossing the ice age boundary, suggested the protracted lower level (2a) should have shown more stratigraphic breaks.[15]

Geologist Vance Haynes, who has played a major role in American archeology, visited Meadowcroft for two hours in 1976. He believed that pluvial sediment made it habitable only after stream subsidence between 11,050 and 10,050 BC, slightly bending his upper boundary for humans in America. He failed to note that the shelter stood fifty feet higher than Cross Creek and nearly sixty miles south of the Wisconsin glacier's most southern reach. Besides, Meadowcroft is not an open site subject to periodic sedimentation. It displays continuous and abundant signs of occupation in the "uninhabitable" period. During human occupation, Cross Creek flowed probably fifteen to thirty feet higher than today, allowing easier access.[16] To discredit an ice age origin for lower level (2a), Haynes further proposed that coal and groundwater contaminated carbon samples, which inflated the resulting dates. Yet no coal seams run in or near the site. The nearest outcrop of coal is five miles north.[17]

Haynes accepted dates above the middle third of level (2a), but charged that only those dates below conflicted with other data (for example, flora and fauna of a post ice age deciduous forest), even though there was no evidence of an anomaly. According to Haynes' opponents, what they really conflicted with was his 1969 dogma that middle-Paleo- Indian evidence failed to meet his strict criteria. He felt the early Paleo-Indian was purely theoretical.[18] In 1964, he was more tolerant and admitted there were good indications of cultures in the New World earlier than 10,000 BC, the maximum age for the Llano (another name for Clovis) culture, which he said had no undisputable progenitor.[19]

He also dismissed Adovasio's 1978, 14,050-11,050 BC "pre-fluted point populations" and announced the basal archaeology of Meadowcroft was probably no older than Clovis, if that old.[20] Yet Haynes must have been the unnamed critic who confided to Adovasio in September of 1987 that he had not meant to impugn (2a) carbon-dates, but only suggested that they should be examined.[21] However, Dillehay's January 1997 demonstration of the Monte Verde campsite, complete with bolas (stone balls) and child's footprint, appears at last to have converted Haynes, among those present, to human habitation of the New World before Clovis.

The Smithsonian's 17,650 BC carbon-date of carbonized cut-bark basketry in lower level (2a), looked too conservative due to a different process at a different lab. *Dicarb Radioisotope* in Gainesville, Florida, using charcoal samples from immediately below the basket produced dates of 19,430 and 19,120 BC. Irene Stehli of Dicarb reported absolutely no contamination of any sort.[22] After twenty years of carbon-date testing and retesting, Adovasio could reiterate there was absolutely no evidence whatsoever for particulate or non-particulate contamination.[23]

Another geologist, Jim Mead of Northern Arizona University, granted that carbon-dates did indicate occupation during the Wisconsin glacial maximum, but pointed out the inconsistencies of recovered plant and animal remains.[24] Stuart Fiedel, uncritically honoring Haynes and Mead's strictures, expressed surprise at a deciduous forest fifty miles from the Laurentide ice sheet.[25]

Adovasio's article, *Yes Virginia, It Really Is That Old: A Reply to Haynes and Mead*, blistered Haynes' critique. Haynes' Clovis primacy syndrome assumed there was coal where none existed. He was also naive while inspecting local sedimentation and geology, failing to see an exact match of lower (2a) flora and fauna with local Wisconsin-age flora and fauna when the climate approximated the present.[26] Stratum (2a), through the course of 16,940 years, accumulated 220 feet of sediment. A sterile layer of soil and carbon lenses, the latter from the twenty-ninth and twentieth millenniums BC, divided it from earlier Stratum I. A series of seven lower (2a) carbon-dates range from 17,650 BC to 11,290 BC, obviously from the ice age. Roof debris sealed it from middle (2a), which spanned 11,000 to 9000 BC, at the end of the ice age. More roof debris sealed the middle from the upper layer, which ended at 6000 BC, completely post-ice age.[27]

Just as the Meadowcroft controversy seemed forever settled, Kenneth Tankersley and Cheryl Ann Munson teamed up to point the finger at level (2a) age again. They asserted that "vitrinized wood" (coal) was present and potentially contaminative, inflating carbon-dates. They elaborated that quaternary wood, which natural wildfires turned into charcoal, is difficult to distinguish from coal in some instances.[28] To this, Adovasio, Donahue, and Stuckenrath replied that no vitrain had ever been seen anywhere near the site. All parts of two recorded fragments of vitrinized wood lacked any evidence of a wood-type cellular structure. No one, they repeated, suspected contamination for any of the sequence except level (2a), whose aberrance would be unlikely.[29]

* * *

Controversy regarding the antiquity of cultures in the Americas is not confined to the buried remains of primitive peoples. South America contains a wealth of megalithic structures and, although most are attributed to the more recent cultures of the Mayan, Inca, and Aztec, an ancient city in the Andean Altiplano adds to the continuing controversy of American prehistory. The stone city of Tiahuanaco mysteriously belongs to no known culture. According to Andean mythology, those who built it were taught the ways of civilization by another, more advanced, race of people.

Chapter 15
The Stone at the Center

- Dating of Tiahuanaco
- Bennett's Statues
- Carvings of Extinct Animals
- Puma Punku - The Port of Tiahuanaco
- Lake Titicaca

Outside Egypt's Giza plateau, the long abandoned city of Tiahuanaco may be the most famous ancient ruin of the world. Located in the Bolivian Andes, it lays 12,500 feet above sea level in the northern most section of the South American Altiplano. Fifteen miles north is Lake Titicaca, the highest navigable lake in the world.

Tiahuanaco was built using stone blocks, some weighing more than 100 tons. The Spanish, who discovered it in 1535, were deeply impressed by its megalithic architecture. Decorated by figures with square faces and eyes and rectangular mouths, its unique style of art is carved into its ancient monuments, statues, and walls. Unfortunately, Tiahuanaco became a quarry to the Spanish, who erected churches and other colonial structures as faraway as La Paz, removing possible clues to its origin and culture.

The original name of the city was *Taypi Kala*, which means "the stone at the center." Its current name has many interpretations. According to Luis Valcárcel in *Etnohistoria del Perú* (Lima, 1959), Tiahuanaco means

Satellite View of the Bolivian Altiplano

"the place where the Earth forms and the water." Yet others suggest *Eternal City, Children of the Tiki* or *the Jaguar, City of the Water* and *Town of the Children of the Sun.* Tiahuanaco could also be derived from Tiwanaku, which means *This is of God.*

The principal ruins at Tiahuanaco consist of six structures, all of which are close to each other. It is formed by the remnants of the Acapana Pyramid, the Kalasasaya, a subterranean temple, a palace, a building of unknown purpose, and a wall.

The Acapana is a step pyramid aligned perfect with the cardinal directions. Most of its andesite covering was removed for construction in La Paz. Its interior is honeycombed with passages and incorporates a system of weirs to direct water from a tank above to a stone canal surrounding the pyramid. The true function of this waterway is unknown.

The Kalasasaya or "Place of the Vertical Stones" is built in stockade fashion with twelve-foot high columns. Each of the columns is carved into human figures. At its northwest corner stands a squared archway named the *Gateway of the Sun.* In its southwest corner rests a large statue simply referred to as "the idol."

Archeological research at Tiahuanaco, during the past 50 years, suggests that it was first occupied around 1500 BC. According to radiocarbon dates from samples collected during the 1950s, 1980s, and 1990s[1], the city reached its peak somewhere between 100 and 900 AD with a population of 70,000 to 90,000. At one time there were as many as 500,000 inhabitants who lived in the surrounding valleys.

Gateway of the Sun (carved from a single block of stone)

Tiahuanacan culture collapsed around 1000 AD and the city was abandoned, although a remnant population continued to work raised fields in the area. There are various theories to explain its disappearance. Severe drought, as was proved to be the case in the collapse of Mayan culture, is a likely candidate.

Not all scholars, however, believe this is all there is to Tiahuanaco. Some theorists think another culture existed before 1500 BC and was responsible for its construction. Its megalithic monuments, statues, plazas, palaces, and unique artwork are out of place and out of time. In such an inhospitable area two miles above sea level, it seems unlikely anyone would want to live there. However, there is only circumstantial evidence, at best, to support any theory of extra-ancient habitation.

Dating of Tiahuanaco

Tiahuanaco's first investigator, and possibly the most controversial, was Arthur Posnansky (1873-1946), an Austrian born engineer who dedicated fifty years to its study. During his early life, he managed a river transport company on the Amazon River and sympathized with Bolivia during the Brazilian/Bolivian war. When Bolivia surrendered, he fled to Europe but returned several years later, and by 1903 settled in La Paz close to Tiahuanaco. He was a photographer and filmmaker, as well as amateur archeologist and author. The result of his archeological work in the region was published in 1945, *Tiahuanaco: The Cradle of American Man*. He passed away a year later.

Posnansky at Tiahaunaco in 1945

Posnansky's theories of prehistoric origin are based on the Gateway of the Sun. Carved from a single block of andesite granite, ten feet high and twelve feet wide, it stands in the northwest corner of the temple Kalasasaya and faces east into the rising sun. When found, it was broken in half and toppled. Restoration work brought it back to its original position in 1908.

Its upper portion is deeply carved with intricate designs of human figures, condors, and other animals. Centered at the top of the gate is the sun god, with beams of light emanating from his face in all directions. He holds a staff in each hand with tears etched in his cheeks, but it is an incomplete work. Figures flanking the centerpiece are, themselves, unfinished.

Posnansky's dating of Tiahuanaco is based on astronomical calculations of the earth's tilt of axis. If viewed from earth, the planets of our solar system travel across the sky in a line called the "plane of the ecliptic." The Earth is tilted on its axis in respect to this plane of which its resulting angle is known as the "Obliquity of the Ecliptic." The earth's axis varies slowly between 22 degrees, 1 minute to an extreme of 24 degrees, 5 minutes. This cycle repeats itself from one extreme to the other over a 41,000-year period. The present angle is 23 degrees, 17 minutes.

Since the gateway bisects the rising sun on the vernal equinox and the cornerstones of the Kalasasaya enclosure on the winter and summer solstice, it must have been intentionally aligned to the sun when built. Today, however, it does not align perfectly and is slightly offset to the southeast. Alignments of the gateway and Kalasasaya temple are based on a tilt of 23 degrees, 8 minutes, 48 seconds. This means that if it were erected in perfect alignment, it would have been built 17,000 years ago. Astronomers of Posnansky's day, Hans Ludendorff (Astronomical Observatory of Potsdam), Friedrich Becker (Specula Vaticana), Arnold Kohlschutter (Bonn University), and Rolf Muller (Institute of Astrophysics at Potsdam) verified the accuracy of Posnansky's calculations.

Not everyone agrees with Posnansky's dating, but this theory also has its contemporary supporters. According to Javier Escalante, Director of the Bolivian National Branch of Archeology, it is clear that astronomy was central to the Tiahuanaco culture:

> We know that the Tiahuanaco civilization had a great and vast understanding of astronomy, clearly demonstrated in the extremely precise astronomical based solar and lunar calendars. Their knowledge of astronomy is also reflected in their architectural designs. Each temple and structure served as an astrological observatory plus, their architectural dimensions guided by their command of astrology converted these structures into physical representations of calendars.[2]

Bennett's Statues

During the early 1930s, William Clark Bennett (1905-1953) of New York's American Museum of Natural History excavated an area east of the Kalasasaya Temple and discovered the interior of a subterranean temple. Within this temple he found two large stone statues, one beside the other.

The first statue depicts a man sporting a beard and is referred to by some as the mythical Viracocha. The second is simply known as "The

Friar." The first statue stands seven feet tall with the arms crossed over a body-length shirt decorated with pumas. It depicts the physical traits of a man with large saucer-shaped eyes beneath the thick dash of his eyebrows, a straight, narrow nose and oval mouth, with rays of lightning carved on his forehead. A thick mustache encircles his mouth to join a sharply pointed beard. Strange animals are etched about his head. Serpents climb the statue on both sides. For some, it looks like a sculpture of the mythical thunder-god, Viracocha.

The second statue, the Friar (also known as the Bennett monolith) is much larger. It measures twenty-four feet tall, weighs fifteen tons, and is carved out of red sandstone. The lower half of its body is carved with what look like fish scales, but are actually fish heads upon closer inspection. Winged figures, similar to those found on the Gate of the Sun (but with curled tails), adorn the upper body. In his hands are unidentified cylindrical objects.

A third large stone statue stands in the southwest corner of the Kalasasaya Temple next to the Gateway of the Sun. Covered with hieroglyphic style engraving, it is nearly seven feet tall.

Carvings of Extinct Animals

Toxodon

Macrauchenia

Artwork carved into the Gateway of the Sun (referred to as a frieze) is said to be a calendar, but has never been deciphered. Etched into this frieze are a number of animals such as condors and jaguars, but the relief outline of two animals appears to be that of the extinct toxodon and the South American elephant.[3] These were originally described by Posnansky in his four volume set. Forty-six toxodon heads have been identified on the Gateway. It has also been found in other works of Tiahuanacan art, such as recovered pottery fragments and three-dimensional sculptures. Others, such as Michael Cremo, have corroborated his observation:

There are also sculptures in some of the temples in Tiahuanaco that resembles elephants. And, of course, elephants don't live today in North or South America, but over 10,000 years ago, they did.[3]

Graham Hancock, author of *Fingerprints of the Gods*, also states that an elephant's head is visible on the statue.[4]

Besides the elephant and Toxodon, two other extinct animals have also been identified in the calendar frieze, the Shelidoterium, and the Macrauchenia. The Shelidoterium is a diurnal quadruped and the Macrauchenia is an animal similar in size to a horse with distinct three-toed feet.

The artwork of the frieze is unique in that, as you move closer to an object, you can see it is comprised of smaller objects, in and of themselves whole objects. For instance, standing ten feet away you can see an elephant's head but when you move closer, say to two feet away, you can see the elephant head is comprised of two birds standing face-to-face.

However, not everyone who has seen it believes it is an elephant. Professor James Bailey of Lewis & Clark College (Portland, Oregon) offers a different explanation:

> This is a carving of a *parrot*. It looks like an elephant until you are told that it is a parrot and then it is very obvious that it is a parrot. Here's the reason: the carving looks like an elephant in profile with a head curving into a trunk crossed by a tusk. The carving is actually the profile of a parrot's head; the elephant's eye is the parrot's nasal opening, the elephant's trunk is the parrot's upper beak, the elephant's tusk is the parrot's lower beak. What looks like the front part of an elephant in profile is actually an entire parrot's head in profile. Of course, someone could respond: "Well, you think it looks like a parrot because that's what you want to see." Fair enough. But what's more likely, that it's an incongruous, extinct elephant carving from 10,000 years ago or a more recent carving of an existing, common indigenous species?[5]

Although a parrot may be a more likely animal to carve today, no one really knows when the figures were actually carved.

Puma Punku – The Port of Tiahuanaco

A mile from the principal ruins at Tiahuanaco lies a jumbled mess of seemingly tossed about blocks of stone. The site is called Puma Punku, meaning *Door of the Puma*. Archaeologists speculate that these gigantic, bluish-gray stones were dressed by quarrymen, prepared for assembly but never erected, and the construction for which they were intended was never completed. However, another equally valid speculation is the buildings were completed but toppled by a natural catastrophe.

The quarry for these blocks is located on the western shore of Titicaca, nearly ten miles away. It is not known how these blocks were moved and placed.

The ruins at Puma Punku (Photo by David Hatcher Childress)

Among these ruins are a collapsing, four-part building and a massive T-shaped structure. The T-shaped structure is composed of enormous blocks, one of which may weigh over 400 tons. Other blocks scattered around the site are easily between 100 and 150 tons. Large metal clamps shaped like a block "I" (called tenons) curiously hold some blocks together. Researchers believe that this is perhaps one of the earliest uses of metal for structural purposes. Analysis performed with a scanning electron microscope has determined that these tenons are comprised of a copper-nickel alloy and poured into shaped-slots already carved into the rock. This of course, required a portable smelter. According to archeologist, Neil Steede, they are an anachronism:

> **In order to fuse copper and nickel you need to have a temperature of 3500 degrees. Our own civilization only came up with this technology in the 1930s. Yet here, at now what we are considering to be the most ancient city on the face of the earth, we have that type of technology.[6]**

Tiahuanaco is one of only three places in the ancient world to use metal I-clamps to join cut blocks (the others being ancient Egypt and Angkor Wat in Cambodia). Strangely enough, the Bolivian Andes is an area where current historical theory denies an iron age.

Tenon joints at Puma Punku (Photo by David Hatcher Childress)

The official purpose of Puma Punku is unknown. Based on the pattern of structures (as suggested by Posnansky), it looks like the remains of a pier. No other fitting explanation has yet been offered. This finds consideration by some archeologists, such as Eduardo Pareja, from the Bolivian National Institute of Archeology:

> One of the theories postured by the engineer, Posnansky, was that the lake was, at least, level with it. It was a port to the west of Puma Punku, where we have a T-shaped area where they disembarked. Archeological evidence of the Ts does exist and we do not discount the theory that the water could have risen to this level creating a port.[7]

If the T-shaped structures were a pier, they would obviously have to be at the shore. The closest body of water today is Lake Titicaca, fifteen miles from Tiahuanaco, and 100 feet lower than it needs to be.

Lake Titicaca

The meaning of the name Titicaca is uncertain. One possible translation is *Rock of the Puma*.

Straddling the border between Bolivia and Peru at 12,500 feet above sea level in the Andes Mountains, Lake Titicaca is the world's highest navigable lake and the second largest lake in South America. Covering 3,200 square miles, it extends in a northwest-southeast direction for 100 miles, and at its widest point, is 50 miles across. A narrow channel called the *Straits of Tiquina*, separates the lake into two bodies of water, one small and the other quite large (the Huinaymarca and Chucuito). Peruvians refer to these as the *Pequeno* and *Grande*.

The Titicaca basin is a vast area spanning 22,400 square miles and includes twenty-five rivers. It surrounds the lake, most of which is located in the Altiplano (high plain). Being the deepest point of the Altiplano, most of the rainwater from the surrounding region drains into the lake. Forty-one islands, some densely populated, rise from the lake's waters. The largest is located just off the tip of the Copacabana, Bolivia.

The lake's depth averages between 100 and 600 feet, with a maximum of 1,000 feet in its northeast corner. Water levels vary seasonally due to the summer rains and dry winters. Because of its saline content, it is considered neither a fresh nor saltwater lake.

The level of the lake was much higher during prehistoric times. At one point (30,000 years ago), a vast lake covered much of the Bolivian Altiplano because of increased levels of precipitation. Recent analysis of core samples from the bottom of Lake Titicaca have shown that tropical South America has endured alternating periods of heavy rainfall and severe drought during the last 25,000 years. The lake itself has dramatically risen and fallen because of these climatic changes.

Previous research of Lake Titicaca typically involved core samples from areas near the shore. Stanford geologist, Robert B. Dunbar and his multi-institutional team have taken samples from deeper water for a new study, hoping to get a better picture of climatic changes. From their data, they composed a history of the lake.[8]

Fifteen thousand years ago, a dry period began and lasted for the next 2,000 years, causing Lake Titicaca to drop significantly. For the next 1,500 years after that, the lake overflowed again only to be followed again by another 1,500-year dry spell then another 2,500-year period of heavy rain. Drought caused the lake level to fall sharply again 8,500 years ago, and rise again 7,500 years ago during another period of heavy rainfall.[9]

In 4,000 BC, extreme drought occurred, lasting for a thousand years, and lowered the lake to 250 feet below its current level. The drop was sudden (within 200 or 300 years) and reached its lowest level in 25,000 years. In 2,500 BC, the lake began to rise again and eventually reached the level it is today.[10]

To explain this multi-millennium pattern of climatic change, scientists turned to climate studies of the Atlantic Ocean and found a correlation between temperature and precipitation. Periods of falling surface temperatures, with centuries of heavy rain, match the history depicted in the core samples that were studied.[11]

During August of 2000, the remains of what is thought to be a 1,000 to 1,500-year-old temple were found at the bottom of the lake. A team of thirty researchers, backed by *Akakor Geographical Exploring*, and led by Italian Lorenzo Epis, discovered a 160 feet wide temple, a terrace for crops, a pre-Incan road, and a retaining wall 2,600 feet long. These new discoveries are located between the town of Copacabana and the Island of the Sun and Island of the Moon.[12]

In 2001, anthropologists Charles Stanish of the University of California at Los Angeles, and Brian Bauer of the University of Illinois at Chicago, discovered sites on the Island of the Sun and Island of the Moon that predate the established time table for Tiahuanacan culture. The 185 archeological sites that Stanish and Bauer have identified are believed to be on the trail of a popular pilgrimage for ancient South Americans, as long ago as 2,500 years.[13]

Tiahuanaco – A Continuing Mystery

There is no hard evidence (in other words, carbon-dates) to support a habitation at Tiahuanaco before 1,500 BC. Of the twenty-nine published samples, the oldest date is sample ID GaK-194 at 3530±120.[14]

Despite this, Tiahuanaco is still a mystery, and the port of Puma Punku, a hope to those who want to believe. The evidence, though circumstantial, is there. If it really were a port, according to the research performed by the Stanford group, it would have to have been built sometime during the last period of heavy rainfall before 4,000 BC. If one entertains this idea, why not 17,000 years ago, as the carvings of extinct animals and Posnansky suggest? After all, as Posnansky noted, certain parts of Tiahuanaco were deeply buried under sediments and, because they were immersed for a long time, a thin layer of lime deposits covered the ruins. (Some argue the lime deposits may be due to a lubricant used in block transportation since the Andean people were without the utility of the wheel.)

It is at least possible since advanced civilization did exist in prehistoric South America. Although the Egyptians are well known for their traditions of mummification, they were not the first. A sophisticated fishing tribe called the *Chinchoros*, that lived on the north coast of modern day Chile, was embalming their dead as early as 5,000 BC.[15] They disassembled the deceased, treated the internal organs to prevent decay, and then reassembled the severed parts. Wood was often added for support along the spinal column, arms, and legs. The chest and bowel cavities were filled with fiber or feathers, and then the body was coated with clay where artists painted or sculpted. Adults of both sexes were mummified, as were infants and children. Although important individuals received more elaborate work than others, a proper burial was everyone's right.

Insufficient Excavation

Science keeps pushing back the time for the first Americans. The Folsom culture (9000 BC) was thought to be the first, then Clovis (11,000 BC), and now the date drops back even further with finds from the works of Dillehay and Goodyear. There is also Caral, Peru, a true city in every sense of the word, excavated and dated by Ruth Shady Solis, which pushes the date of South American civilization back to 2600 BC. With the Chinchoros, the date rolls back another 2400 years to 5000 BC.

For all that have been discovered and uncovered in Tiahuanaco and the Lake Titicaca Basin, there is still not enough evidence to convince the skeptics, but there is much more work which needs to be carried out. According to Eduardo Pareja of the Bolivian National Institute of Archeology, very little is known about the area:

> **I believe it's more important to work in Tiahuanaco because only 3.5% of this area has been excavated and we still have 96.5% of the area that needs to be investigated.**[16]

There are other megalithic sites in the Andes besides Tiahuanaco. For example, forty-five miles north of Cuzco, at the north end of the Sacred Valley along the Urubamba River is *Ollantaytambo*. It guards the entrance to the narrow Urubamba Gorge. Besides the gigantic Sun Temple, six large stones, made from red porphyry (a very hard rock), face the river each weighing fifty tons. The stones were quarried across the Urubamba River two hundred feet below the temple and three thousand feet up the opposite slope – an incredible feat involving the efforts of thousands of workers.[17]

According to world explorer, David Hatcher Childress, it is proof that the Incas did not build the structures. The Incas inherited the structures and added to them or maintained them with smaller stones (see upper right area in the picture on the next page).

Sun Temple at Ollantaytambo (Photo by David Hatcher Childress)

David Hatcher Childress and friend on top of an abandoned gigantic block
(Photo by David Hatcher Childress)

Is it enough to say that archaic Indians of the Altiplano organized themselves into a cohesive group advanced enough to build a spectacular city of stone? Or is this simply admitting that no one really knows who built it? History has its own answer.

During the sixteenth century, explorers commissioned by Charles I of Spain set out in search of gold (as had others before them). When they reached the city of Tiahuanaco, they found only ruins. From the local Indians, they learned that sacrifices were brought to the feet of the giant geometric stone statues. They also learned that the Incas had been there a hundred years or more before them and had found the city already destroyed and deserted for a very long time. When asked about the origins of the city, the Indians only knew of a tradition. They claimed that, according to myth, unknown giants had built the city in a single night after the flood. The giants ignored a prophecy of the coming of the sun and were destroyed by its rays, and their palaces were reduced to ashes.

Chapter 16
Andean Genesis

- The Spanish Conquest
- Origins of the Inca Empire
- Inca Gods
- The Legend of Viracocha
- Incan Adaptation of the Viracocha Myth
- South American Myths of Civilization

Prior to the sixteenth century, there is very little written history for the people of the Andes and the Bolivian Altiplano, only oral tradition and myth. Through archeological investigation, however, it is believed the first complex societies began on the west coast of Peru around 3,500 BC. Then, during the next several thousand years, they began to domesticate animals (particularly the llama and alpaca) and systematically endeavored to plant and harvest crops. By 500 BC, the customs of the Tiahuanaco and *Huari* people flourished and became the dominant culture of the region. Its dominance lasted for nearly a thousand years, with its decline as mysterious as its rise. When expansion of the Inca state reached the Altiplano in the thirteenth century, they found it abandoned and already in ruins with only a remnant of its people occupying the area.

At its peak, the Inca Empire extended along the Pacific Coast and Andean highlands, from the northern border of modern Ecuador to the Maule River in central Chile. Their domination of the area, however, was short-lived. Almost a hundred years earlier, the Spanish had discovered the New World and now wanted its riches. In 1532, Spanish explorer Francisco Pizarro and 180 soldiers landed on the coast of Peru.

The Incas applied a peculiar association on meeting the Spanish. Just as the Aztecs of Mexico had associated the Spanish explorer Hernán Cortés with their god, Quetzalcoatl, they believed Pizarro to be their creator god, Viracocha. As history recounts, it turned out to be a grave mistake, enabling the Spanish to infiltrate the heart of the empire and plan their conquest accordingly. The story, however, is not that simple.

Inca civilization in some ways was more advanced than Western Europe. Inca physicians were practicing trepanation (drilling a hole in the skull to relieve pressure) while their European counterparts were practicing "bloodletting" for most every ailment. They built a vast road system throughout the empire consisting of two north-south roads. One ran along the coast for about 2,250 miles, the other ran inland along the Andes for a comparable distance with interconnecting links. Tunnels and suspension bridges (made from vine) were also erected. A relay service was used where couriers carried messages to and from leaders in the form of knotted cords. Their technology and architecture were highly developed, and included irrigation systems, palaces, temples, and fortifications.

The Spanish Conquest

When Pizarro landed in Peru in 1532, all he knew of the Incas was, that according to legend, they possessed fabulous wealth. His twin objectives were to loot the empire and to force its people to accept Christianity and Spanish rule. The Conquistadors arrived at a most opportune time. Atahualpa and his half brother Huascar both claimed the throne after their father, Huayna Capac, died in 1525 without formally naming his successor. Although Capac's priest named Huascar as the new ruler, a civil war erupted between the two brothers and lasted until 1532. When Atahualpa's forces captured and imprisoned Huascar, he was forced to witness the slaughter of the royal family. Hundreds of men, women, and children were killed so Atahualpa could reign without further challenge.

Atahualpa's bloody power play disrupted the ordered Inca society, and the natives, looking for a savior, hailed Pizarro as a son of their white-skinned God, Viracocha. They believed he was sent to avenge Huascar and his family. The sound of his cannon added credence to this false identity since Viracocha controlled thunder. So, the conquistadors marched and looted their way across the country. They met no resistance from the intimidated and demoralized Incas.

However, when word of the Spaniards' conduct during their trek to Cajamarca reached Atahualpa, he

The Spanish Conquest

demanded the thieves return the goods they had stolen. Instead, they sent him a priest, Brother Vicente, who began to teach Atahualpa western religion. The catechism lesson ended abruptly when Atahualpa hurled a bible on the ground. At this the offended Spaniards (who the night before had been whipped into a religious frenzy by Pizarro) attacked and slaughtered the unarmed natives. The Inca warriors stationed outside the city scattered before the onslaught of the Spanish artillery. Atahualpa was taken captive and held for ransom. When he learned that Huascar was promising the Spanish more gold for his own release, the ruthless Atahualpa secretly ordered his brother's death.

During the next nine months, a roomful of gold and silver was delivered to Pizarro to secure Atahualpa's safe return to the throne, but the Spaniard had no plan to release his prisoner. Pizarro knew that to disrupt and conquer this society, he would have to kill the Inca leader.

After a mock trial at which Atahualpa was found guilty of trumped-up charges, Pizarro offered him a choice. He could elect to be burned alive as a heathen or to be strangled as a Christian. When the Inca ruler chose the latter, he was baptized Juan de Atahualpa in honor of St. John the Baptist, tied to a stake and garroted (a stick tucked under the noose is twisted by the executioner to strangle the condemned). Pizarro and his men gave the Inca a full-scale Catholic funeral.

Although too late, the Incas did finally realize the Spanish were not the Viracochas. But why were the Incas so eager to accept a foreign people so readily as their god? The short answer is that it was important to their culture, beliefs, and history, and they were ready for prophetic fulfillment because of civil war. The long answer requires a review of Inca origins, its religion, and the legends of Viracocha.

Origins of the Inca Empire

According to José de la Riva Agüero, a pioneer of Peruvian culture during the first half of the twentieth century, Tiahuanaco was originally the cradle and home of the Inca Empire. The Inca themselves were once the ruling priesthood, the upper class of Tiahuanacan society, but were forced to leave for the Cuzco Valley by encroaching militant Aymarans. Fernando Montesinos, the seventeenth century chronicler, wrote that the priest kings of Tiahuanaco (los amautas) fled the country, trying to save the cult of their gods. They fled northward to the mountain valleys inhabited by other Quechuan tribesmen where they later established the Inca Empire.

The Aymarans remained in the Tiahuanacan region and founded the kingdom of Colla. To this day, the Aymarans live in the Lake Titicaca region, and have preserved the heritage of their ancient migration and suppression of the people who were driven from the city.

Legend explains migration of the Tiahuanacan priesthood with the story of four pairs of brothers and sisters. They were created by Viracocha to rule the world, and left the cave of Mountain Pacaritambo in search of fertile land to sustain life. As they moved towards Cuzco, the group became smaller. Rivaling brothers confined one brother to a cave; two others were turned into stone. The only surviving brother, Ayar Manco (Manco Capak) with his sister and wife Mama Ocllo and his brothers' wives, founded the city of the World Pole (center of the world) in the name of Viracocha, the Creator and Inti the Sun God.

In the fifteenth century, the Incas incorporated the Colla Kingdom into their empire and regained possession of Tiahuanaco. They regarded the area surrounding Titicaca as their former home, and revered

Viracocha as a god who had told them to build the city of Cuzco. Mythology related to Viracocha would later take on an important role in the Inca religion.

Inca Gods

The principal deity of the Incas was Viracocha, the Creator God. He became the cultural hero of the Inca and was said to have brought culture to people, then set off into the Pacific Ocean, promising to return. Although he was the prime deity, he was invisible and considered not to live among the people. Later, Viracocha would also become known as *Pachayachachic*. Originally, Pachayachachic was a sky god of the Lurín Valley in central Peru whose name was later given to the sky god of the Inca.

Inti, the sun god, was thought to be Viracocha's representation in the physical world. He was the main god of Inca State religion, which might have been a nature totem of the Quechua, or a god of another tribe that assimilated into Inca culture. Another significant deity in the Inca pantheon was the thunder god *Illapu*, who was distinctive from the Tiahuanaco sky god, but was named after a thunder god of the central Peruvian tribes.

The Incas were tolerant of the beliefs of their conquered subjects as long as the worship did not interfere with the new duties laid upon them by Incan religious leaders. The Incan pantheon was also forced on them over the pre-existing deities, and was considered of greater importance.

The Legend of Viracocha

As with any tale passed down through oral tradition, there are various renditions of the Viracocha myth. In general, they all agree on major points. He was the creator of the world who destroyed it by a flood, recreated it, and taught civilization to mankind. Viracocha means, "sea-foam," and is also referred to as Lord Con Ticci Viracocha and Pachayachachic. He was also a storm god and a sun god that wore the sun for a crown. He wandered the earth as a beggar and wept when he saw the plight of the creatures he had created. The Incas "have the tradition he

Viracocha

was a man of medium height, white and dressed in a white robe like an alb secured round the waist, and that he carried a staff and a book in his hands."[1] (An alb is a long, white robe with sleeves tapered to the wrist.)

In the beginning, Viracocha emerged from the void and created the heavens and the earth. Some say he rose from Lake Titicaca at the dawn of time and then went to Tiahuanaco to perform the act of creation. The first world that he created he destroyed by fire. In creating the second world, he made the animals and a race of giants who lived in eternal darkness, for there was yet no sun. He created giants, as the story goes, to see whether it would be well to make real men of that size.[2] These giants enraged Viracocha, so he turned them into stone and flooded the earth until all life was destroyed. A variation of this describes how two people, a man and woman, survived the flood by hiding in a box and were carried to their destination (Tiahuanaco) by the receding waters.

After the flood, Viracocha created a New World. In this world, he fashioned people out of clay from the earth at Tiahuanaco (another version says stone) and gave them the breath of life, languages, songs, and seed to sow. (In the version were the two survived, they were forgiven.) After they had been cultured, he spread them around the world through underground passages. Another version claims he painted them how he wished them to look (such as long or short hair, clothing color, etc.) and buried them to await the command to animate. In yet another variation, he delayed creating the sun, moon, and stars until the people he created were ready to awake.

Viracocha called on his helpers (smaller Viracochas) and told them to go forth in different directions to prepare places for the new humans to occupy. A variation exists here where the smaller Viracochas called forth the people to see to it that they multiplied and followed the commandments they were given. Viracocha traveled the land, calling each group into life as he entered their land, after which he taught them how to live.

In a variation where they were to check on the people, the smaller Viracochas traveled south and southeast. His two sons went northeast and northwest while Viracocha himself traveled due north. If tribes were found to be rebellious, they were turned into stone as punishment. At Pucara, forty leagues north of Cuzco, Viracocha called down fire from the sky on those who disobeyed his commandments.

In Cacha (a province), Viracocha called the inhabitants in the area to emerge. These people, however, came out armed since Viracocha was unknown to them. They rushed him with weapons raised, ready to kill. When Viracocha saw them coming, he instantly caused fire to fall from heaven, burning the a mountain near the people. When they saw this (the volcano), they realized his power and feared they would die. After throwing their weapons to the ground, they went straight to Viracocha, and knelt before him. Viracocha saw their repentance, gave the volcano three blows with his staff, which put it out forever. He then told the people that he was their maker. So to remember their origins and the miraculous activities, the Canas Indians built a majestic huaca (which means a shrine or idol) at the place where Viracocha rained fire from heaven.

Arriving at last at Cuzco and the seacoast, Viracocha gathered his two sons and all the little Viracocha, and spoke to those he created, foretelling of the events to come. He said that people would come claiming they were Viracocha, their creator, but they were not to believe them. However, in time he would send his messengers who would protect and teach them. Having said that, they walked west over the waves of the ocean toward the setting sun, until they disappeared from view.

Another myth of Viracocha exists that is clearly of Inca origin. This second myth confirms the migration of the priesthood from Tiahuanaco to Cuzco and the establishment, as well as expansion, of the Inca Empire. It appears that they composed their historical studies and rules on these ancient Tiahuanacan myths. Most likely, the Inca customized the original Viracocha myth for their own ideological purposes.

Incan Adaptation of the Viracocha Myth

When man was first created, he was a wanderer, naked and behaving like an animal in all ways. Viracocha decided to civilize man, so he looked around to find a people that would be good leaders. He found only a small group, eight in all, that would do. These people were the *Ayar*. They were very intelligent, able to build crude huts and make clothing of leaves without the aid of a god.

The leader of the tribe, Ayar Cachi, was an obnoxious man. He threw giant stones and made loud cries that frightened away the animals so the people, unable to find prey, would go hungry. He vented his anger by beating his brothers and sisters. His three brothers, Manco Capac, Ayar Oco, and Ayar Ayca and one of the sisters, Mama Ocllo, wanted to be rid of him. So they tricked him into entering a cave, allegedly to save a llama. While he was deep in the cave, they covered the entrance with stone, climbed the mountain above it, and pushed its peak into the valley below so their brother would be trapped forever. Every once in awhile, the earth roars and shakes as Ayar Cachi tries to escape. According to legend, this is why there are so many earthquakes in the region.

Because of their ingenuity, Viracocha decided he had found the people who would teach all other how to be happy and prosperous. He sent for the Ayar and taught them the ways of civilization: sharing and cooperating, growing plants, building houses, making weapons, weaving cloths, and worshipping him for all he has taught. Then he sent them into the world to teach the people. As their reward, they and their descendants would rule, making sure their subjects followed his ways.

He gave them a golden rod and ordered that a great city be built in his honor which should be named Cuzco, meaning the "Navel of the World." At various points along their journey, they were to strike the ground with the rod, and where it sank is where they would build. Cuzco became the source of a new life for all people. When they finally reached the spot where the rod sank into the ground, they named it *Huanacauri*, which means the Place of the Rainbow, because it was a place of great promise. The inhabitants of the valley, however, were fierce and did not want civilization. When they attacked, Mama Ocllo killed the first warrior, ripped out his lungs, and inflated them into bloody balloons to terrify the advancing throng. Sickened by the sight, they fell to the ground and begged forgiveness.

Later, they gathered the people and told them of their commission from Viracocha; convinced not only by their gruesome act, but also by their beautiful clothes and golden earrings. Surely these people had something to teach them. They decided to cooperate in building a society.

After seven years, people dressed in the most beautiful clothes (so their words would carry more power) were sent out from Cuzco to tell others what they had learned. In this way, the knowledge of the Incas was spread from group to group, and civilization was brought to many.

South American Myths of Civilization

The people of the Andes are not alone in their claims of taught civilization. The story is widespread. The Aztec, Maya, Tarascos, Muyscas, and Chibchas cultures of Central and South America all held similar beliefs.

Quetzalcoatl

The God, Quetzalcoatl, was worshipped by the Aztecs of Mexico and was a teacher of the arts, a wise lawgiver, the virtuous prince, the master builder, and the merciful judge. He was a white man with long dark hair, a flowing beard, and wore a strange dress. With his helpers, he made roads, civilized the people, and then disappeared. He forbade all that was wrong: the sacrifice of human beings and animals, wars, fighting, robbery, and all forms of violence. He came from the east and returned to the east, stating that he and others like him would someday return.

As a bearded man that wore a robe, Kukulcan appeared in Maya culture with twenty of his bearded followers. He was one of four brothers, three of whom had died or left. He trained the people in the arts of peace, and had various structures built at Chichen Itza. Under his rule, the nation enjoyed peace and prosperity. His teachings and activities were similar to those of Quetzalcoatl. He left Yucatan toward the west.

Curicaberis, also known as Surites, brought the Tarascos (of Michoacan in Mexico) out of barbarism. He devised their calendar, similar to the Aztecs and Mayas, and set up their form of government. At sunrise, in the town of Cromuscuaro, he instructed the people in the ways of civilization. He also established a feast for the resurrection from death called *Zitacuarencuaro*, and predicted that white men would arrive in this country. He left, promising to return at a future date.

Bochica (from the Muyscas or Chibchas cultures of Colombia), also known as Nemterequetaba, Xue, Chimizapaqua, Zuhe, and Sua, appeared from the east to form communities and establish laws among the people. He was a white man with a long beard, dressed in a robe, and ruled with equity for many years, teaching the people to build and farm.

John Fiske

American philosopher and historian, John Fiske (1842–1901), a science reconciler of orthodox religious beliefs, recognized there were many myths of an all-destroying flood, partly due to a misperception of local inundations. It was also partly based on the acceptance of biblical scripture through early Catholic and Protestant missions. (He cites S. Baring-Gould, *Legends of the Patriarchs and Prophets*, 1885, pp. 85-106.) He also points out that, despite the unimaginative and rather scanty American stories, there is a fundamental resemblance between myths of the Old World and New World. There are solar myths and myths of the storm curiously blended with culture-myths as in the cases of Hermes, Prometheus, and Kadmos. The American parallels to these are to be found in the stories of Michabo, Viracocha, Ioskeha, and Quetzalcoatl. He quotes Daniel Garrison Brinton (*Myths of the New World*, 1896, page 160):

> As elsewhere the world over, so in America, many tribes had to tell of .... an august character, who taught them what they knew, – the tillage of the soil, the properties of plants, the art of picture-writing, the secrets of magic; who founded their institutions and established their religions; who governed them long with glory abroad and peace at home; and finally did not die, but, like Frederic Barbarossa, Charlemagne, King Arthur, and all great heroes, vanished

mysteriously, and still lives somewhere, ready at the right moment to return to his beloved people and lead them to victory and happiness.

These stories, of a full-bearded white man (such as Quetzalcoatl) passing on the rudiments of civilization to the aboriginal Americans, were at first credited to pre-Columbian visits by Europeans, such as the Vikings of the tenth century. After a scientific study, he claims such notions are trifling and states that:

> These legends are far too numerous, they are too similar to each other, they are too manifestly symbolical, to admit of any such interpretation. By comparing them carefully with each other, and with correlative myths of the Old World, their true character soon becomes apparent.[3]

It seems Viracocha was "God Most High" to the Aymara and the other peoples of the Andes. Their myth is proportional to the Hebrew and Mesopotamian story of creation. It is an Andes Genesis. There is a creation, a flood, the beginning of civilization and, at its center, the ancient city of Tiahuanaco. Tiahuanaco was their Eden, their "Pacarina," the holy place of human emergence.[4] Similar to Eden in the Valley of Tabriz, the Lake Titicaca Basin was a microclimate where the crops of two cultures (Umasuyu and Urcosuyu, mountain and lake) could be grown. According to Alan Kolata in *Valley of the Spirits: a Journey into the Lost Realm of the Aymara*, the Aymara Indians organized society and their habitat in sacred geography and symbolism. In Aymara cosmology, their world was divided in two: *Urcosuyu* and *Umasuyu*. Between these two ecological and conceptual poles (the people of the mountains and the people of the lake) was the *taypi*, the crucial zone of convergence. The taypi that connected these different social and physical parts of the world was Lake Titicaca itself.[5] Tiahuanaco was the stone city at the center.

The irony behind all this mythology is that, like the biblical Garden of Eden, the Andean Pacarina *really did exist*. Mythology it seems, as Heinrich Schliemann once proved when he found the city of Troy, is sometimes based on fact. In its proper perspective it may simply be a way of keeping the old legends alive by spinning shining heroes where only frightened men and women existed, or lauding glorious wars where murder was the issue. Perhaps it is the making of gods from those who already knew the ways of civilization.

Chapter 17
The Iberian Connection

- Searching for a Clovis Progenitor
- Solutrean & Clovis Technology
- Expanding Glaciers and Crossing the Atlantic
- Genetic & Language Clues
- Long-Lost White Brothers
- Theoretical Chaos

In the wake of such remarkable discoveries as Meadowcroft, Pedra Furada, Hueyatlaco, Allendale, Cactus Hill, Monte Verde, and the Bluefish Caves, a growing number of scientists have abandoned the Bering Strait land migration theory as a single source for populating the Americas. A coastal migration route is now gaining acceptance. According to the Smithsonian Institution's Anthropology Outreach Office (*Paleoamerican Origins*, 1999), new evidence suggests that a seafaring people did in fact move along the Pacific Coast into Alaska and northwestern Canada. By 14,500 BC, and perhaps much earlier, they migrated south to Peru and Chile. Archaeological evidence in Australia and Japan indicates that boats were in use as long as 25,000 years ago and possibly even 40,000.[1]

Most coastal areas remained un-glaciated during the ice age, making the theory at least believable. Also, offshore sea routes would have supplied abundant sources of food, as well as fast, relatively safe journey.

It would have been a most effective way to travel. Early coastal sites in Canada, California, Peru, Ecuador, and Chile, dated at 10,000 and 12,000 years old, suggest this may have been the case.

Coastal migration, however, doesn't explain the traces of Middle Paleolithic activity within the continent's interior. Could these ancient seafarers be the ancestors of the Clovis culture? The missing link of the American Paleolithic (a progenitor to the Clovis culture) remains an important issue.

Searching for a Clovis Progenitor

One possible candidate for a Clovis progenitor is found on the Russian steppe lands in Eurasia. The Kostenki culture (part of the Eastern Gravettian culture of Cro-Magnon) was specialized mammoth hunters. They existed from 28,000 to about 10,000 BC in Central and Eastern Europe. Their oldest settlements were located in eastern Eurasia, and it appears they migrated eastward over time.

The *Borshevo* region, of the Don Valley in the Russian Steppe, contains 20,000-year-old sites with artifacts bearing some likeness to Clovis. Bifacial projectile points, end scrapers, side scrapers, borers, and blades associated with animal remains, including mammoth, have been found. At various sites, burned bone was present in hearths similar to those found at Murray Springs near Sierra Vista, Arizona. The 25,000-year-old sites of Pavlov and Dolni Vestonice in Eastern Europe also exhibit Clovis-like curiosities. Mammoth was used for everything from food to housing. Beveled bone points (tools for shaft straightening) and cylindrical ivory pieces found there are also similar to what is seen in Clovis assemblies. Red ocher was also used in burials. Yet the creation of Venus statuettes, other elaborate artwork, and mammoth huts are prevalent in this culture and are not found in the New World. This makes it difficult to accept Kostenki as the Clovis progenitor.

No direct cultural ties can be made to Clovis in Siberia, but there are finds worth noting. On the upper Ob River, in a site called *Tomsk*, end scrapers, flakes, blades, and prismatic cores have all been found among burned mammoth remains. Further east, in the middle Yenisei region, are several mammoth graveyards. Afontova Gora II and Kokorevo II contain bifacial tools, side scrapers, end scrapers, flaked points, notches, backed blades, burins, borers, retouched flakes, bone points, polishers, awls, needles, ivory spheres, and antler shafts. Both sites produced grooved bone points characteristic of microblade cultures though no microblades were ever found. Mal'ta and Buret I, on the upper Angara River, contain evidence of structures, cache pits, a grave containing red ocher and ivory, art objects, beveled bone projectile points, as well as flaked tools, and blades. Again, microblade technology was not found, yet the red ocher grave resembles a Clovis gravesite at Anzick, Montana.

Discoveries in Dyuktai Cave (dated to be 13,500 years old), on the Aldan River in Siberia, include bifacial projectile points, oval and triangular knives, wedge-shaped cores, multifaceted burins, large side scrapers, small end scrappers on blades, and retouched flakes. All were associated with large animals including mammoth. In 1982, it was believed there was no obvious connection between Dyuktai dwellers and Clovis because of the small blades and wedge-shaped cores discovered, but others thought there could be. They existed in Siberia from 30,000 to 11,000 years ago. The Berelekh site (dated at 12,200 years old), at Yakuria, Siberia, presents red ocher, microblade technology, bifacial flaking, and ivory foreshafts. And according to Goebel and Slobodin (1999), they were specialized mammoth hunters.

The *Denali* culture of Alaska lived south of the Brooks Mountain Range in central Alaska. Similarities between the Denali and Siberian tool kits are so great that some have suggested they are part of the same assemblage. According to Hamilton & Goebel (1999), their tradition appears as early as 10,600 years ago (and possibly 1,000 years older than that) at Swan Point. The "core-and-blade" tradition, as it has been referred, appears at sites like Swan Point and Healy Lakes, Campus in the Tanana Valley, Panguingue Creek, Tangle Lakes, and Gallagher in northern Alaska. All of these sites contain characteristics that point to Dyuktai origins. Clearly they made it across the straits to Alaska. Yet their tools do not resemble Clovis technology.

The *Nenana* culture of Alaska is represented by tool industries found at Dry Creek, Orion Portage, Walker Road, Moose Creek, Mesa and Owl Ridge, which consistently date between 11,300 and 11,000 years ago. Nenana points were small, triangular, or teardrop-shaped projectiles.

Although no fluted points are found among these sites, some researchers suggest the Nenana were a regional precursor and that fluted points developed slightly later in New World cultures.

Goebel and Slobodin discovered that fluted points have been found in Alaska at several sites:

- Girls Hill - 4,440 years old
- Putu (stemmed and fluted points) - 5,700 years old
- Bonanza Creek - 700 to 1,800 years old
- Batza Tena - 1,800 to 2,160 years old
- North Fork on the Koyukuk River - 12,300 years old.

All were found in the foothills or north of the Brooks Range. However, these sites are chronologically too late to represent any pre-Clovis occupation, except for North Fork. Most of the Alaskan fluted points appeared about 8,400 years ago.

Other sites located in the far west provide insight into early Alaskan finds. At Charlie Lake Caves in Canada, in an area once ice-free, short fluted points associated with bison are dated to 10,500 years ago. Similar finds have been discovered at Sibald Lakes, Canada. A 9,700-year-old shell refuse heap at Namu in British Colombia exhibits aquatic mammal remains associated with microblades. Other stemmed-point technologies indicate a west coast, southern migration by the Denali tradition. A settlement at Vermillian Lakes, Canada, suggests that this culture possibly engaged in sheep domestication 10,700 to 9,600 years ago. Stemmed-points were also found at Smith Creek Cave in Nevada dating to 10,600 years old. At Winache, Washington, fluted points and bone shafts have been found directly on an ash layer 11,200 years old. In Anzick, Montana there is an adolescent burial 10,600 years old that contains red ocher, bone tools, and a cache of large bifacial, preform projectile points similar to the Clovis style. Although the evidence strongly suggests the existence of two distinct tool traditions in the west, sites like Borax Lake, California confuse the matter with tools representing both Clovis and stemmed-point traditions.

It seems obvious that two distinct cultural traditions, the Denali and Nenana, existed in Beringia during the latter parts of the ice age. The Denali came from the Dyuktai complex of Northeast Asia. This culture most likely evolved into the stemmed-point tradition (and its varieties) and migrated south along the western coast of North America. Linguists have associated this tradition with the Nadene language family. While it remains unclear where the Nenana complex originally appeared, some have suggested a link to the Kostenki culture of the Russian Steppe.

Today the earliest fluted points still appear in the southern half of North America. This suggests a northern migration by people who crafted these fluted point projectiles.

Why does the Nenana tradition in Alaska, similar to Clovis in so many ways, lack characteristic fluting? Perhaps fluting was a New World adaptation, or perhaps the Nenana is a tradition separate from Clovis altogether. Or perhaps it had nothing at all to do with Siberian-Alaskan migrations.

One of the more recent and remarkable observations in American prehistory is that archeologists and anthropologists have found no technical similarities relating Clovis culture to any Asian-Paleolithic cultures. If Clovis culture's origin were indeed Asian, as the Alaskan-Siberian land bridge theory suggests, it should be expected that Clovis tools and weapons would resemble those found in Asia. They don't. They do resemble a culture that existed in Western Europe, the Solutrean, which existed 24,000 to 16,000 years ago. They share bone-shaping techniques, pebble-decorating artistry, and the unusual tradition of burying stone tools in caches filled with red ocher.

More than twenty years ago, Dennis Stanford (curator of anthropology at the Smithsonian Institution) argued against the theory that peopling of America occurred only after 10,000 BC.[2] A proponent of an Atlantic migration theory, he focused on several obvious facts. Clovis points were found in significant numbers in Southeastern regions of the United States, and none were found on either side of the Bering Strait. He also noted that Clovis and Solutrean projectile points were wider, flatter, and thinner than Asian points, therefore showing a stronger Atlantic (as opposed to Pacific) connection in the same 20,000 year range. According to Stanford, not everything in Solutrean is found in Clovis, but everything in Clovis is found in Solutrean.[3] He also contends that Clovis points have never been found in Siberia, while those in Alaska have come from the U.S.

With that technology simultaneously existing in Europe, it is easier to believe that it was brought over than developed independently. He believes there was no antecedent to Clovis point technology, and that it appeared in America fully developed.[4] In October 1999, at the *Clovis and Beyond Conference* in Santa Fe, New Mexico, he put forth his theory of an east coast origin of both Clovis and Solutrean points, suggesting migration across the Atlantic Ocean.

Solutrean & Clovis Technology

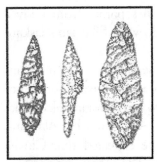

Solutrean Points
Leaf, Shouldered, Laurel

The primary connection between Clovis and Solutrean cultures is their technology, the way in which they created projectile points, blades and other tools from stone and bone. According to Stanford, Clovis and Solutrean blades are virtually indistinguishable.[5] Stanford is not alone. Archeologist Kenneth Tankersley of Kent State University claims there is no question about it. There are only two places in the world and two times that this technology appears – Solutrean and Clovis (Europe and America).[6] Michael Collins, research associate with the Texas Archaeological Research Laboratory at the University of Texas in Austin and director of the Gault site, also agrees. Gault excavations have produced Clovis style projectile points, point preforms, blades and cores, burins, and small engraved stones. These artifacts bear a striking similarity to cultural material recovered from Upper Paleolithic sites in Western Europe.[7] Collins has identified eighteen general and technical similarities between Clovis and Solutrean cultures.

Fifty engraved stones (primarily geometric symbols) found at the Gault site provide another tantalizing clue. Only two other sites in North America have produced engraved stones besides Gault, the Wilson-Leonard site in Texas and the original Clovis site in eastern New Mexico. Engraving was common among European Paleolithic cultures, particularly small, flat engraved stones called *plaquettes*. Some stones also display geometric symbols although these were typically painted. Collins speculates that some of the engraved shapes could be representations of plants or perhaps animals impaled by spears.

Bruce Bradley, an independent archeologist working under his own auspices (*Primitive Tech Enterprises, Inc.*) in Cortez, Colorado, is an expert in the reproduction techniques of Stone Age tools and projectile points. He also believes the Solutrean technique of working flint into a two-sided blade is identical to the Stone Age flint blades found at some American sites. The blades that early Asian migrants created were completely different in concept, as well as method of manufacture. He contends that these shared features can only mean a shared source.[8]

Those who embrace the Atlantic migration, or "out of Iberia" theory, speculate there might have been an early maritime people living in Paleolithic Europe who routinely traveled to America (such as vikings, a much later example). Although canoes or other sailing vessels would not be preserved in the soil because they were constructed from wood, French archaeologist Abbé H. Breuil noted the depiction of a boat with a sail in La Mouthe cave. Dennis Stanford also believes it is not too far-fetched. Even with skin boats, favorable winds and strong currents could have propelled Europeans to America in as little as three weeks.[9]

Expanding Glaciers and Crossing the Atlantic

First defined in 1867 at le Solutré Village in the Sâone Valley near Mâcon, France, it is believed the Solutrean culture arose untraceably from Gravettian culture. This culture, although defined at *la Gravette* rock shelter in the Dordogne Couze Valley, was centered hundreds of miles northeast in Moravia where it developed delicate flint work passed on to Solutrean heirs. When forced from Central Europe by expanding glaciers, they slowly migrated east to the Black Sea and Russian steppe, quickening cultural development in those regions. They then doubled back through the Mediterranean to Spain and France.[10]

Advancing glaciers pushed Western European inhabitants south by 18,000 BC. Scandinavia, the British Isles, the Low Countries, and France (to forty miles south of Paris) became uninhabitable when the glacier reached its maximum in 16,500 BC. Unrelenting for another 5,000 to 6,000 years, the glacier prevented reoccupation of northern Europe.

Survivors of many groups crowded into campsites south of Saint-Sulpice-de-Favières in southern France, particularly in the Bay of Biscay and coastal areas of the Iberian Peninsula.[11]

This hybridizing density of people, in itself, created physical and cultural vigor as well as tension. Is it possible that dislodged groups, in constant view of the sea, felt compelled to coast the glacier while feeding on marine life, perhaps following migratory birds that foretold of land. Michael Johnson, one of the principal investigators at Cactus Hill, thought so.[12] Solutrean mariners would also have had additional guidance if Isaac Newton Vail's theory was correct; disintegrating rings around the earth, like Saturn's stratospheric ice crystals, created a 'canopy effect,' reflecting land far ahead. According to the theory, this phenomena would have existed as late as the fourth millennium BC.[13]

Lawrence Guy Straus, of the University of New Mexico, opposes the North Atlantic migration theory.[14] Straus and his predecessor, P.E.L. Smith found no Solutrean tradition of seafaring in their research. However, Emerson Greenman from the University of Michigan found canoe, kayak, and dug-out type craft painted in red and black in the Spanish caves of La Pasiege, Castillo and La Pileta. They included midship gunwale peaks that characterize Beothuk vessels of Newfoundland. If mariners did launch from the Atlantic shore, they would have journeyed up the Bay of Biscay to skirt the edge of the glacier and launch from the French coast. It would have been 150 miles closer to Newfoundland than it is now because of lower sea levels.

When Greenman discovered Sandia points, he referred to them as Solutrean, specifically Solutrean *Montaut,* which is north of Dax in the extreme corner of Southwest France. He also noted that most North American point-types, between the end of the last glacial period and the first and second cold phases, are also present in the Solutrean regions of France and Spain.[15]

Smith and Straus disagree and argue that fluted points were not so unique in Solutrean areas of France and Spain.[16] Their debate, however, according to their academic opponents, is rhetorical and based on personal beliefs. There is no physical proof. Skin and wood boats, of course, would not have survived the past 12,000 to 20,000 years.

Although similarities certainly exist, there is no concrete proof in the Americas to suggest Solutrean culture existed. Settlements, distinctly

Solutrean, have not been found. Other scientists believe the Solutrean alternative is such a radical departure that it might take years to evaluate adequately, but there is other evidence to view. Skeletal remains also hint at a mystery, a genetic one.

Genetic & Language Clues

Tucked away for the past forty years in the National Museum of Anthropology in Mexico City, are twenty-seven skeletons excavated during the late 1950s. One day, Dr. Silvia Gonzalez of John Moores University, Liverpool, England, decided to investigate. Knowing the remains had never been properly tested, she took a small sample from five of the skeletons to be dated with the latest radiocarbon technique. Director of Oxford's Radiocarbon Accelerator Unit, Robert Hedges performed the analysis with surprising results. A perfectly preserved skull and near perfect skeleton from a woman was dated to be 13,000 years old. According to Gonzalez, the date is accurate. The results have been peer reviewed and accepted for publication in the *Journal of Human Evolution*.

The most intriguing aspect of the skull was not that it was 13,000 years old, but that it was long and narrow. It was also Caucasian in appearance and typical of Western Europeans today. According to Dr. Gonzalez, that is the most likely case. They were definitely not Mongoloid in appearance and were from somewhere else. Whether they were actually European is, at this point, undetermined.[17] However, Gonzalez believes it is quite possible that dolichocephalic man existed in North America well before the arrival of Native American Indians. With respect to the age of *Peñon Woman*, as the skeleton has been named, one of two ideas explains her existence in America. Either she was descended from a much earlier migration of Caucasian people from Asia, or from the Cro-Magnon people of Europe.

Recent mitochondria DNA studies of existing Native American Indian populations have shown similarities to populations in Asia and Siberia, but there are also unique American characteristics, giving possible evidence for diverse migrations. Five lineages for mtDNA were discovered, four of which can be traced to Asian sources, but the fifth linage, simply called "X," appears not to have an Asian origin. Found in

Europeans, the first variant of "X" suggests Eurasia as a possible origin, although thousands of years of disease, famine, and intermarriages has probably influenced the genetic signature of Native American Indians.[18]

The *Buhl Woman* of Idaho (dated to 8750 BC), with a round head and wide face, clearly resembles modern Indians. However, a younger Nebraskan and a pair of Minnesota skulls, ranging from 6850 to 5950 BC, look either European or south Asian. *Spirit Cave Man* (7450 BC), discovered in western Nevada near Fallon in 1940, looks Mediterranean. *Wizards Beach Man* of Nevada (7250 BC) is likely a mixture of India, Polynesian, and Norse. The younger *Kennewick Man* (6050 BC) looked European to some and Ainu, or perhaps Polynesian, to others, based on his dentition (Sudnadont as opposed to Sinodont).

Christy G. Turner II, Regents Professor of Anthropology at Arizona State University, has greatly contributed to the studies of dental anthropology, archaeology, human evolution, and the peopling of America (as well as Japan, Asia, Siberia, Australia, and the Pacific Islands). His research, in the southwestern United States and the Aleutians, has shed new light on microevolution and cultural change in specific human contexts. Through his meticulous studies of dental structures, Turner has made a major contribution to understanding the prehistoric movements of peoples over the earth.

In 1981, Turner noticed that all Paleo-Indians known to him exhibited North Asian *Sinodonty* (a term he coined) meaning shoveled or double-shoveled incisors, single-root upper first molars, and three-root lower first molars. To him, this confirmed a Siberian origin and Bering land-bridge theory. It also contrasts with Sudnadonty of the Archaic Caucasoid in southeast Asia and Europe who lived from the Atlantic coast west to Lake Baikal in southern Siberia.[19]

Everyone did not look European during the waning years of the ice age, but some of the earliest Paleo-Americans certainly did. South American anthropologists have been as surprised as their North American counterparts to find Pleistocene skeletons other than Siberian, Mongolian, or North Chinese types. Brazilian skulls, dating back to the ice age, resemble no current race. Curiously, skeletons of mastodon-hunters in Peru look Neanderthal, unlike native Peruvians today.[20]

Language clues also suggest a transatlantic, European connection. Pre-Indo-European speech persists in the earliest dialects of the Algonquin Cree language, specifically *th*, *n*, and *y*. It is similar to Euskera before its Indo-Europeanization as modern Basque. Before spreading across Manitoba and Saskatchewan to Alberta, the Algonquin Cree peoples lived on Hudson Bay and its southern extension, James Bay. Original speakers of this language in America would not initially have colonized the arctic region during the severe glacier, but would have preferred campsites on rivers in Pennsylvania, Virginia, the Carolinas, and Mexico.

The mounting evidence of an early European migration does not convince all anthropologists and archeologists. Professor Chris Stringer, Director of Human Origins at the Natural History Museum in London, believes that most prehistoric humans were dolichocephalic (long-headed) regardless of their origin.[21] If true, this is perhaps more mysterious than an Atlantic crossing. Why were they longheaded? And what became of "long-headed" man?

Long-Lost White Brothers

In *Life Among the Piutes*, Sarah Winnemucca tells the curious story of her people meeting white men for the first time. Her grandfather, chief of the Piute Nation, was camped near Humboldt Lake with a small portion of the tribe when a party, traveling eastward from California, was seen. After hearing the report that white men with hair on their faces had been seen, the Chief jumped up, clasped his hands together, and cried aloud, "My long-looked for white brothers have come at last!" He immediately gathered some of the leading men and went out to meet his long-lost white brothers. He approached them several times. Each time the white men (in fear it is assumed) kept their distance and soon passed out of the territory. Disappointed, he hoped they would come again the next year. Then he sent for the entire Piute Nation and told them an ancient legend of the white man.

According to Piute tradition, in the beginning of the world there were only four people, two girls and two boys. One girl and one boy were dark and the other pair was white. The Indian forefather and mother were only two and the current Indians were their children. Everyone was happy. For a time everyone got along well, but disagreement arose and, to the dismay of the parents, they fought. After a while and much prayer, the parents saw that they must separate their children. "Depart from each other, you cruel children - go across the mighty ocean and do not seek each other's lives," they said. So the light girl and boy disappeared and their parents saw them no more. They were grieved, but they knew their children were happy. As time went on the dark children grew into a large nation. The nation that sprung from the white children would sometime send someone to meet and heal all the old trouble.[22]

The Klamath Indians of the Pacific Northwest also hold a tradition about white men living long ago in North America. At the end of the Civil War, a chief named Lalek told a story to a young Union soldier about how his ancestors lived in stone houses, and that white men ran wild and lived in the forest. According to the chief, this was before the 'stars fell,' so long ago that no one could count the years.[23]

The Oglala Sioux also contend that, in the northern areas, there lived tall white men. As told by John G. Neihardt in *Black Elk Speaks*, their traditions state that in the northern regions lived the great white giants.[24]

In his book *Red Earth-White Lies*, Vine Deloria tells the traditions of Native American Indians and how their oral records of history display no memory of a migration from Siberia or anywhere else from across the ocean. He also explains a theory by Werner Muller from his book *America-The New World or the Old*, which describes how Cro-Magnon originated in the northern parts of North America and migrated along the glacier's coastline to Western Europe.[25]

Muller argues that early origins of some Indian tribes can be based on architecture, astronomy, and calendar recording. According to his theory, four diverse groups of people lived in the far northern areas of North America very early in time. Three of the groups were the ancestors of the Salish, Sioux, and Algonquin Indians. The fourth group was white-skinned, bearded and cruel, and, as in the Winnemucca's Pauite story, unfriendly to the Indians. As a result the Indian groups moved south to avoid contact with this malicious tribe.[26]

Muller insinuates that a climatic catastrophe occurred (the stars falling) most likely involving the ice age, which forced the Indian tribes to migrate south separately. The Salish moved to the Pacific Coast, the Sioux to the Plains, and the Algonquians went

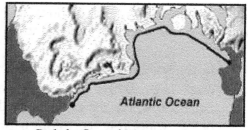

Path for Coastal Migrations in the North Atlantic

eastward to the region of the Great Lakes and beyond. The white-skinned people made their way across the North Atlantic to modern Scandinavia and Western Europe. Muller places their migration at 42,000 BC with the beginning of the interstadial of the Wurm glaciation, the beginning of the ice age.[27]

In support of his American Cro-Magnon theory, Muller cites the Calaveras skull. It was found in Calaveras County, California 130 feet below the surface, embedded in a gravel layer beneath rock composed of compacted volcanic ash. The ash was created from tertiary eruptions in the Sierra Nevada. Gold miners found the skull and, when discovered (February 1866), its credibility was unquestioned.[28]

Deloria cites the opinions of well-known scientists, such as the renowned evolutionary biologist, George Gaylord Simpson (1902-1984), in support of the theory. In *Mammals and Land Bridges*, Simpson reviews the evidence and theories concerning mammalian migrations across continents. He states that, based on the history of mammals, a wide-open corridor that would allow the wholesale exchange of animals is rare. He also argues that wherever herbivores migrate, carnivores will follow and is critical of any theory postulated on scanty evidence:

> The postulation of land bridges on the basis of one or a few mammals is thus very uncertain. Unless there is reasonable possibility that their companions have not been discovered, a theoretical bridge based on such evidence is probably unreal.[29]

He defines the term "land bridge" as a relatively restricted link between two landmasses and further states that:

> In the whole history of mammals there are exceedingly few cases (e.g., Lower Eocene between Europe and North America) where the evidence really warrants the inference of a wide-open corridor between two now distinct continental masses.[30]

Simpson does accept the theory of land bridges, but is practical in his ideas. Mammals, including man, need a reason to migrate from one area to another, and many barriers exist even though a bridge is available. Animal migrations are a much more complex matter than some television documentaries would have you believe. Believing that animals and man trekked to America from Siberia, simply because the land was there to walk on, is entirely presumptuous.

Deloria also believes that scientific writers have ignored Simpson's conclusions for several decades and he believes that this supports Muller's Canada to Europe migration theory. This leaves little scientific comfort to scholars who adopted the Bering Strait land bridge idea as a means of populating the Americas (animal as well as human).[31]

Windover Pond

One of the more important finds, if not *the* most important, came in 1982 when a construction crew was clearing the way for a new road through a swamp near Titusville, Florida. In a small pond, located in the Windover Farm subdivision, workers discovered a skull as the backhoe they were operating scooped out a load of peat. After three years of excavation and more than twenty of research, a gold mine of information was gained in understanding prehistoric America. Led by Glen Doran of Florida State University, the excavation team unearthed the skeletal remains of 169 people aged at death from six to seventy years old (seventy-five skeletons were relatively intact) and ninety nearly complete, human brains. Carbon dating revealed that these graves were created 8,100 years ago, with the youngest being 6,900 years old.[32]

The Windover people were not the primitives most would guess. They were quite the opposite. Artifacts of wood, bone, and seed that were made into jewelry and tools, revealed that they were a complex society. Indeed, woven cloth was discovered that served as a burial shroud for those that were sunk into the bog. Eighty-seven cloth fragments were recovered that revealed five different methods of fabric making. Some were woven as tightly as a cotton t-shirt. The burial clothes were especially fine, suggesting there was a special status attached to their passing. James Adovasio, director of the Mercyhurst Archeological Institute in Erie, Pennsylvania and an expert in ancient textiles, believes from the evidence that they were an egalitarian society.

DNA analysis performed by University of Florida molecular biologist, William Hauswirth revealed that these people were a specific and small subset of modern American Indians that did not interbreed with other tribes. Recent DNA testing, performed by Dr. Joseph Lorenz at the Coriell Institute for Medical Research, has produced far more intriguing results.

Lorenz studied tissue samples from five of the excavated brains. He was searching for haplotypes (a specific DNA pattern) that would confirm they were, indeed, Native American. None of the samples did. The first two samples looked European, as did the last three, although they were slightly different.[33]

Theoretical Chaos

All this scientific debate and the puzzling evidence about these 'first Americans' have thrown the archeology and anthropology communities into fevered disagreement. In December 2000, *National Geographic Magazine* made the muddle 'official' by publishing a twenty-seven page article that explained archeology's state of affairs. It surveyed the sites, the evidence, and personal interpretations. Entitled *The Dawn of Humans: Hunt for the First Americans*, Michael Parfit asserts there is theoretical chaos in the realm of the American archeologist. The evidence is diverse and sometimes scanty, but strong enough to open the field to new ideas.

Parfit covers the 14,500 year-old finds at Monte Verde, Chile; Cactus Hill (Virginia), 18,000 years old; and Meadowcroft (near Pittsburgh)

20,000 years old. He also tells of a unique discovery made in northern Florida's Wacissa River. Tools, crafted from mastodon ivory, have been unearthed from the river beneath four feet of mud. Under the direction of David Webb, curator of vertebrate paleontology at the University of Florida's Museum of Natural History, the scuba equipped excavation team has recovered many finely crafted tools: projectile points, a spear tip carved from ivory thirteen inches long, and several daggers made from the bone of an extinct Pleistocene horse.[34]

He also supports the theory of European migration of ice age peoples as put forth by Dennis Stanford and Bruce Bailey. Like Solutrean points, Clovis projectile points are wider, flatter, and thinner; distinctly different from the narrow, thick points found in Siberia, Alaska, and Idaho. Of course there are those who are strongly opposed to a European migration, such as Lawrence Straus an expert on Solutrean culture, but others smell the proverbial smoke. Michael Collins, Director at the Gault site in Texas, thinks there is enough smoke concerning the Iberian connection that someone should look for the fire.[35]

DNA evidence is just as puzzling. Genetic markers from the mother's side support an Asian heritage, but others match those that are common today in Europe and central Asia. Of course, the Siberian people that were responsible for the migration to Alaska may have died out, but it may also be the case that Europeans found a more direct route to America in the north Atlantic.[36]

This puzzling state of interpreting the past exists all the way down the Americas. At the southern tip of South America in a place called *Tierra del Fuego*, the archeological record shows that people were living there as long ago as 6,500 BC. When the European explorers first arrived they found four different groups of people, that spoke two separate languages, in a fairly small area of land. Argentinean archeologist, Jose Luis Lanata, describes it as a puzzle that may contain many different combinations.[37]

Physical anthropologists agree. Although there are a few prehistoric skeletons to base a theory on, results suggest that America was a diverse land. Those skeletons do not resemble the Native American Indians of later times, but they do resemble Polynesian and Japanese Ainu. This, according to Doug Owsley of the Smithsonian Institute, would be consistent with multiple migrations of various people over a long period of time.[38]

Those who have been researching the first Americans, the archeologists, physical anthropologists, as well as DNA experts and linguists, disagree on basic elements of the story. The tale is obviously complicated.

A Puzzling Picture

Based on the available scientific and historical evidence, the Siberian-Alaskan migration theory, as an exclusive method of populating America, is highly questionable. In fact, a quick glance at the raw data suggests just the opposite. (*See maps on pages 328-329.*) The densest areas for fluted points and archeological sites are in the eastern third of the United States. Since ancient people migrated either by foot or by boat, the densest areas would logically be the points of arrival. Further migration would continue outward in all directions as the population grew which, of course, could take thousands of years.

It is also clear there is no obvious, direct host to Clovis culture anywhere in America, yet an indirect link to Europe exists. Clovis tool technology (how they created tools, particularly spear points) is nearly identical to a particular Cro-Magnon culture of Europe, the Solutrean. This is an enigma, which for us presents even more questions. Who were the true natives of America? Where is the point of origin for these people? Curious examples exist.

As we have seen, the mound building, oblong-headed Adena culture was replaced by the more modern looking Hopewell with no descendents remaining of the former. According to the history of the Iroquois Nation, prehistoric giants were enemies to Native American Indians. They also no longer exist. Could it be the Americas had their own source of mankind and that these giants, this white-skinned tribe, really did make their way across the Atlantic to Europe as the Piute legend explains? Some archaeologists admit that evidence suggests they appeared from nowhere in Western Europe with fully modern behavior.

One of the most striking facts regarding American prehistory is that all great civilizations, those who built with stone in monumental fashion, are found in Central and South America, such as the peculiar city of

Tiahuanaco. Likewise, the oldest settlement dates also come from those areas (Pedra Furada in Brazil and Hueyatlaco in Mexico). Both are 30,000 years old or older. Did modern peoples spread from Europe to the Americas some 20,000 years ago as the proponents of the Clovis-Solutrean connection suggest? Or did the first cultures of Cro-Magnon migrate from North America, via the North Atlantic, to Europe, as Muller believes? There may be no greater mystery.

In his National Geographic article, Micahel Parfit addresses the Atlantic and Pacific migration theories with equal weight. He also quotes five Native American Indian legends from the Piute, Pomo, Cheyenne, Yuchi-Creek, and Yamana tribes, but does not refer to them in the body of text. Silently, he points a finger at the people who were there to witness history. Perhaps he is hinting that they may know something.

Wherever they came from, the case has been made for the existence of civilization as long ago as 40,000 years when Cro-Magnon appeared on the shores of Western Europe. With the historical context now set, we can move on to solving the mystery of the giants and the story behind the Genesis story of creation.

Chapter 18
Myth & Shamanism

- The Myth in All of Us
- Building A Paleolithic Worldview
- Archaic Cosmology and Shamanism
- Mystical Numbers Seven and Nine
- Origins of Shamanism
- Evidence at "The Three Brothers" Cave

You may be thinking it is an odd approach to mix the prehistory of the Americas with that of the Near East. Historians who espouse an 'invetionist' approach to cultural development would certainly think so. Although some contact with other cultures in unavoidable, they believe any given culture, as a general rule, invents their own traditions and develops their own knowledge. Diffusionists, on the other hand, believe knowledge is transmitted from one culture to another, and in its ultimate form, from an ancient 'mother' culture of which all others cultures descend – commonly referred to in scientific circles as 'hyperdiffusion.' Advocates of these two opposing views often vigorously disagree. Although proof is hard to come by, linking cultures of the Western hemisphere with those of the East, a number of scholars and researchers see evidence that is worth investigating, such as the case with the Clovis/Solutrean connection.

Neither inventionism nor diffusion can be proven wrong since it is not possible to know exactly, and consistently, what happened when. On one hand, it is difficult to believe that people would forget their traditions when they migrated from one region to another. On the other, there are no detailed records describing prehistoric migrations so inferences must come from the archeological evidence, which may or may not tell the whole story. In reality, ancient history and prehistory is a wobbling house resting on the shifting sands of evidence and interpretation. It is a ship made of mostly theory and part fact sailing uneasily in uncharted waters somewhere between science and speculation. So looking at trends and significant facts is the place to start.

One curious fact that Chris Stringer has pointed out is that nearly all of the prehistoric skulls excavated are dolichocephalic. This is the case regardless of the continent. Another curious fact is that most cultures that made the transition to what we call civilization all have similar mythologies. Although scientists have a tendency to heavily discount myths and oral traditions, they are a part of history as much as official documents from any given period of time.

The Myth in All of Us

Mythology has always played a role in culture. Even today, we wrap stories around significant events, possibly to make them seem bigger than life, or perhaps to remind us of their importance so the next generation will continue the tradition, or maybe both. A case in point is Christmas. It is a religious holiday celebrating the birth of Christ (even though it is academically accepted that his birth was actually in late October or early November). Yet individually and as a society, we celebrate it on December 25th and wrap it in myth, nearly overshadowing its true significance. There is no reason to continue with the mythological aspect of it, but we do. We don't believe it, but we behave as if we *want* to believe. It is a mythical part of our culture and has survived into the twenty-first century.

We go out of our way to believe in Santa Claus and enjoy doing it. We tell our children Santa Claus will bring presents on Christmas Eve. "Santa is hungry from all the work he has to do early Christmas morning, so it is hospitable to leave him cookies and milk," we explain to our children. As our children set the table with cookies and milk, we watch and smile.

After bedtime, we put the milk and cookies back where they belong (or eat them) leaving a few crumbs and dribble of milk in the bottom of a glass. Their joy on Christmas morning, because Santa has eaten his treat and left his gifts, becomes our joy. Somewhere near the human age of reason, (ten or so) our children discover that Mom and Dad are behind the feats and treats of Santa. Yet, they continue to believe and reproduce the myth. And when they become adults, the cycle moves to the next generation. There is Easter, Thanksgiving, and national mythologies as well, such as Abraham Lincoln, George Washington and Independence Day, each with their own story wrapped around a core of fact. Myth, it seems, is a by-product of the human experience.

The story of Christmas and Santa Claus is well-known and pervasive in society, but there are many other modern examples; from Star Trek's *Trekkers*, to the medieval world of trolls, magic, and armor. These reach deeper into the human psyche and its affinity for myth and myth creation. The *Belegarth Medieval Combat Society* has chapters in seventeen states and one in British Columbia. Although activities are centered on simulated combat (actually a sport), much work is devoted to costume and alternate identities; most enthusiasts have an alias, like Leod MacGregor, Goat, Soth, Sir Winfang, Arioch, and so on. It is common for some of the members to have watched the film "Lord of the Rings" thirty times or more. Although fun and games is obviously a large part of it to the casual participator, precisely why this happens and why some immerse themselves so deeply may never be known. Perhaps the more radical enthusiast dislikes the worldview that society has created for him or her and prefers an alternate. The point here is not to judge or psychoanalyze, but to display how powerful the mind is as a creative force and how worldviews can develop quite naturally.

Everyone has a worldview, a way of relating his or her existence to the external conditions of society which surround us all, even if one's worldview is simply 'I need to make money to live.' Ultra-basic and purely capitalistic, it is still is a worldview. An individual's worldview stems from an innate need to explain everything.

Although nonexclusive, the people of the western world base their worldview on several variations in Christian doctrine. The human mind, however, is rarely that simple. There is coexistence within the mind of other beliefs. One can spend vast energy in a mythical way of life, but at the same time, embrace the doctrines of Christianity. From the civilizations of ancient Sumer to those of the Belegarth Medieval Society, mythology helps to forge a worldview so our species can accept its place in this world.

The human being is obviously quite complex and multidimensional. This is, no doubt, a function of higher consciousness. Being anatomically human, prehistoric man was no different. From the evidence of his artwork and funerary rituals, it is clear he had higher consciousness.

Building A Paleolithic Worldview

We can never know precisely what went on within Paleolithic settlements 40,000 years ago or within the mind of Paleolithic man. By the sheer simplicity of life, as well as evidence left behind, a reasonably educated guess can be offered. The first bands of humans, unfortunately, did not have the benefit of any progenitors for their worldview. They had to develop it themselves, through their senses and by their experiences. Try to image how you would think if you grew up living in an environment with no television, radio, newspapers, books, or no modern technology whatsoever. Your sole purpose in life was to find enough food to survive another day, all the while living in a pristine forest or grassland and subjected to the elements every day of every year. Maslow's hierarchy of needs surely comes into play; physiological needs and safety are paramount, as is perhaps, belongingness. Innate pressure to fulfill these biological needs must play a significant role in molding the first worldview of man; animals, to kill for food and shelter, and female companionship to fulfill biologically based emotional needs. This can also be said for the needs of woman. It is just a mirror image. It is doubtful the biological-emotionally based relationship between man and woman has ever changed. It is no wonder Paleolithic paintings, engravings, and carvings depict animals and women.

"Venus" statuettes were carved in such numbers that it is clear, due to their pervasiveness, that they were important in a cultural and religious way. It is also safe to say that women were just as important to Paleolithic men as they are to modern men, and vice versa. No relationship is ever perfect, but, as it is today, it must be the case they worked together.

According to the archeological record, mankind developed tools and technologies over many thousands of years to become successful in his fight for survival. Banded together in larger groups, with the ability to hunt abundant wildlife successfully (and often store meat in natural refrigeration pits), life was a little bit easier, enough so for him to deliberate his place on Earth. Of course, it may also be the case that man, by his very nature, searches for meaning regardless of his success.

The most amazing and inspiring aspect of life must have been the sky, the rising and setting of the sun, as well as the nighttime stars. Even today, knowing what the stars really are, we often gaze in awe and wonder. And of course there is land, a place where life is "lived out." There can be no doubt that man was acutely aware of his surroundings; the majesty of mountains, the refreshing waters, the change of the seasons, and its affect on wildlife. He also knew the habits of his prey, when to hunt and how to disguise himself within the natural terrain. It must have been obvious to him that nourishment came from the land on which he lived much more so than it is today (at least in comparison to industrial societies). The cave proposed an interesting element; being underground, it proved to be a sanctuary from the harsh elements of winter. From these most obvious aspects of nature, the levels of his world were three: sky, ground, and cave (or underground).

Archaic Cosmology and Shamanism

From Mircea Eliade's *Shamanism: Archaic Techniques of Ecstasy* and David Lewis-Williams' Shamanic explanation of cave art, a Paleolithic cosmology (and perhaps theology) can be developed with a reasonable degree of likelihood. No religion, be it ancient or modern, can be completely new and abolish the past. A synthesis of the most crucial elements can turn into a new belief system. While it is true that prehistoric documents go back no further than the Neolithic, nothing justifies the assumption that during the millennia that preceded the earliest stone age, mankind did not have a religious life as intense and as various as in the succeeding periods.[1] It is almost certain some of that man's earliest religious beliefs were incorporated into later mythologies and belief systems.

The earliest known cosmology of man uses a "World Pillar" metaphor to rationalize physical reality. The sky is seen as a tent, the Milky Way, a seam with stars serving as holes for light to shine through. Sometimes the gods open the tent to look at the Earth below (an explanation for falling stars). In the middle of the sky, the North Star, referred to as "Nail Star" or "Sky Nail," secures the celestial tent. In their cosmology, the Pole Star was the "World Pillar." It served as a link between heaven and earth.

Its imagery and terminology is found across cultural barriers: the Samoyed, Chuckchee, Koryak, Lapps, Finns, Estonians, Turko-Altaians, Mongols, Kalmyk, Buryat, Kirgiz, Bashkir, Siberian Tatars, Teleut, etc.[2] Symbolism of the "World Pillar" is also seen in more advanced cultures, such as Egypt, India, China, Greece, and Mesopotamia. In ancient Babylon, man himself in the form of a ziggurat, palace, or temple, often formed the link between heaven and earth. This man-made "Cosmic Mountain" symbolizes the "World Pillar." In ancient Mesopotamian beliefs, a central mountain called the "Mount of the Lands," joined heaven and earth. Eliade concludes that this cosmological concept was a universally dispersed idea related to the belief in the possibility of direct communication with the sky (or God).[3]

The idea of a cosmic mountain as the center of the world is based on symbolism of "The Center," which predates the rise of the ice age civilizations of Asia.[4] It appears that, in the very beginning, any sacred place, which was the site of religious and physical realities thought as not part of this world (usually originating from the sky), was a "center." It was where communication between ground and sky occurred and in archaic cultures, it was normally used to send offerings to the celestial gods. The Siberian Tatars, as well as the Yukat shaman (with seven levels in their mystical journey), climbed a mountain with seven stories and at its summit was the polestar in the naval (center) of the sky.[5] The ziggurat with its seven stories, represented the seven planetary heavens or depicted the colors of the world as it did at the Ur ziggurat, a man-made cosmic mountain that was symbolic of the cosmos.

Complementary to the "Cosmic Mountain" is the "World Tree." Cosmologically, it rises from the center of the Earth at the umbilicus (or navel) and connects the three cosmic regions of sky, ground, and underground. It represents the universe in its state of continual regeneration as well as the sky and planetary heavens. In archaic tradition, it also represents sacredness of the world. Its fertility and lasting relationship was related to creation, fruitfulness and initiation, as well as the concept of absolute reality and immortality. Therefore, the "World Tree" was a tree of life and a representation of immortality.[6] Symbolically strengthened, it also represented the well of life and the master of destiny. This idea of the "World Tree" is quite old. It is found among many primitive cultures and was part of their lunar and initiatory symbolism.[7]

Through the ages, various cultures have further expanded the "World Tree." In particular, southeastern influences contributed to mythologies in central and north Asian peoples. The "Cosmic Tree" and "Book of Fate" are introduced from more developed civilizations, in the idea the "World Tree" lives and gives life.[8] The cosmological representation of the tree-bird (or tree with a bird at its top and snake at its roots), typical of central Asian cultures as well as those of ancient Germany, is presumed to be of Oriental origin. However, this symbolism was already expressed on prehistoric monuments.

Another theme of distant origin is that of the "Tree" associated with the "Book of Fate." Among the Osmanli Turks, the "Tree of Life" has a million leaves, and on each leaf is written the fate of each human. Each time a leaf falls a man dies. The Ostyak people believe the gods look for the child's future in a "Book of Fate." According to legends of the Siberian Tatars, seven gods inscribe the destiny of newborn infants into a "Book of Life." Although occurring in different cultures, all of these images are taken from the Mesopotamian concept of the seven planetary heavens, which are viewed as a "Book of Fate."[9]

Shamanism has been found typically among nomadic hunter-gatherer people, such as those found in Siberia and central Asia. These cultures were composed mainly of hunters-fishers or herdsmen-breeders. One hesitates to refer to totemism in addressing shamanic cosmology, but rather a mystical relationship between man and his prey. These relations were fundamental in hunting societies. Religions found in Siberia and central Asia were, in structure and form, similar to that of the Indo-Europeans. Both have the same importance of the Great God of the Sky (or atmosphere) and the same absence of the goddesses, which are more characteristic of Indo-Mediterranean peoples. They also depict the same function credited to the "sons" or "messengers," and the same exultation of fire. It is typical in their cosmology for lesser divine beings (messengers and sons of God) to occupy intermediate levels, while the Supreme Being rests at the top.[10] In this we have the cosmological source of Enoch's

Watchers and why those who lived on mountains were considered angels (messengers) or sons of God.

The Shaman

A person does not choose to be a shaman, rather he or she is chosen through a mystical experience involving a dream, sickness, or other similar circumstance. Most commonly, the shaman is chosen by a divine or semi-divine being. Principal to the act of becoming a shaman is an initiation ceremony involving suffering, death, and resurrection,[11] by which the shaman enters the spirit world to embark on a mystical journey. In a dream state, the future shaman usually journeys to the "center of the world," or "seat of the cosmic tree" and "Universal Lord."[12]

It is doubtful the shamans created the cosmology, mythology, and theology of their respective cultures. Rather, they used it as an itinerary for their spiritual journeys from one cosmic region to another (earth to sky or earth to underworld).[13] His journey is one of gathering information to improve the life of an individual or the tribe in general. He does this by entering a trance and communicating with the spirits of the deceased, demons, and spirits of nature. It is noteworthy to state that the shaman differs from the "possessed" person because of his ability to communicate with the 'spirits' without becoming their instrument and subject to their will. Although the mastery of fire and magical flight are among the shaman's talents, he is not to be confused with magicians and sorcerers found in other cultures throughout the world. The shaman's magic is particular, and defined within the cosmology and theology set forth by his culture.[14] He knows the mystery of breaking through to sky or underground.

'Helping spirits,' most of which are of animal form, often attend his journey. He has immediate and concrete experiences with these spirits, sees them face-to-face, and talks and prays with them, sometimes in a secret language. (The secret language is actually the animal language and originates in animal cries. It occurs in almost all shamanic-based cultures.) He solicits them, but does not control more than a few. The presence of a helping spirit in animal form (or incarnation of an animal spirit by the shaman through masks, actions, or dances) is another way of displaying that the shaman can abandon his human condition and is able to "die."

Each new shamanic séance represents the shaman's death and resurrection.[15]

The shaman's drum is different from all other musical instruments because it makes an ecstatic experience possible. They understood and used the power of rhythm and sound to connect with the magic of "the sacred." Dancing to the beat reproduced the shaman's journey to the sky.

It is believed that the first drums appeared sometime between the Paleolithic and the Neolithic periods, around 8000 BC. The drum itself comes from a branch of the "Cosmic Tree" which the Lord fell for the express purpose of making its shell. Its symbolic meaning is obvious from the underlying ideology. There is communication between sky and earth by way of the "World Tree," or perhaps more precisely, by the axis that passes through the center of the world. Climbing the ritual birch tree, he effectually reaches the summit of the Cosmic Tree. And since the shell of the shaman's drum is taken from the wood of this tree, the shaman, by his drumming, is magically projected into the vicinity of the cosmic tree (i.e. to the center of the world) where he can ascend into the sky.

There are many styles of drums. Among them are found the most important symbols, such as the "World Tree," the sun and moon, and the rainbow. They depict a microcosm of the perceived world and its three zones – sky, earth, and underworld. This symbolism shows the means by which the shaman carries out the breakthrough from plane to plane and establishes communication with the world above and below.[16]

The shaman's ornament-laden costume gives him a new and magical body in animal form. The bird, stag (reindeer), and bear are typical of the shamanic costume, but the bird is the most common. The same aerial symbolism is found across the world in connection with shamans, as well as sorcerers and mythical beings.

Snakes are also a common feature of the costume. The Siberian shaman wears a caftan, a full-length garment with elbow-length or long sleeves, from which hang ribbons a foot wide and three feet long, called *kulin* (or snakes). The Buryat costume displays two sticks ending in horse heads and encircled by bells. Thirty snakes, made of black and white pelts, hang from the shoulders and reach the ground, topped by an iron *casque* (a visor-less helmet) with three points that resemble deer horns. The Altaic costume displays a quantity of ribbons and kerchiefs sewn to its frock representing snakes, some of them being shaped into snakes' heads with eyes and open jaws.[17] Masks are not typical in shaman rituals. The costume itself is a mask, but may be regarded as adopted from a mask originally.[18]

The shaman's costume also proclaims the special status of its wearer, who symbolically died and returned to life. It is crafted to resemble a skeleton. Certain iron objects that mimic bones, at least partially, gave the appearance of a skeleton. This summarizes and re-actualizes the initiatory drama of death and resurrection. The theology behind this is that the soul lives in the bones. Therefore, resurrection of the individual from its bones is expected.

Tibetan and Iranian customs both embrace excarnation (exposing a corpse to be devoured by dogs and vultures). For the Tibetans, it was important for the body to be transformed into a skeleton as quickly as possible. In Iranian custom, the bones were placed in an *astodan* (the place of bones) where they awaited resurrection.[19] Examples of this have found their way into biblical stories. A legend of the Gagauzi tells that the Adam of *Genesis* gathered bones from various animals and prayed to God to animate them to provide wives for his sons.[20] There is also the famous vision of Ezekiel, where bones from the whole house of Israel reassembled themselves and once again were covered with flesh by the spirit of the Lord.[21]

Mystical Numbers Seven and Nine

Identification of the "Cosmic Tree," with its seven branches and the seven planetary heavens, is unquestionably due to original influences from Mesopotamia. Ascent to the sky along the axis of the world is a universal and archaic idea. It occurred much earlier than the idea of traversing the seven celestial regions, which probably spread through central Asia well after Mesopotamian speculations on the seven planets. It is also known that the religious value of the number "3," which symbolizes the three cosmic regions, preceded the value of the number "7." The supreme omnipotent being rests in the seventh level where the Sun also lives. (The belief in a celestial supreme god is also indigenous and very ancient in central Asia and the Arctic.) Although the number seven represents an Oriental and recent influence, the belief of the sons of god, who live in intermediate levels, is ancient. According to Eliade, it is likely that shaman ideology played some part in propagating "7" as a sacred number. The Ostyak and Lapp shamans eat mushrooms with seven spots to enter the trance.[22]

The myth of the rainbow (with its seven colors), as the road of the gods and the bridge between sky and earth, doubtlessly existed in religious beliefs of Mesopotamia, and is also found in Japanese tradition. Furthermore, the seven colors of the rainbow have also been incorporated into the idea and symbolism of seven heavens. Traditions of this are found in India and Mesopotamia, as well as in Judaism. The rainbow surrounds the Throne of the Supreme Being of which symbolism has persisted in the art of the Christian era, well into the Renaissance. The Babylonian ziggurat was sometimes represented with seven colors symbolizing the seven celestial regions, and he who climbed it reached the summit of the cosmic world.[23]

Origins of Shamanism

According to Siberian Yakut tradition, the first shaman, with a body made from a mass of snakes, possessed extraordinary power. In his pride, he refused to recognize the supreme God. So in judgment, it rained fire. A toad emerged from the flames, and from this creature arrived the demons, which in turn supplied the Yakut peoples with their exceptional shamans. Here there is the dual conception of good and evil, probably drawn from Iranian influences. It may be the case, however, that this legend deals with the origin of black shamans who were reputed to have relations only with the underworld and devil.[24]

Most myths concerning shamanic origins put forward the direct intervention of God or his representative, the eagle, bird, or sun. In his initiatory dream, the shaman is carried to the Cosmic Tree where the top is the domain of the Lord of the World. Sometimes the Supreme Being is represented in the form of an eagle, and in the branches are the souls of the future shamans. This cosmology reveals complex symbolism crystallized around a celestial divine being with the idea of magical flight to the center of the world or "World Tree."[25]

According to Arctic and central Asian tradition, the first shamans really flew through the clouds on their horses and performed miracles their present-day descendants are incapable of repeating.[26] Findings in many other traditions show friendship with animals and understanding of their language, representing a paradise association. In the beginning (in mythical times), so the story goes, man lived at peace with the animals and understood their speech. It was not until after some primordial catastrophe that man became what he is today: mortal, gendered, required to work to feed himself, and at enmity with the animals.[27]

In this paradise age, human beings could easily rise to the sky and uphold familiar relationships with the gods. After the catastrophe (at the dawn of time), communications between man and the gods were interrupted. Only certain privileged beings, first of which were shamans, preserved the power to connect with the upper regions. Shamans had the power to fly and to reach the sky through the "central opening," whereas the rest of mankind could only pass on offerings. Also, the shaman's privileged status was primarily due to his ability for ecstatic experiences.[28] Eliade believes the cosmological symbolism of the dwelling and the experience of shaman's ascent, confirms, though in another aspect, this archaic myth.

In the Oceanian region, the "Tree of Life," in whose branches the souls of infants are perched, is also a very old myth. In their mythology, the creation of the world is a result of a conflict between two gods of opposite principles: feminine (cosmologically lower and represented by the waters and the snake) and masculine (the upper region, the bird). During the struggle between these two gods, the "World Tree" (a primordial total) is destroyed, but its destruction is merely temporary. It created an archetype of all creative human activity and is destroyed only that it may be reborn. The supreme god *Mula Djadi Na Bolon* (he who has his beginning in himself), the creator of the universe and of the other gods, lives in the most distant heaven. He became like all the supreme gods of primitives, in that no sacrifices were offered to him. His adversary, a cosmic snake, lives in the subterranean world that will finally destroy Earth.[29]

Another central Asian myth also depicts influence from Indian peoples. The Mongolian god, Ochirvani, in the form of the eagle *Garide*, attacked the snake *Losun* in the primordial ocean, wrapped it around Mt.

Sumeru three times, and then finally crushed its head. According to Eliade, symbolism of the center was a natural part of ancient Indian spirituality. It seems probable that Mesopotamian influences also reached India and the Indian Ocean.[30]

Evidence at "The Three Brothers" Cave

Funerary rites, cave paintings, engravings, and evidence of induced trance (although circumstantial) all attest to a belief system of some kind existing within the cultures of Cro-Magnon. But were there actually shamans as defined by Mircea Eliade within ice age cultures? We will never know for sure, but it is logical to assume the cosmological foundations, at least for shamanism, reach as far back as the hunter-gatherer cultures at the end of the ice age. The cave of *Le Trois Freres* (The Three Brothers), however, suggests it is even further.

In 1914, Count Begouen and his three sons discovered a cave in the French Pyrenees. In honor of his boys, he named it Les Trois Freres. Inside this cave, a long, narrow passageway ends in a large hall covered with paintings of mammoths, bulls, stags, woolly ponies, and bison, with spears flying towards these beasts. Christened "The Sanctuary," one chamber contains paintings, which includes over thirty bison, ten horses, and four ibexes. At its center is a man-bison holding aloft a bow and presumably dancing. A hidden corner leads to a sunken corridor, followed by a twisting, long, narrow passage that leads to a ledge fifteen feet above the cave floor. Painted on the wall exists a bizarre, black figure that is thirty inches tall and unlike anything ever found. The figure's legs are human, yet the body and forearms are those of an animal. Its genitals are also human, but in the position of those on an animal. Its head and face are reindeer-like, but may depict a man in a mask. The antlers, however, are decidedly those of a reindeer. Abbe Henri Breuil, the famous French archeologist and pioneer in the study of Paleolithic art, named this 16,000-year-old painting "Le Sorcier" (the Sorcerer).

The Sorcerer is painted in a unique area of the cave. No other paintings exist on the wall, and an outcrop of rock hides the opening from where the figure is painted. A squatting individual with a torch could cast light from a seemingly invisible source on the image. His spoken words would seemingly come from nowhere, providing the illusion that God himself is speaking. Although the artist that created the Sorcerer must have used fire to light up the wall, no trace of soot has ever been found.

Some speculate the Sorcerer represents the Animal Master (the one who controls the hunt and multiplication of game), a ceremonial leader whose purpose was to increase the game while meditating on the mystical relationship between humans and their natural environment. Beasts were considered to be willing participants in a sacrificial act bound by a covenant. Joseph Campbell (1904-1987), prolific author of comparative mythology, has suggested that these early hunters were coming to terms with the strangeness of a world in which one must kill to survive. A guilty conscience probably developed when they saw the animals they had killed come to life in their dreams (possibly for revenge). To prevent this, rules were made, and a mythology emerged in which animals willingly gave themselves if a proper protocol was followed. Hunters had to engage the 'spirits of the game' in rituals, think as the animals thought, honor their gods, thank the animals for their sacrifice, sing their songs, and dance their dances. If this was done properly, and if meat and skin were taken reverently while not violating the animal's soul, the Animal Master would take the souls of the slain back to the dark womb of Mother Nature where they could be regenerated.

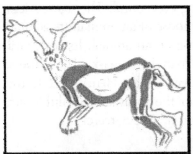

Sketch of the "Sorcerer" at the Three Brothers Cave

Interestingly, the sketch of the Sorcerer is similar to certain traditions of Native American Indians. The Navajo, in particular, still tell the story of a people called the *yenaldlooshi* who are animal shamans. From a young age they are taught to be both man and animal. To what purpose seems to be lost to history. Yet, the Navajo still consider them to have supernatural powers.

A little inferring puts forth the Sorcerer as the earliest rendering of the Celtic god *Cernunnos*, the Stag Lord. His image is portrayed on a rock carving from Val Camonica in northern Italy. He is standing with a horned serpent and a male worshipper, presumably his companions. Later images depict him seated in a somewhat half-lotus position. His name was preserved for posterity on a stone carving unearthed in Paris. It shows this god with antlers and on each hangs a torc. The name Cernunnos is carved in Roman letters literally meaning "The Horned One."

Another famous Gallo-Roman image shows a bearded Cernunnos wearing a mantle and torc and holding a large sack of coins, which flow downward in abundance. Standing beneath him is a stag and bull, while above is a rat. Another image of Cernunnos is from an inner plate of the Gundestrop Cauldron (a vessel found in a Danish bog allegedly used for catching the blood of sacrificed victims) where he appears as a horned deity. In his left hand, he holds the ram-headed serpent. In his right is the magical torc. At his left flank are a stag and bull, with boars and mythical creatures on his right. Others, however, believe the Gundestrop deity is almost certainly Rudra, the earliest form of Shiva.

Cernunnos is a complex and powerful god. From his early origins as a God of the Hunt, he became associated with animals, abundance, good fortune, fertility, and virility. But he has far less to do with fertility and sexuality than is assumed in popular fantasy, for he is a god of hunting, culling, and taking. The goal of a hunt is the death of the prey and sometimes even the hunter himself is killed in that pursuit. Thus, Cernunnos is also the Lord of Death and Guardian of the Gateway to the underworld (metal and snakes are

Replica of Cernunnos

chthonic symbols) who presides over the great seasonal festival of Samhain (corresponding to Halloween). His purpose is to purify through selection or sacrifice, so powers of growth and fertility may progress without stagnation.

* * *

With the religions of Siberia, central Asia, and those of the Indo-Europeans, we have the introduction of the Great God of the Sky and the dual conception of good and evil. Following in its path come the familiar symbolisms of biblical fame, the "Tree of Life," the number three (a trinity), and the seven heavens. However, these traditions are relatively new and belong to burgeoning cultures of the Neolithic.

It is unlikley that shamans created in its entirety the cosmology, mythology, and theology of their respective cultures. There is evidence that they borrowed, at least some ideas, from a pre-existing culture that lived throughout Europe and may have been centered in the Mediterranean. A culture that was already ancient when the first shaman took his first journey into the spirit world.

Chapter 19
Clash of Cultures

- Searching for the Tree of Knowledge
- The Mother Goddess of Old Europe
- The Patriarchal Culture of Indo-Europe
- Mesopotamia in Transition
- Mystery of the Halil River People

If Paleolithic cultures used hallucinogens in ritual ceremony, then there must be an explanation for their use. We know natural narcotics, stimulants, relaxants, and hallucinogens were discovered by primitive man and have been in use from the beginning. Brewing beer, for example, reaches at least as far back as the culture of ancient Egypt.

With social taboos attached to the use of narcotics, it is not a typical research topic for the academic world. However, in 1975, Terence McKenna (1946-2000) received a self-styled degree in Shamanology in the Department of Natural Resources from the University of California at Berkeley. He made altered states of consciousness his lifelong study. Although highly controversial, his views are not without merit and provide insight into certain aspects of archaic cultures.

His idea of a Paleolithic worldview centers on a partnership with nature which is, in general, agreeable with shamanic beliefs systems in early cultures. He contends that man's inclination to form dominant social hierarchies was temporarily interrupted during the ice age by adding *psilocybin* (a hallucinogen typically found in a certain mushroom) to his diet. Thus, male dominance was chemically interrupted by psilocybin, allowing a style of social organization called "partnership" to emerge. This occurred during the period when language, altruism, planning, moral values, aesthetics, and music (everything associated with humanity) emerged. At the end of the ice age, mushrooms became less available because of climatic change, and as a result were absent from the human diet. This allowed the previous tendency of dominant male hierarchies to re-emerge.

McKenna also puts forth the notion that Paleolithic society was orgiastic, making it impossible for men to trace their lines of male paternity. As a result, there was no concept of 'my children' for men; it was 'our children' meaning 'we, the group.' This orgiastic style worked itself into the effects of higher doses of psilocybin to create a situation of frequent boundary dissolution. According to McKenna, that's what sexuality is about on one level, and what psychedelics are about on another level. With the ending of this orgiastic, mushroom-using style of existence, a very neurotic and repressed social style emerged which is now widespread and typical of western civilization.[1]

Searching for the Tree of Knowledge

In his book, *Food of the Gods: the Search for the Original Tree of Knowledge*, Terence McKenna digs into the archaic evidence of drug use in ancient cultures. As hunter-gather societies tested all different types of plants for consumption, they came across a particular *coprophilic* (dung loving) mushroom, *stropharia cubensis*. Free from nausea producing compounds, stropharia cubensis contains psilocybin in concentrated amounts, and is widespread, occurring throughout tropical regions wherever the Zebu cattle graze. Psilocybin is a hallucinogenic compound ($C_{12}H_{17}N_2O_4P$) found today in 186 different mushrooms. McKenna believes this mushroom is the 'Ur Plant' (man's umbilicus to the feminine consciousness of our planet) which, when the Paleolithic cult of the 'Great Horned Goddess' was intact, transferred to us such knowledge that we were able to live in an equilibrium with nature.[2]

Although his theory seems to be a throwback to the counter-culture of the 60's and sounds a little extreme, it is not without evidence. At an archeological site in Non Nak Tha, Thailand, bones of the Zebu cattle have been found coincident to human graves dating to 15,000 years ago. Stropharia cubensis is also common in that area of Thailand today. At Tassili n'Ajjer (in the Sahara desert of southern Algeria), pictorial evidence is more convincing. Rock paintings depict shamans dancing with fists of mushrooms and mushrooms sprouting from their bodies. One instance shows them running joyfully, surrounded by the geometric structures of their hallucinations. These earliest known shamans, accompanied by large numbers of grazing cattle, were priests of the *Round Head* civilization, which existed from 7000 to 5000 BC. A painting from the late Round Head period shows images of the dancing Horned Goddess, typical of ice age Europe some 10,000 years before. Certainly the goddess and her accompanying theology was part of their worldview.[3]

In the middle of the tenth millennium BC, the remarkably advanced Natufian culture appeared in Palestine. With them came an explosion in the size of settlements, arts, and crafts, as was documented by archeologist James Mellaart. Sometimes schematic, at other times naturalistic, their art was worthy of Paleolithic France. Although European archeologists link this culture with settlements of Old Europe, McKenna is convinced that their origins are African. Skeletal evidence from Jericho (robust, long skulls), where the Natufian culture reached its peak, as well as a similarity in pottery to Sahara-Sudanese ceramics, supports African migration. Pottery of this type has been found near the Egyptian-Sudanese border in a context suggesting domesticated cattle were present.[4]

According to Mellaart, everything at Çatalhöyük indicating plant husbandry must have had a long prehistory elsewhere. Çatalhöyük's host culture surely existed where wild ancestors of these plants were native (presumably in hill country), a long way from the man-made environment on the Konya plain. Çatalhöyük also preserved traditions that seem archaic in a fully developed Neolithic society, such as the art of cave wall painting and reliefs modeled in clay or shaped into plastered walls. Their naturalistic representations, in a wide range of expressions, preserved the remains of an Upper Paleolithic heritage:

- Figurines of animals, human figures, and deities(including the goddess)
- Finger impressed clay designs like 'macaroni'
- The use of geometric ornament (spirals, meanderings, and others) carved on seals or transferred to woven materials
- Modeling of animals wounded in hunting rites
- Red ocher burials (symbolizing blood of the womb)
- Amulets in the form of a bird-like goddess with exaggerated buttocks
- Certain types of stone tools
- The preference for dentalium shells in jewelry

These archaic aspects are also traceable in other Mesolithic and Neolithic cultures (Natufian, as one example), but nowhere are they so pronounced as in the culture at Çatalhöyük. They introduced the beginnings of agriculture and stockbreeding, which is the basis of our civilization. Yet, their culture had no great impact on latter cultures of the area.[5]

McKenna finds his answer in why Çatalhöyük left no legacy in a theory of cultural replacement by Indo-Europeans. The theory was developed at UCLA by Professor of Archeology, Marija Gimbutas, and made popular by Riane Eisler in her 1989 book, The Chalice and the Blade.

According to the theory, the cultural pattern to emerge in the fourth millennium BC was that of a cavalry and wheel driven society from regions north of the Black Sea. In three waves of invasion, between 4,500 and 2,500 BC, from the Russian Steppe lands, an Indo-European culture conquered new lands. They were patriarchal, pastoral, mobile, and war oriented. It effectively replaced the more matriarchal, egalitarian, and peacefully existing culture, except for the southern and westernmost fringes of Europe.[6] After this period, the predominantly male deities of Indo-Europeans replaced the older female deities. What developed after 2,500 BC was a blending of the two cultures that eventually became the historical Europe we recognize today.[7]

Cambridge archeologist, Colin Renfrew offers another explanation with his Kurgan wave theory of Indo-European language diffusion. He claims that Çatalhöyük was the point of origin of the Indo-European language group, and the area most likely to be involved in inventing agriculture. To support his views, he cites the linguistic findings of Vladislav M. Illich-Svitych and Aron Dolgopolsky. Dolgopolsky's student, Sergi Starostin, argues that 7,000 years ago, Indo-Europeans borrowed a massive number of words from the north Caucasian language of Anatolia, and therefore concluded that Indo-Europeans did not establish Çatalhöyük. They would have migrated there during a much later period. And since they borrowed so many words, Anatolia must be the home of the Indo-European language.[8]

Recent genetic findings by Luigi Cavalli-Sforza and Allan C. Wilson also support a close relationship among speakers of Afro-Asiatic and the Indo-European languages. It seems that populations with linguistic roots in Africa had been living on the Anatolian plateau well before the appearance of Indo-Europeans.

According to McKenna, the legacy of Çatalhöyük was suppressed because of the culture's association with the ancient Horned Goddess. Its orgiastic and psychedelic-based religion was despised by this new and dominate Indo-European culture. It became anathema with a formal ecclesiastic ban.

The Indo-Europeans arrived suddenly and without warning. With the domestication of the horse and invention of the wheel, their tribes moved south of the Zagros Mountains for the first time. They brought with them pillage and plunder and trampled beneath their hooves the last great partnership civilization. Plunder replaced the cooperative and mushroom use came to end. For those who survived and were assimilated, the human god-king replaced the goddess.[9]

McKenna believes it is impossible not to see, in the cult of the goddess and the cattle cult of the late Neolithic, a recognition of the mushroom as the third and hidden member of a "Shamanic Trinity." The mushroom was seen as much a product of cattle as are milk, meat, and manure. It was recognized very early as the physical connection to the presence of the Goddess. According to McKenna, this is the secret that was lost some 8,000 years ago at the eclipse of talhoyuk.[10]

From the archeological evidence, we know that fire swept through Çatalhöyük (excavation levels V and VIA) around 6500 BC, and the city was abandoned. McKenna assumes this was the result of a conquering force, making it clear the age of undefended cities and partnership were ending. From that point forward, the Goddess religion and her partnership-based social structure would suffer slow erosion and fragmentation in favor of the dominating culture of Indo-Europeans.[11] The surviving people of Catalhoyuk sought refuge elsewhere; some migrated to the island of Crete where they continued their cattle cult. According to the theory, Minoan civilization began around 6000 BC with a small colony from Anatolia. With them came the Goddess and the agrarian technology that classifies these settlers as Neolithic.

For the next 4,000 years, a steady technical progress in ceramics, weaving, metallurgy, engraving, architecture, increasing trade, and development of a jubilant artistic style became characteristic of Minoan culture. There were no signs of war. The economy prospered and the arts flourished. Even when the island came under Achaean dominion during the second millennium BC, the Goddess and the way of life she symbolized held fast.[12] A mixing of cultures created what has become known as the *Minoan-Mycenaean* culture.

The particular environment created by the Minoan-Mycenaean religion was one of realism and sensual celebration, whose values were represented in the snake-handling Minoan Goddess of nature. Minoans depict her with bare, full breasts and handling a golden snake. According to McKenna, scholars following Shamanic convention see in the snake a symbol of the soul of the deceased, and (like Persephone who rules the underworld) a shamaness of great power whose mystery was already thousands of years old.[13] However, this last element of the old culture did not last.

With the obscurity of the Minoan civilization of Crete and its mysteries, mankind crossed a watershed into a progressively more vacant and ego-dominated world, whose forces were coming together into patriarchy, male domination, and monotheism. The great society of plant relationships of the Old World's past declined into a mystery and the esoteric pursuits of wealthy travelers and the religiously obsessed.

As the mysteries of the Old World faded, the phonetic alphabet spurred a general consciousness to a way of life stressing the spoken and written language. Culture, in general, moved away from pictographic awareness and the psychedelic mushrooms. This reinforced the emergence of the dominator culture. Western civilization as we know it had begun.[14]

Terence McKenna argues for the use of mushrooms containing psilocybin in prehistoric Africa and Asia Minor, based on pictorial and circumstantial evidence. He also sets forth the idea that the birth of cognition was in the grasslands of Africa, and may actually be the original, generic religion of all mankind. Furthermore, he believes that all religions in the ancient Near East can be traced to a Goddess cult and cattle worship, whose archaic roots go back to an ancient rite of eating psilocybin mushrooms. This rite induced ecstasy, dissolved the boundaries of ego, and reunited the worshipper with the personified vegetable nature of earthly life.[15] Although his views are driven by his own research into hallucinogens, he is not alone in his assessment of the past.

The Mother Goddess of Old Europe

A European "archeo-mythologist," named Marija Gimbutas, spent a lifetime in a cross disciplinary search for prehistoric truth. Through mythology, folklore, history, and archeology, she pieced together the story of a great culture that existed from 40,000 to 3000 BC. Growing up in Lithuania, she was familiar with the traditions of the Goddess *Laima*, the 'spinner' or the weaver of life. She remembers how the women would offer gifts of towels and woven articles to her. At night, she would often check on her believers by peering through a window.

Although Lithuania was Christianized during the fourteenth century, it remained predominantly pagan for the next several hundred years because of the missionaries' lack of language skills. The Goddess remained a part of Eastern European culture in some areas as late as the nineteenth and twentieth centuries. Fascinated by the culture she grew up with, Gimbutas focused her early studies on linguistics, ethnology, and folklore.

In 1942, Gimbutas received her Master's degree from the University of Vilnius in German occupied Lithuania and, four years later, her PhD from University of Tubingen in Germany. Both were in archaeology. Her dissertation focused on ancient and pagan religions, symbolism, burial rites, and beliefs in the afterlife. It was published in Germany in 1946.

Born during a time when Lithuania was as much pagan as it was Christian, Gimbutas had a unique perspective on Europe and its history. For years, she worked in excavations in southeastern Europe and the Mediterranean, and began to develop a theory of a culture that was once, long ago, prevalent in the land. So, when the excavation team she worked with began to unearth small sculptures of women (so prevalent throughout Europe as we have already seen) she had an easy time grasping their significance. Gimbutas alone unearthed at least 500 sculptures. As the work continued in Yugoslavia, Greece and Italy, the evidence mounted as did her confidence of the theory she was considering.

In 1955, she was named Research Fellow of Harvard's Peabody Museum. A year later, in Philadelphia, she presented her theory to the world for the first time. In 1956, she published *Prehistory of Eastern Europe* and in 1958, *Ancient Symbolism of Lithuanian Folk Art*, the first of many books. In 1963, she accepted a position at UCLA and continued to direct excavation at various European sites. In 1974, with the evidence she needed, she published *Gods and Goddesses*. The original title was *Goddesses and Gods of Old Europe*, but the publisher (most likely for marketing reasons) ordered it to be changed. Eight years later it was published in a second edition under her original title. During her career, she published several other works. In 1991, she published her final book *Civilization of the Goddess*, the culmination of her life's work. She passed away on February 2, 1994 at her home near Los Angeles.

Her story of prehistoric European peoples is also a tale about a clash of cultures and, specifically, the defeated culture of the Mother Goddess. Today, Europe is composed of many different ethnic groups with an assortment of languages. It is a widely held theory, however, that all these ethnic groups were once a single group called Indo-Europeans with a single language. Gimbutas' research provides evidence that before these Indo-Europeans dominated the lands, another completely different culture existed, a culture she refers to as the "Great Goddess" or "Mother Goddess" (the culture McKenna refers to as the Great Horned Goddess). It was a culture that was egalitarian, yet focused on the maternal as a foundation for their cosmology. According to Dr. Gimbutas:

> The earliest civilizations of the world were all matristic. The Goddess worship was there. In China, in the Near East, in Europe, in Americas, so we can say that this is a universal Goddess in the very beginning. And perhaps I

should add that the sovereignty of motherhood has decided the earliest development of social structures and religion.[17]

She refers to this culture as 'matristic' or 'matrifocal' and not matriarchal – for the fact the latter implies dominance.[16] It was a balanced society. Women were not so powerful that they usurped the masculine role. Men had their own power and position, and performed their own duties for the benefit of the family and clan. According to Gimbutas, it was a communal society and communistic in the best sense of the word. Goddesses were actually *creatrixes*, and in fact were creating from themselves, whether it was items for the household or a child.[18] She refers to the deity they worshipped as the "Great Mother Goddess."

During the 1960's, new dating methods gave her a better perspective on just how long-lasting this culture really was. Symbols and sculptures suggest that it was in existence as long ago as 35,000 years, but its climax was between 8000 and 3000 BC. Parts of the female body, specifically the creative or life-giving parts, are typical in Paleolithic art.

Gimbutas believes they had a completely different worldview, and that their natural artistic expression had nothing to do with pornography. For example, the vulva was one of the earliest symbols to be engraved. It was symbolic in that it related to growth and the seed. In some Paleolithic art, next to the image of a vulva is an image of a branch or other plant design, or within it, a seed or plant. This style of symbolism was very long lasting and continued for 20,000 years or more.[19]

Goddess Figurines

In chapter eight, we discovered the European cultures of the ice age carved "Venus" figurines. Gimbutas believes the term "Venus," used to describe these figurines, is a poor choice of words. Venus evokes the idea of beauty. They were not beauties and typically lacked facial features. She believes these figurines were the epitome of the Mother Goddess and depicted birth, regeneration, and death.

Many types of goddess figurines appeared in the Paleolithic, as well as the Neolithic, but they did not form a Pantheon. In essence, they represented different functions of the same Goddess. The deity was nature itself; the nature that is giving life, taking life, and life regenerating. These were the three important functions of the Goddess, which is the natural cycle of life. Perhaps this is the origin of the common term we use for natural occurring phenomena, "Mother Nature."

Neolithic figurines with accented breasts were typically carved with a bird's head. Paleolithic figurines also have large breasts with bird heads. From this, it was clear to Gimbutas that they were the same type. The vulture, owl, crow, and raven were also common. They, however, were symbols of death. Figurines that were carved as a stiff, white goddess depicted death. Some "death" figurines were carved as if wearing a mask and were associated with the vulture.

Here we have a connection to the vulture depictions of Çatalhöyük. These types of figurines were prolific and lasted from 25,000 years BC until the beginning of the Bronze Age.

Cultural Sophistication

Over the course of their history, there was stunning development for this culture from the simple to the really sophisticated, especially in architecture and the construction of temples. Some buildings were two stories tall with painted walls. Nearly 140 wall paintings adorned the dwellings at Çatalhöyük. They were finally published in 1989, twenty-five years after Mellaart's excavation. At first, archeologists disbelieved the settlement's sophistication.[20] The paintings depict otherwise.

For Gimbutas, the vast amount of beautiful pottery and sculptures discovered during years of excavation, was overwhelming. Surprised by the complex design of Goddess culture settlements, she was convinced the older civilization was more advanced than the more recent culture. As her work continued, she began to recognize patterns of repetition in their iconography, especially in the bird and snake goddess. Their religion became clear.

Religion and Politics of the Goddess

Religion has always played an important role within culture, modern as well as ancient. The goddess culture was no different. Their cosmology was based on the 'water bird' and the 'cosmic egg.' In the beginning, the world began by the waterbird bringing the egg. The egg split, one part became earth and the other part became the sky.

The temple was the focus of religious life. Beautiful artifacts were produced for their shrines and the goddess. Evidence suggests that they were grateful for sustenance the earth provided and gave to the Goddess in thanks. The high priestess and queen were the same person within a hierarchy of priestesses. Women were more honored because new life came from them and as a result had more influence in the religious life. They ran the temple and performed rituals at births, deaths, and the change of seasons.[21]

As does McKenna, Gimbutas also believes that, in their rituals they incorporated the use of mushrooms or other hallucinogenic plants. According to Gimbutas, this knowledge still existed in rituals like *Eleusis* in Greece where psychedelics clearly were used. From their portrayal of mushrooms, it can be assessed that it was sacred. From Minoan engravings on seals, for example, poppies were often displayed. Poppy seeds have also been found in Neolithic settlements. So it seems they were aware of what they were collecting and using. Possibly, they were growing poppies like other domestic plants.

Some scholars believe the Goddess religion was a simple fertility rite. Gimbutas responds to this by calling it a silly criticism. She believes that people who say so are usually not knowledgeable and have never studied the subject. There is no question that fertility was important to the continuity of life on earth, but the religion was about life, death, and regeneration. They were not a primitive people.[22]

There can be no doubt the birth of a child is, indeed, a true miracle of life and those who were able to give birth were very special. This mystery of giving birth and the woman herself, may be the origin of the shaman and Goddess cosmology. Geoffery Ashe, a British scholar of shamanism, believes the oldest form of the word "shaman" is referring to a female. The female group, he believes, practiced ancient shamanism.[23]

Dr. Gimbutas' findings, based on the physical remains and what can be deduced in mythology (mythology reflects their social structure), suggests that political life was regulated by an avuncular system (derived from the word uncle). The rulers of the country were the queen, who was also the high priestess, and her brother or uncle. The man (either the brother or uncle) shared in her authority. Its existence was expressed in classical mythology where sister-brother couples of female goddesses and male gods were often encountered.

It is presumptuous to suggest that this was just a woman's culture and there were no male gods. In their art, the male is less represented, but the male gods did exist. In all mythologies, for instance in Europe (Germanic or Celtic or Baltic), there is the earth mother (or earth Goddess) and her male companion next to her.

There are other 'god' couples like the Goddess of Nature, the regenerator, who appears in the springtime and gives life to all animals and plants. In Greek mythology she was Artemis and was called the Mistress of Animals. She had her male counterpart called the Master of Animals. According to Gimbutas, these representations appeared in Çatalhöyük 8,000 years ago and throughout prehistory. In their culture and religion, there was a balance between the sexes.

Sacred Script of the Goddess Culture

The Goddess culture of Old Europe was not without a written form of communication. This peaceful, agrarian civilization developed a near uniform language of symbols that reached from Ireland to Turkey. Elements of a 'sacred script' have been discovered in eastern and central Europe. Attempts have been made to decipher it, but sentence structure and phrases have not yet been ascertainable. During the Bronze Age in Cyprus and Crete, the script persisted and was similar to what existed in the fifth millennium BC. Some of it has been preserved, but there are no clear links due to the sudden end of their culture. Gimbutas believes it could have been a syllable-based script and would have developed into something more structured if it were not for the culture's destruction. Today, scholars continue to research this script with hopes that it will someday be deciphered.[24]

The difficulty is that this pre-Indo-European language is studied very little. Substrates of the languages are studied in Greece and Italy, but the only words that can be reconstructed are place names like *Knossos*, which is in fact, an Old European name. 'Apple,' for example, is also pre-Indo-European. Little by little, linguists discover what words are not Indo-European. Names for seeds, various trees, plants, and animals are easily deciphered. There also exists several pre-Indo-European names for the same thing such as 'pig,' and both were used. Some languages use pre-Indo-European, others use Indo-European names, or both.[25]

The Patriarch Culture of Indo-Europe

The matristic society of the Great Goddess began to develop into an urban culture especially in the *Cucuteni* civilization, which is modern day Romania and the western part of the Ukraine. Cities in the population range of ten to fifteen thousand were evident by 4000 BC, but they did not survive because of a new invading culture that Gimbutas defines as Indo-Europeans (also known as Kurgans or Aryans). They became the forefathers of Western Europeans.

Where did they come from? Around 7000 BC in south Russia (east of the Black Sea and North of the Caucasus Mountains), a Neolithic culture developed that was based more on animal husbandry than agriculture. By 6000 BC they had domesticated the horse. (Areas north of the Caucasus Mountains contain numerous horse bones.) Men grew to importance in their culture because they had to control large herds of horse and cattle. Horses provided mobility as well as food. From the sixth millennium BC on, weapons of war (such as long daggers) began to appear in the archeological record. Ownership concepts developed. Cattle stealing began as did wars with neighboring groups.

By 4000 BC, art and sculpture in Europe changed drastically. New gods were introduced, and a new style in social administration developed. Settlements were built on hilltops. Burials rites became typical of those from the Russian steppe lands. They were confined to males with weapons and symbols of power, such as the horse-headed scepter. In 4000 BC, the spear became their first god which, according to Gimbutas, eventually evolved into the thunderbolt of Zeus.[26] Culturally, across Europe everything changed.

It was a clash of two different cultures, religions, and ideologies. The new Indo-European gods were male and appeared around 3000 BC. There were three primary gods: the god of the shining sky, the thunder god, and god of the underworld. The dagger symbolized the god of the shining sky, the thunder god, an ax, and the god of the underworld, a spear. Symbolism of this new culture was very different, and was reflected in its social structure. This new social structure was patriarchal within the psyche of the warrior. Every god was a warrior. Their female goddesses became brides, wives, or maidens without any power or creativity, and were beauties like the sun maiden.

Dominance was an intrinsic part of their culture. These semi-nomadic people had weapons and horses. In the Goddess culture of Old Europe, there were no weapons for warfare. Their weapons were for hunting. In Old Europe, the culture was agrarian. People lived in one area for a long time. The new dominating culture was the opposite. With horses, weapons, and small families (who are more mobile) they began to dominate.

When the invading warriors arrived, they established themselves high in the hills, sometimes in places with difficult access. But if, and how much the older culture defended themselves is difficult to tell. What is clear is that they were defeated. There is evidence of immigration and flight from war, confusion, and shifts of population. They fled to such places as islands, forests, and hilly areas. In their settlements, there is also evidence of murder.[27] By 4000 BC, the patriarchal culture was well on its way to being the established culture.

Europe later became a hybridization of these two diverse cultures, which is evident by their mythology. Their ideas reached the Mesopotamian plain and were seen in Sumerian and Semite stories. Gilgamesh dethroned Lilith (Adam's mythical first wife). Eve took the blame for paradise lost and the Goddess was dethroned. Athena of Greek mythology was hybridized and became militarized, but still kept some of her former qualities. Behind her was an owl, and on her shield was a snake, in the tradition of Old Europe.[28]

The ideology of separation between body and soul developed from this patriarchal culture. Later, through Christianity, it was spread throughout the world. The 'here and now' world was rescinded in favor of the after life. Life became transcendent, as opposed to the imminence it had in the Goddess culture.

Mesopotamia in Transition

During the sixth millennium BC, two cultures lived side by side in the Mesopotamian Valley. One culture occupied the north and the other the valley's southernmost areas between the Tigris and Euphrates Rivers. The earliest settlements arose in the north within the Kurdistan Mountains. In the Tel Halaf area, a culture emerged around 6000 BC that created various types of ceramic art, including a fine and distinctive style of pottery. To scholars, these earliest Mesopotamians were known as the Halaf culture. They were farmers and artists, and relied on natural rainfall for their crop. (Referred to as dry farming, that is, without the aid of irrigation.) Emmer wheat, barley, and flax were their primary crops, but they also herded cattle, sheep, and goats.

Stone houses from this culture were excavated and produced exceptional pottery, jewelry, sculptures and obsidian tools. From the evidence, a clearly complex prehistoric society existed whose trade contacts within their communities allowed them to amass considerable wealth.

Besides finely painted pottery, they also baked small clay female figurines in the tradition of the Great Goddess. These distinctive clay figurines, with large thighs, buttocks, and breasts, were found throughout their shrines. The figurines depicted a long braid over the top of the head and their eyes were often large and slanted. Two particular figurines, dated to 5,000 BC and found in the Upper Tigris Basin at *Arpachiya* and *Chagar Bazar*, display the exaggerated female characteristics found at Çatalhöyük and in ice age Europe. One figurine contains traces of paint, suggesting that its arms and legs were decorated with jewelry. Its breasts also appear to be painted or tattooed. Both figurines are on display at the British Museum.

During the past 15 years, *Tell Sabi Abyad* in the upper Balikh Valley of northern Syria, has been a focal point of excavation aimed at clarifying the chronology, settlement organization, and ecology of late Neolithic societies in the region. Emphasis has been on the Halaf period of the late sixth and early fifth millennium BC. In 1988, one of the largest Halaf settlements in the

Halaf Figurines

region was discovered and has provided clues into their origins, supported by a series of twelve radiocarbon dates.

According to archeologists, the absence of sterile soil within the layers of excavation suggests a continuous and uninterrupted sequence of occupation. The Halaf culture, it appears, gradually emerged out of an earlier local Neolithic tradition, most likely the Samarran. Around 5200 BC, a major innovation occurred; a technique of creating finely textured and highly artistic ceramics painted with designs in black, red, and white on a buff background.

Excavations have also provided a detailed picture of a Halaf settlement. Over 2,400 square feet have been excavated, revealing the evidence of multi-roomed and possibly, multistoried rectangular buildings. It may be that they were accessed from the roof similar to Çatalhöyük. Subsidiary annexes and other circular structures called *tholoi*, surrounded these buildings. They were made from rectangular blocks of loam and pisé, with some walls built on a stone foundation. The outer wall contained a facade with regular, buttress-like supports protruding in all sections. These structures most likely provided strength for an upper story, but may have been purely ornamental or symbolic.[29]

Roots of Sumer - The Ubaid Culture

By 4500 BC, the Ubaid culture, whose origins were from the Zagros Mountains, expanded its influence northward. About the same time, the Halaf society ended as a vibrant culture. Whether they were assimilated or conquered by the Ubaid remains unknown. Either way, the Halaf culture faded into obscurity and their characteristics were never seen again in the region.

The Ubaid people lived in small settlements, typically along rivers. Their temples were platform-like and built from mud-bricks at the village center. They were used only for ritualistic purposes.

A shift in social organization occurred around 4000 BC. Archeologists and anthropologists refer to this transition as the beginnings of the Uruk culture and the seeds of Sumerian civilization. During this transition, society became distinctly stratified. In other words, ranks or classes were created between certain groups of people, each having a different function and level of social power.

It appears the elite demanded tribute from their subjects. This was not only to meet their own needs, but also to support craftsmen and laborers engaged in constructing temples and fortifications. By the late fourth millennium, Uruk had become the largest city in lower Mesopotamia and covered nearly 250 acres.

The First Kingdom

By 3000 BC, Uruk was entering its early Dynastic period. Most of the population now lived within the city. A tributary economy was replaced by a household economy, where people took part in large extended families; for example, Gu'abba in Lagash had as many as 4,000 adults. Temples themselves constituted a household although many others were dominated by leading families. No longer self-sufficient, the common people contributed their labor in exchange for the necessities of life. The elite now controlled, not only the production of, but also the distribution of goods. The first kingdom was born. And it's authority, according to their cosmology, was handed down from the heavens by God himself.

By 2500 BC, Uruk's expanse covered a thousand acres and boasted a population of 40,000. The first ziggurats were built so city rulers could communicate with their gods. Artisans supplied the elite with luxury goods, while the common people used crude, mass-produced earthenware. A diversity of grave goods epitomized the growing chasm between the privileged few and the masses. Judging from the 4,400-year-old neighboring Royal Tombs of Ur, those privileges included the right of kings to have their servants sacrificed and buried with them.

It is unknown precisely what happened to the Halaf culture, or how the Ubaid made the transition into a stratified society and became the Kingdom of Sumer, but it is clear they did. Like Çatalhöyük, their culture left no legacy in any other people.

Possible Migrations of Indo-Europeans
Based on Linguistic and Archeological Evidence

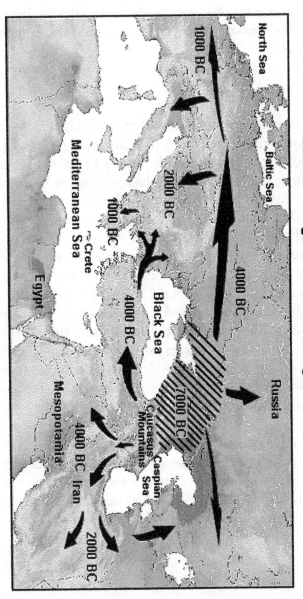

A *Slow Process*

Over the course of her life's work, Marija Gimbutas painstakingly reconstructed the process by which Old Europe was replaced by the new "western" civilization. She begins with the fact there was no copper in the regions north of the Caucasus where these patriarchs came from. This leads to the theory that the cavalry equipped Indo-Europeans were aware of the metal technology, which existed in the fifth and fourth millenniums BC south of the Caucasus Mountains. Seizing those areas would have been an obvious choice of expansion. There was a radical change in social structure on the Mesopotamian Plain which spurred the beginnings of civilization. Is it coincidence the great patriarchs of Western Civilization first appeared on the Mesopotamian Plain when Indo-European ideology first began to spread?

This radical change in culture was not a simple function of wars and conquest. The process was quite slow and far more complex. It likely required the establishment of a new social order and the slow process of assimilation for those who became subjugated. However, from the very beginning, warfare had been an important method of replacing the Old European partnership culture with the new king-centered society. Yet, the events that triggered this change were fairly sudden. What developed over the next millennia was a blending of the agricultural based old system and the hierarchical administration of the new. The result: civilization and the Kingdom of Sumer were born. It was believed to be the first civilization mankind had ever developed.

Mystery of the Halil River People

In 2001, a flash flood in southeastern Iran near the Halil River exposed ancient graves packed with beautiful stone pottery. According to the *Smithsonian*, police confiscated hundreds of finely worked stone vessels carved with the images of animals and decorated with semiprecious stones. The local villagers had discovered the graves first and had been taken advantage of the opportunity. Since the vessels were not scientifically recovered, their age and origin remain open to debate. However, Iranian archeologist *Yousef Madjidzadeh* strongly believes most were made more than 4,000 years ago, and that the society who crafted them predates ancient Mesopotamia.[30] This discovery and the massive architecture and quarries near the town of Jiroft has opened a new chapter in Iranian and Middle Eastern prehistory. It seem an unknown society flourished between ancient Sumer and Harappa in the Indus river valley. According to Madjidzadeh, the now desolate valley was once home to a thriving and literate community and refers to it as nothing less than the earliest Oriental civilization. Some of these artifacts, although typically devoid of carving, have turned up in the royal tombs of Ur, the Sumerian city of Mari, and the Arabian peninsula.

Although scholars are hesitant to make a connection, the Halil stoneware is not the first ever discovered to predate civilization. In Egypt, at the Step Pyramid in Sakkara, as well as Giza, stoneware of a similar nature was discovered during the waning years of the nineteenth century. The Cairo Museum holds some of the most unique and remarkable stone artifacts of Egyptian civilization. A little-publicized fact concerning these artifacts is that there were 30,000 of them found in chambers underneath the Step Pyramid.[31]

Sir William Flinders Petrie (1853-1942), the first archeologist to investigate the Giza Pyramids in 1880 was amazed by the level of Egyptian technology. In his book *The Pyramids of Gizeh*, Petrie describes abundant evidence for the use of tube drills and saws tipped with jewels, tools which were used to cut granite. In his book, *The Giza Power Plant* Christopher Dunn, a forty-year veteran of the machining and precision manufacturing industry, is adamant that the inner chambers of the Great Pyramid, as well as the stoneware, were made with the use of precision machinery.

Although the late Dr. Gimbutas has been accused of being too female centric in her approach to prehistory, the evidence supports her theory of a more sophisticated civilization many thousands of years ago – sophisticated enough, it seems, for them to be heralded as gods.

Chapter 20
Symbolism of the Serpent

- Archaic Belief Systems
- Kundalini Yoga: Wisdom of the Serpent
- Gnosticism and the Universal Self
- Serpent Symbolism in Ancient Egypt

During her lifetime as an archeologist, Marija Gimbutas discovered a recurring motif in the prehistoric art of Europe; the bird and the snake. Both of these animal images were symbols of the Mother Goddess religion of Old Europe. The abstraction of the serpent, a simple spiral, was a central pattern and commonly used as ornamentation. With an origin going back 25,000 years and possibly as old as 40,000, this artistic style continued as a principle means of religious expression until 2500 BC.

As the new patriarch based worldview, with its 'gods of heaven' cosmology, spread across the land, the symbols of the old religion began to lose their influence. The last bastion of the old culture survived in Crete within the civilization of the Minoans.[1] However, traces of the Goddess religion have managed to survive in serpent symbolism and entered the legends and myths of historic Europe.

According to Gimbutas, Hera was one of the most honored of the Greek Goddesses and is likely a descendent of the prehistoric Snake Goddess. Homer referred to her as 'cow-faced.' The Egyptian Hathor (goddess of love and fertility) was also a cow, but was also described as the primeval serpent that ruled the world.[2]

Caduceu Emblem
of the Medical Profession

Although the religion of the Goddess was overthrown, her symbols of power remained and were, not surprisingly, combined into new ways of thinking. Sometimes they were adopted by the original cultures of our western civilization. All new religions borrow from the older ones as their movements spread across culture boundaries. The icons are obvious in their proper historical context. The bird has made its way into Christianity as the 'dove' of the Holy Spirit. The serpent has also upheld its prominence. Now it is more of a mystique, partly because of the notorious viper from the biblical tale of Adam and Eve.

These are our symbols and they span the length and breath of mankind's history. They were common in prehistoric and archaic systems of belief; the Christian Gnostics of the first century, and even today with Kundalini yoga and its associated spiritualism and philosophy.

In western civilization today, being a 'snake' has negative connotations implying deception and trickery, but at one time it meant something entirely different. It used to be a symbol of regeneration, healing, and wisdom. Even Moses himself displayed the snake as his symbol of power in confronting the Pharaoh of Egypt and his magicians.

Archaic Belief Systems

In archaic belief systems, from ancient Germany to central Asia and Siberia, from cultures of the Minoans to the Celts, the serpent or snake played a significant role in shamanic and cultural symbolism. From ancient Greece to India and China to Europe, as well as the Aztecs, Hopis, and other cultures in the Americas, the symbol of the snake crosses every path in myth, culture, and history of man.

Snakes evoke fear and repulsion in western societies. Yet, to this day, they oddly remain a part of our culture, most noticeably in the medical profession's iconography. The *caduceus*, modeled after Hermes's badge of office, depicts two serpents winding their way up a winged pole. (As a messenger of God Hermes escorted souls to the underworld.) A wooden staff with a single snake coiled around it symbolizes *Aesculapius*, the Greek physician who was deified after death. But the origin of this symbol most likely does not reside in ancient Greece.

"Serpent Lord Enthroned"
Cylinder Seal from Sumer, 2200 BC

The oldest available evidence suggests the caduceus comes from ancient Sumer during the late third millennium BC. A cylinder seal[3] from 2,200 BC entitled *The Serpent Lord Enthroned* shows the deity in human form sitting on his throne before a smoldering altar. Caduceus emblems, less the pole, border him. Another seal from the late third millennium reveals a male figure sitting on a throne. Opposite him is a female figure and between them, a tree heavily laden with fruit. Next to the female figure in the familiar "S" pattern, writhes the serpent Nabu[4], the god of intellectual activity (wisdom) and writing.

There is also literary evidence in ancient Sumer referring to symbolism of the serpent. In the oldest recorded story known to mankind, *The Epic of Gilgamesh*, the serpent springs from a well, eats the 'plant of youth,' sloughs off its skin, and disappears again, thus robbing the hero of his chance at immortality. Although no editorial provides meaning for the snake's theft of the plant, it is clear from the story the serpent became immortal by doing so, and Gilgamesh did not.

Sumerian Cosmology and Mythology

Sumerian mythology is diverse with a pantheon of gods. In it we see the blending of the old world and the new. This was a result of various stories having been assimilated from other cultures, and traditions that developed over a long period of time.

In Sumerian cosmology, the primeval sea, Abzu, existed before anything else, and within that, the heaven An and the earth Ki were formed. The boundary between heaven and earth was a solid vault, and the earth was a flat disk. Within this vault lies the gas-like Lil' (atmosphere). The brighter portions formed the stars, planets, sun, and moon.[5] Each of the four major Sumerian deities is associated with one of these regions. An, god of heaven, may have been the main god of the pantheon before 2500 BC, although his importance gradually waned.[6] Ki is likely to be the original name of the earth goddess, whose name more often appears as Ninhursag (queen of the mountains), Ninmah (the exalted lady), or Nintu (the lady who gave birth). It seems likely that these two were the progenitors of most other gods.

In the first days, all things needed were created, as told in the Epic of Gilgamesh. Heaven and earth were separated. An took Heaven, Enlil took the earth, while Ereshkigal was carried off to the netherworld as a prize, and Enki sailed off after her. Enki consumed the plants (Ninhursag's children) and so was cursed and received one wound for each plant consumed.[7]

In the prologue to Gilgamesh, a huluppu tree was transplanted from the banks of the Euphrates into a garden in Uruk by Inanna. Here she finds "...a serpent who could not be charmed made its nest in the roots of the tree. The Anzu bird set his young in the branches of the tree, and the dark maid Lilith (Adam's alleged first wife) built her home in the trunk."[8] At Gilgamesh's death, his family and friends weighed out their offering to the gods. Among them was Ningizzida, the god of the serpent, the "Lord of the Tree of Life," to whom they offered bread.

In another Mesopotamian myth, Tiamat is a large female dragon personifying the saltwater ocean, the water of Chaos, and the primordial mother of all that exists, including the gods themselves. Her consort is Apsu personifying the freshwater abyss that lies beneath the Earth. From the union of saltwater and freshwater, the first pair of gods were born: *Lachmu* and *Lachamu*, who were parents to Ansar and Kisar and grandparents to Anu and Ea.

In the creation epic *Enuma Elish* written around 2,000 BC, their descendants started to aggravate Tiamat and Apsu, so they decided to kill their offspring. Ea discovered their plans and managed to kill Apsu while the latter was asleep. Tiamat flew into a rage when she learned about Apsu's death and wanted to avenge her husband. She created an army of monstrous creatures, which was to be led by her new consort, Kingu, who is also her son. Marduk, born in the deep freshwater sea, defeated Tiamat. He cleaved her body in half, and from the upper portion, he created the sky and from the lower half, he made the earth. From her water came forth the clouds, and her tears became the source of the Tigris and the Euphrates. Kingu also perished, and from his blood Marduk created the first humans.

On a donation record (stone tablet) from the Kassite Period of Mesopotamia (1,202-1,188 BC), there is a listing of gods in pantheon hierarchy. (Symbols of the gods were carved on the tablets to protect the records.) At the top of the tablet are symbols of the three heavenly gods: Sin (moon), Shamash (sun), and Ishtar (Venus) in order of their position in the heavens. They are surpassed by the supreme triad of Anu (sky), Enlil (air) symbolized by their horned crowns, and Ea (freshwater from the abyss) symbolized by a scepter carried by a goatfish. Below them are the emblems of Marduk, patron-god of Babylon, identifiable as a pointed hoe placed on a stand and the serpent-dragon, which guards the underworld of the gods. The same dragon carries the scribe's stylet (a slender, pointed instrument), which is the emblem of Nabu, Marduk's son.

It is difficult to arrive at a precise, dictionary-style definition of serpent symbolism from Sumerian mythology. Yet it is certain that their cosmology was similar, in some respects, to the archaic shamanic cosmology: sky, ground, and underworld. Some elements even describe a "Tree of Life," similar to central Asian and ancient Germany tradition. Yet there is more substance, more gods for the Sumerian. It is likely that these Mesopotamians were adding to an existing cosmology, that of the

Mother Goddess and the earliest gods of Indo-Europeans. A blending of these two cosmologies resulted in the creation of a pantheon.

As for the serpent; immortality, regeneration, and wisdom appear as its primary features At least one of those traits has made its way into the Christian Bible. Jesus himself advised his disciples, "I send you forth as sheep in the midst of wolves: be ye therefore *wise as serpents*, and harmless as doves" (*Matthew 10:16*).

Serpent symbolism, as we have discovered, has had long history in archaic beliefs systems. However, several questions remain: What idea is at the core of serpent symbolism? In what way does the serpent represent wisdom? More to the point, perhaps, exactly who or what is the serpent?

For the Great Mother Goddess, the snake was a seminal image. It was life and energy. They didn't worship the snake itself. They worshipped the energy which is its movement: spiraling, and coiling. Interestingly, this philosophy of energy and worship has survived to this day.

Kundalini Yoga: Wisdom of the Serpent

Kundalini Yoga, the *Yoga of Awareness*, has existed for a very long time and is still practiced worldwide. Training courses are available from a multitude of sources. One of the most prominent is the *3HO Foundation* (Healthy, Happy, Holy Organization), whose motto is, "You have a right to be healthy, happy, and holy. It is your birthright."[9]

The word itself, Kundalini, means "the curl of the lock of hair of the beloved." According to Shakti Parwha Kaur Khalsa in his book, *Kundalini Yoga, the Flow of Eternal Power* (Perigee 1998), "It is a metaphor, a poetic way of describing the flow of energy and consciousness that already exists within each one of us. These practices enable you to merge with, or yoke with, the Universal Self. This merging of individual consciousness with universal consciousness creates a divine union called yoga."

Mark Amaru Pinkham, an author on the subject, is a master who studied under Swami Muktananda Paramahamsa and Sri Mata Amritanandamayi. In his book, *The Return of the Serpents of Wisdom*, he believes that throughout history, several individuals have realized the reason and goal of human existence. By using spiritual disciplines these masters have united the male and female values within themselves. They have raised their inner "fire serpent" of consciousness from its seat (located at the base of the spine, the Kundalini) and awakened the realization of love in their hearts.[10]

People who reach the goal of "all spiritual paths" become androgynous serpents of wisdom. More precisely the *I am* of the individual has united with the infinite spiritual self. *I am that, I am everything,* and *my Father and I are one* continually echoes in their hearts. In symbolic terms, this means the eagle (spiritual male principle) has joined with the snake (matter, ego, or female principle) and together they have become a Serpent of Wisdom.[11]

More succinctly, the Kundalini is the "Serpent Mother" that everyone has; the inner female soul of man in the shape of a serpent (also referred to as psychophysical energy or divine serpent energy of the Self) coiled at the base of the spine and a great reservoir of creative energy.

Through the proper practice of yoga, this 'serpent' can be uncoiled and mounted through spinal 'chakras' (dimensions of consciousness, usually described as discs or wheels; there are seven) toward the head, bringing forth infinite wisdom. Using certain breathing techniques and meditation, the serpent power progresses upwards until it reaches the top of the head. On its way, it engages or stimulates the charkas. An experienced practitioner of Kundalini yoga may be able to direct it to any one chakra or all of them progressively (even through the top of the head).

Origins of Kundalini

One story describes the origins of Kundalini as being linked to the Hindu myth of the Ganges River. The Goddess Ganga, life force of the river, once lived on Mount Kailash and flowed demurely for the sole pleasure of the gods. At the request of *Bhagiratha*, a powerful king and sage, she came to earth, then went to the netherworld to rescue the tormented souls of the sons of Sagar. Since then, the Ganges is believed to flow in the three worlds of heaven, earth, and netherworld, and is known as the *Three Path River*. This journey of the Goddess Ganga, from heaven to the netherworld, symbolizes the origin of Kundalini and its descent through the various chakras of the body resting in the netherworld (the pelvis).

There it remains coiled like a serpent until it ascends into the higher chakras during one's spiritual awakening.

Another possible interpretation is that Ganga represents divine knowledge which, with its strength of purity and illumination, has the powers to uplift all, both living and dead, toward the heavens. Bhagiratha gave this knowledge, originally available only to the gods, to mankind through his devotion to Lord Shiva who helped him to receive this knowledge. He passed it on to mankind for their eventual salvation.

In another Hindu myth, particularly of southern India, the Nagas (Serpent in Sanscrit) were a primeval race of divine serpent-people, half human and half snake. They were believed to have lived in palaces and the underground city of Bhogavati. The Nagas were considered the protectors of springs, wells, and rivers. They brought rain (hence fertility), but also disasters, such as floods and drought. Important in religion, Naga depictions are commonly found adorning temple walls and stairways. Since temple ceilings were made of wood, therefore susceptible to fire, these gods of rain were often depicted lining the ornate roofs of temples.

Pinkham believes the origins of these Serpents of Wisdom can be traced to the dawn of time, when only an unlimited ocean of consciousness existed. This infinite ocean was the "androgynous, unmanifest Spirit of God." The Hindus refer to this Spirit as Shiva or Brahman. According to Pinkham, from this spiritual sea came a brilliant dragon, the first Spirit form, the first Serpent of Wisdom. According to Jewish and Christian theology, this "ocean" and "consciousness" can be likened (although not entirely) to *Genesis* 1:2 when "the earth was waste and void; and darkness was upon the face of the deep and the Spirit of God moved upon the face of the waters."

He further points out that this concept of a Primal Serpent, although referred to by different names, was realized around the world as a Serpent Goddess, the Serpent on the Tree, the Plumed Serpent, the Azure Dragon, Shesha, Ammon Kematef, Kneoh Agathodaemon, Ea, Enki, Kon or Kan, and the Serpent Son. This Primal Serpent was the first tangible form of the Spirit of God and the instrument of His powers including creation, preservation, and destruction. It also included His Divine Mind, the wellspring of all knowledge and wisdom.[12]

In the opening lines to the biblical *Genesis*, we read, "darkness was on the face of the deep." The word used for deep is *ta-home* and came from the Babylonian word Tiamat. Tiamat was the serpent mother of the world.

If serpent cosmology was as widespread in archaic times as the evidence suggests (and Pinkham reiterates), then the question must be asked: What happened to it? According to Pinkham, during the rise of Christianity, those who espoused the serpent's wisdom were forced into clandestine orders or retreated into eastern cultures that welcomed their ancient rites and practices. They were not welcome in Christian culture. Nearly 2,000 years ago, within the burgeoning Christian Church, there was a struggle between orthodox Christianity and a faction of believers who preferred mixing ancient knowledge and tradition with the growing Christian movement.[13]

Gnosticism and the Universal Self

In 1945, an Arab peasant named Muhammad Ali al-Samman made an astonishing discovery in Upper Egypt while digging for *sabakh*, a soft soil used for fertilizing crops. A red earthenware jar was uncovered that contained thirteen papyrus books bound in leather. Unimpressed by the find (he was hoping for gold), he dumped them next to his stove to be used as kindling. A dubious fellow, Muhammad was under suspicion for murder (in avenging his father's death). In fear of the police searching his house, he asked a local priest to keep one or more of the books. A history teacher somehow obtained one of the books and, suspecting it had value, sent it to a friend in Cairo. This attracted the interests of the Egyptian government who bought one of the books and eventually confiscated another ten and a half.

Upon deciphering, the books were discovered to be a set of fifty-two texts, including non-canonical versions of gospels: *The Gospel According to Thomas, Gospel of Philip, The Apocryphon* (secret book) *of John, Gospel of Truth, Gospel to the Egyptians, The Testimony of Truth, The Secret Book of James, Apocalypse of Paul, Letter of Peter to Paul,* and *The Apocalypse of Peter.*

This discovery brought both political and theological struggles of the early Christian Church into a whole new light. These books explained the events in the life of Jesus in a very different way. Others told the story of the origins of man in new terms, different from the usual reading of *Genesis*.

One such text, *The Testimony of Truth*, tells the story of *Genesis* from the viewpoint of the serpent. Known to appear in Gnostic literature as the principle of divine wisdom, the serpent persuaded Adam and Eve to experience knowledge. God then threatens them with death and tries to prevent them from gaining knowledge. Finally, they are expelled from Paradise after achieving it.[14] Another text, entitled *Thunder-Perfect Mind*, contains a poem in the voice of a feminine divine power. Still others contain texts ranging from a quasi-philosophical thesis on the origin of the universe to secret gospels, myths, and mystical practices.

As Elaine Pagels points out in *The Gnostic Gospels*, these texts were virtually unknown for 2,000 years because of their suppression in critical struggles during the formation of the early Christian Church. Until now, only the essays of the victorious Orthodox Church were available. They did write of struggles with heretical movements, but purely from their point of view. Of course heretical theology is labeled from the victor's viewpoint. Those who wrote and embraced heretical teachings did not consider themselves heretics.

Both orthodox and Gnostic teachings accepted the *Gospel of John* in their theology. It is the only canonized Gospel that philosophically describes the relationship between God, Jesus, the Holy Spirit, and man. Gnostics used it as a primary source for teaching. It was opposed by some factions of Orthodoxy, but included because of verses such as 14:6, where Jesus says "I am the way, and the truth, and the life; no one comes to the Father, but by me." So what could be the cause for such a split among early Christians? Simply, it was how they defined and viewed God.

The Greek word *Gnosis*, from which Gnostic comes, has very special meaning. It has been traditionally interpreted to mean knowledge, which is true, but it is not an ordinary knowledge. The Greek language distinguishes between scientific and reflective knowledge. Gnosis refers to a knowledge gained by observation and experience, best described by the word "insight." Therefore, *gnosis* involves an intuitive process by which one comes to know oneself, and to know oneself is to know human nature and destiny. At its deepest level, knowing oneself is to know God, clearly in violation of Judaism's principle foundation that God is wholly other. The Christian Gnostics subscribed to such a view. This was reason enough for excommunication.[15]

Flourishing at the beginning of the second century were the Ophites (a collective name for several Gnostic sects), who regarded the serpent as a symbol of creative wisdom. It was also known as the *Brotherhood of the Serpent*. These sects most likely existed within Judaism before the birth of Christianity. However, not all Ophites agreed on theology. Some held to Jewish principles, others Christian, while still others were anti-Christian. Only the idea and symbolism of the serpent was a foundational belief.

At the end of the second century, Irenaeus[16] (125 - 202) wrote a history of heresy, but did not know the Gnostics under the name of "Ophites." Clement did, and cited another group called the "Cainists" whose name was taken from the object of their worship. Philaster, in the fourth century, believes the Ophites, Cainites, and Sethites were the source of all heresies because of their belief that the serpent was their true origin and was seen as the devil.

These groups declared the serpent of paradise to be wisdom itself, since wisdom came to earth through the knowledge of good and evil that the serpent brought. They exalted Cain and Seth as heroes of the human race, whom they felt were granted this knowledge. All Ophistic circles believed in seven spirits under the dominion of the serpent (a demonic hebdomad). Last mentioned is the son of fallen wisdom, *yalda bahut* (which means "son of chaos"), and from him, continuing in successive generations were Jao, Sabaot, Adoneus, Eloeus, Oreus (or light), and Astaphaeus. They are said to be expressions of the God of the Old Testament. The Ophites claimed that Moses himself exalted Ophis by setting up the serpent, and that Jesus also had recognized it by saying[17] "Just as Moses lifted up the snake in the desert, so the Son of Man must be lifted up, that everyone who believes in him may have eternal life" (John 3:14-15).

According to Theosophists, the Gnostics were not a Christian sect in the common use of the term. Although they believed in a "Christos" principle, their Christos was the "Eternal Initiate" (the Pilgrim) typified by hundreds of Ophidian symbols for several thousand years before the Christian era. Its name was Ophis, who was the same as Chnuphis or

Kneph, the Logos, or the good serpent. A living serpent, representing the Christos-principle, was displayed in their mysteries and revered as a symbol of wisdom. This Christos of pre-Christian thought (and the Gnosis) was not the "god-man" Christ, but the divine ego, made one with Buddhi. Their androgynous iconography can be seen on the "Belzoni tomb" in Egypt as a winged serpent with three heads and four human legs. On the walls descending to the sepulchral chambers of Rameses V, where it is found as a snake with vulture's wings (the vulture and hawk are solar symbols).

> **"The heavens are scribbled over with interminable snakes",
> writes Herschel of the Egyptian chart of stars. "The Meissi
> (Messiah?) meaning the Sacred Word, was a good serpent",
> writes Bonwick in his Egyptian Belief.**[18]

The crowned serpent of goodness was mounted on a cross and formed a sacred standard of Egypt. The Hebrews borrowed it in their "brazen serpent of Moses," the healer and Savior. Therefore, the Ophites referred, not to Jesus or his words, but to Ophis when referring to *John* 3:14. Tertullian, they claim, knowingly or not had mixed up the two. The four-winged serpent is the god Chnuphis, the good serpent, who bore the cross of life around its neck or suspended from its mouth and became the Seraphim (angel) of the Hebrew tradition. In the 87th chapter of the Egyptian *Book of the Dead*, the human soul transformed into Bata and the omniscient serpent says, "I am the serpent Bata, of long years, Soul of the Soul, laid out and born daily; I am the Soul that descends on the earth." In other words, he is the ego.

Serpent Symbolism in Ancient Egypt

During the early 1970's, while living in London, John Anthony West read a novel by Isha Schwaller entitled "Her-Bak." Although unimpressed by the author's writing style, she frequently referred to the symbolist works of Rene Schwaller de Lubicz, her late husband. The book's unique portrayal of Egypt fascinated West, so for eight weeks he visited the British Museum reading Schwaller's work, a French dictionary at his side since it was yet to be translated into English. When finished, he was thoroughly convinced that Schwaller had revealed an untold story of ancient Egypt; it's philosophy and the symbolic way it was expressed in their art and architecture.

Although the works of Schwaller focused on the Egyptian cultural and architecture with a symbolic interpretation of their society, an observation by Schwaller that the Sphinx was weathered by water roused his curiosity. During the 1970's, West, still unaware of any English translations of Schwaller's works, concentrated his efforts on bringing a symbolist view of Egypt to the English-speaking world. In 1978, *Serpent in the Sky* was published introducing Schwaller's view of ancient Egyptian wisdom to the English-speaking world.[19]

Typically, a book concerning ancient civilizations explains the when and where. And for those interested in the subject matter it is fascinating to read the play-by-play details of a society's making. John Anthony West takes a very different approach. A symbolist and a Pythagorean, he expounds upon Schwaller de Lubicz's monumental works and seeks to explain Egyptian civilization through the eyes and minds of the ancient Egyptians themselves, as best as one can from the 20th century.

De Lubicz, after two decades of study primarily at the Temple of Luxor, was able to prove that the accepted dogma of ancient Egypt, and ancient civilization in general, is hopelessly inadequate. His work overthrows nearly every cherished belief regarding man's history, and the so-called evolution of civilization. Egyptian science, medicine, mathematics and astronomy were all of a higher order and sophistication than most modern scholars will acknowledge. Egyptian civilization in its entirety was based upon a complete and precise understanding of universal laws. And this profound understanding manifested itself in a consistent, coherent and inter-related system that fused science, art, and religion into a single philosophy. Furthermore, every aspect of Egyptian knowledge seems to have been complete at the very beginning. The sciences, artistic and architectural techniques and the hieroglyphic system show virtually no signs of development. Many achievements of the earliest dynasties were never surpassed, or even equaled later on. Orthodox Egyptologists readily admit this astonishing fact, but the magnitude of the mystery it poses is skillfully understated, while its many implications go unmentioned.

With the insights of an artist and philosopher West puts together an Egyptian worldview that explains why they built the temples and monuments in the way they did. They were a complex society with a view of the world that integrated mathematics with cosmology, which spilled over into greater aspects of life, such as architecture, rituals, and rites. The ancient Egyptians thoroughly understood human psychology, physiology, as well as the mechanisms of genesis, the nature of numbers, the use and nature of forces, and the human experience following death. Their perception of reality was to become the foundations for Pythagorean geometry.

According to West, "What is today called Pythagorean number mysticism is Egyptian in origin (if not older still) and corresponds to the underlying philosophy behind the arts and sciences of Egypt." One, the number, is the "Absolute" or unity and created multiplicity from itself. So One became Two. Two, in turn, expresses fundamental opposition. He continues explaining through the numeral nine. The single act of the Primordial Scission – One splitting and becoming Two – automatically sets in motion the sequence of whole numbers and of the 'irrationals,' which we represent as diagonals. It brings a new understanding to the ancient Hebrew declaration, "Hear, O Israel: The Lord our God is one Lord" (Deut. 6:4). In other words, he is not necessarily a single being, but is all that there is, the 'absolute.'

As for the serpent, seemingly a unity, it symbolized duality, simultaneously representing the creative and destructive forces in nature. Creative in the sense that multiplicity is created out of unity, destructive in the sense that creation represents the splitting of the Absolute. It represents the intellect, the sense by which man discriminates. In other words, how we break down the whole into its constituent parts. The serpent is an apt choice to represent this concept. It bears both a forked tongue and a double penis.

> Duality, and for that matter intellect, is not only a human but a cosmic function. There is a higher and a lower intellect. Thus, symbolically, there is the serpent that

crawls and the higher intellect, that which allows man to know God – the heavenly serpent, the serpent in the sky. The Egyptians knew perfectly well that snakes don't fly. But there is a deep meaning to their placing the serpent in the air under specific circumstances. The winged serpent, common to so many civilizations, was employed in Egypt as well and played a similar symbolic role.[20]

What West and de Lubicz before him contend is that the Egyptians were highly sophisticated in their worldview and around this abstract thought built a civilization. It is simply a revelation and a defining of God. In taking consciousness, Unity (God) unfolds creating multiplicity and, as a result, the universe exists. Tum, in regarding himself, creates Atum out of Nun, the primeval waters that encircle the earth. It is similar to the 'big bang' theory, except that it views creation as merely a physical force, trivializing and de-spiritualizing the ancient version of the myth. Christianity can be viewed as a later incarnation of this abstract view of reality, only expressed as God the Father, God the Son, and God the Holy Spirit. In the aspect of esoteric cosmology, the virgin may be regarded as equivalent to Nut, the "sky," the virgin matrix of principal substance.

West also puts forth the idea that Egypt was a legacy. They "did not develop their civilization, but inherited it." The earliest pyramids were not so much a process of developing construction skills, but of training. The physical evidence for this claim is in Schwaller's observation that the erosion of the Sphinx is a result of water and not wind and sand, a theory that was substantiated by Geologist Dr. Robert Schoch. Based on the geology, Schoch asserts that the Sphinx is at least 7,000 years old.

So who were the progenitors of Egyptian civilization? Beyond the scope of his book, West leaves us wondering.

The Ages of European Religions

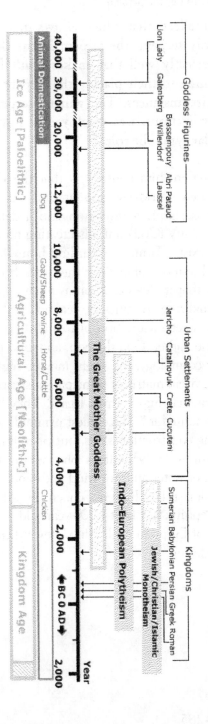

Chapter 21
Adam's Path

- The Genesis Creation Stories
- The Real Adam
- Sons of God – Daughters of Men

In the early part of the twentieth century, the prominent archeologist, Vere Gordon Childe (1892-1957), set forth a breakthrough concept in the history of mankind. According to the increasing evidence, a revolution had taken place long ago. He concluded that this change was not unlike the industrial revolution of his day. Society, in the first half of the twentieth century, was shifting from an agrarian to an urban-industrial based culture. Through his pioneering studies in archeology, he noticed a similar trend some 7,000 years ago. Man's early mastery over his environment was helping him shift from being a hunter-gatherer to a farmer and shepherd. It was a necessary transition. At the end of the ice age, climatic change and the resulting environmental changes drove mankind to meet his corporal needs in new ways.

In 1941 Childe coined the phrase *The Neolithic Revolution* to describe this monumental event. It marked the beginning of western civilization. Effectively, it was the beginning of history. Long ago, for those that witnessed the events, history was remembered as a story often told in mythical fashion. But as communicative advances allowed, it became documentary.

As was the tradition of the time, the beliefs in cultural origins and the saga of mankind were encapsulated in a tale based on the cosmology of the day. Handed down from generation to generation, the accounts of men were easier to remember in the form of a story rather than a listing of events.

The Genesis Creation Stories

There are many creation stories. Every culture has at least one. But that which has had the greatest impact for the western world is found in the biblical *Genesis*. Of all creation stories it is, perhaps, the least mythical. *Genesis* not only describes historical events, but also genealogical records covering nearly 2,000 years from the first identifiable man (Adam) to a royal Egyptian administrator named Joseph. This makes the *Genesis* text unique. It is also distinctive in that women are seldom mentioned; clearly the stories are from the viewpoint of a successive line of patriarchs.

There are really two biblical stories describing the creation of man. The first one occurs in *Genesis* Chapter One, verses twenty-six through twenty-eight. The second is in Chapter Two, verses five through eight. It is generally accepted that these two versions are simply different renditions of the same event. But on closer inspection, it is easy to see that this is not the case.

The first story of man's creation is general. Mankind is created in God's image, both male and female, implying sexual equality. Man is given the rule of all plants and animals, as well as the commandment to multiply and fill the earth. These events are *not* mentioned in the second story. It is quite different.

Man is a specific person named Adam, and is created *before* his female partner. Adam's wife, Eve, is not created in the same way her husband was, but formed from one of his ribs while he slept, implying woman was naturally subordinate. Furthermore, the Garden of Eden was a specific geographic location that exists to this day. So all the elements of this second creation story describes specific events of a particular man.

It makes perfect sense that the *Genesis* author is first describing the general creation of mankind and second, the specific creation (or identification) of an individual for historical reasons. The author's ordering of events is chronologically correct, which also suggests the stories are separate events. And when viewing the two stories as one, the text as a whole is considerably less articulate.

At its essence, the story of Adam is more than a mythical telling of a man's creation. It is the first chapter of a long, documented history, according to the Hebrews, whose ascendants lived on the Mesopotamian Plain during the fourth millennium BC. These historical records were (and are) cherished as the word of God. They were (and are) quite important, committed to memory for thousands of years, and for generations painstakingly copied by scribes. As genealogy records they are complete totaling forty-six generations from Adam to Joseph (father of Jesus), recorded in the *Gospel According to Luke*. All this of course requires that Adam was a living person and not just an analogy for mankind.

Details of the second creation also place a date and context on its occasion. Adam's role was to "work [or till] the ground."[1] In the first creation story, there is no mention of this labor. The sources of food, both plant and animal, were *given* to man by God and imply a hunter-gatherer lifestyle.[2]

This contrast of lifestyles, between the first and second creation stories, strongly suggests that Adam's story occurred during the period of transition from hunter-gatherer to farmer-shepherd, in other words, during the Neolithic Revolution. The *Book of Jubilees* corroborates this Neolithic setting by providing a date of 3760 BC for Adam's appearance in the Garden of Eden.

Concluding that the creation stories in *Genesis* are mutually exclusive events, also agrees with the archeological evidence that man first lived off the fruits of the land as a hunter-gatherer for many tens of thousands of years. Only later, after the end of the ice age and during the Neolithic Revolution, did mankind develop an agrarian lifestyle where he worked the land to subsist.

The two versions of creation have been viewed as a single story due to the interpretation that Adam was the first man created by God. He was formed from the dust of the ground and animated when God breathed the "breath of life" into his nostrils. Why the second creation story was written in this manner becomes an important detail to address.

As David Rohl so succinctly puts it, Adam was simply the first man to be remembered and therefore received the distinction. For that reason he was remembered, but there is more to the story. As circumstance would have it, this time period also coincides with a southerly expansion and the influence of a patriarchal-based society. For the previous 3,000 years, this intrusive culture had been developing in the Russian steppe land based on the strength and leadership of men.

The Real Adam

This raises the questions, "Who was Adam?" and "Was he real?" Some scholars believe the historical Adam may have been King Allum, the first king in the Sumerian kings list, or perhaps the first king of Eridu. He has also been equated with Adapa, the first sage of Eridu. Regardless of precisely who he was, there was something special about him.

We know from *Genesis* that he was not created in Eden, but migrated there from somewhere else. Once there, he married Eve. (Other myths claim his first wife was *Lilith*, who refused to submit to him sexually, therefore was unsuitable.) He and his wife, as the story goes, were banished from the Garden, an event that spurred civilization on the Mesopotamian Plain.

According to O'Brien's translation and interpretation of the Kharsag tablets, Eden was an agricultural settlement managed by a group of people known as the Anunnaki. On occasion, they received migrants and drifters (outsiders) to help with the work. It is not a large leap in reasoning to suspect that Adam was one of these workers taken in by the Anunnaki, *Genesis* 2:15 states that:

The Lord God took the man [Adam] and put him in the Garden of Eden to work it and take care of it.

If Eden was such a wonderful place to live, why was he expelled? (Or perhaps he left on his own accord.) The 2,000-year-old doctrinal answer is that he disobeyed God by listening to the serpent and ate from the Tree of Knowledge. Taken literally word for word, this makes little sense, but when viewed within the proper understanding of religious symbolism, the meaning of events becomes clear.

The Serpent and the Fruit

As we have already seen, the serpent and its symbolism have a long, prolific tradition within the cosmology of mankind. It is part of the oldest of belief systems and was man's first grasp at understanding the spiritual world. From its beginnings as the representation of the androgynous unmanifest Spirit of God, to shamanism and the "Tree of Life," to Gnosticism of the first century and Kundalini Yoga, the serpent has represented immortality, regeneration, and wisdom. But in the Genesis creation story, it represented an opponent who beguiled a man through the implied weakness of a woman.

If the serpent was considered holy in archaic religions, then why was the serpent portrayed as a nemesis? According to the author of Enoch, the son of a serpent named Gadreel led Eve astray. He was a Watcher, and therefore a force of evil in the world. A likely deduction is that Gadreel, possibly a shaman, was associated with an ancient religion represented by the symbolism of the serpent. Perhaps he was a disciple of the Mother Goddess.

How could the serpent have led Eve astray with a piece of fruit? A clue to the answer is that before Adam and Eve ate the fruit, they were naked and unashamed. But afterwards, they were ashamed and strung fig leaves together to cover their naked bodies (to be replaced later by animal skins). Obviously, they knew they were naked before they ate the fruit. They simply didn't care. So what fruit could cause such a change in self-perception? Clearly not an ordinary fruit consumed for nutrition. Much to the dismay of traditional doctrine, there is no other literal explanation except for a hallucinogen such as a psilocybin mushroom, or Belladonna or some other naturally occurring narcotic. Detecting good from evil and unashamed versus ashamed is an ideal way to convey an altered or enhanced state of consciousness.

It is widely known that small doses of hallucinogens cause heightened self-awareness, a state that often borders on paranoia. Also, Adam and Eve knew the fruit was poison and that they would die if they ate it (God told them, the story implies).[3] This, we know today, is absolutely true! It is also the case that in small quantities, most narcotics are not lethal. So, the serpent was also correct in stating that they would not die after eating it because they did not consume enough for a lethal dose.

We have discovered that hallucinogens were ritualistically used in the religion of the Mother Goddess, a tradition that goes back to tens of thousands of years. With that in mind, it is easy to see the story (at its essence) is a rejection of religious beliefs and rituals. For reasons specific to Adam and his descendents, this ancient religion was contrary to his own personal and cultural beliefs. This rejection of, and hostility toward, the serpent, and all it represents by Adam and his culture, is clear in the words of the *Genesis* author:

> I [God] will put enmity between you [the serpent] and the woman, and between your offspring and hers; he will crush your head, and you will strike his heel.

Obviously the author is not referring to an actual snake in this passage, but uses the likeness of a snake, and what it cosmologically represents, as a metaphor.

This enmity, a deep-seated hatred, was real and literal for Adam and his descendents. Why? It is clear from biblical text that Adam and his descendents espoused a culture based on paternity. The culture of those who inhabited Eden was not patriarchal based (as was the prevailing culture throughout Europe and the Near East). Theirs, as a wealth of evidence suggests, was matristic.

Adam was a patriarch. Since Eden was relatively close to the native lands of the Indo-Europeans (Kurgans), it is reasonable that his original home was north of the Caucasus Mountains. After leaving Eden, he made his way onto the Mesopotamian Plain and continued his life according to his own, culturally defined ideals. The rest of the story, and the story of his descendents, is continued in Sumerian and biblical history. They went on to create a kingdom that included the cities of Babylon, Erech, Akkad, Calneh, and Nineveh.

Of course, the story of Adam was written long after his death. Therefore, the telling of the tale is in mythical fashion. As it is with most history, it was written by the victor and, from a particular point of view, that of a patriarch. In the transition from a matristic to a kingdom-based culture, he may have been the first father figure on the Mesopotamian Plain to organize socially. From the perspective of his descendents, he really would have been the first man.

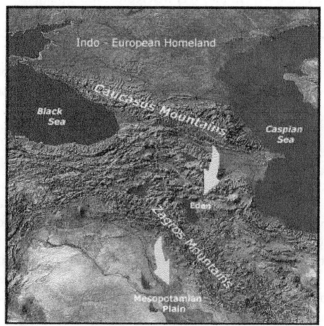

Adam's Path of Migration

Adam marked a beginning point for his descendents and the growing patriarchal based culture of which he helped to create. For posterity, religious conviction, and unity under this new culture's cosmology, he needed to be identified with, and created by, a male god. Generations later, as monotheism replaced polytheistic beliefs, the story was changed to reflect the times. Historical fact faded into story, the result is that he was simply created by God. According to Sumerian mythology, the god "Ea" (the ancient name of the Hebrew God "Yahweh") requested that man only worship one god. This, of course, was not Adam's doing. But as with many cultural heroes, even in contemporary times, fact becomes blurred in myth and the memory of a person often takes on a persona bigger than life.

We also see in the story of the Garden of Eden West's symbolist view from Egyptian thought. Unchecked duality, represented by the serpent, is chaos and nothing more than destruction. It is also significant that the Egyptian serpent, in its 'separator' role of the works of Ra, is vilified under various names. Knowing without synthesizing is to parody God, so the symbol of the serpent may very well represent temptation.

Sons of God – Daughters of Men

It is amazing to discover that the Garden of Eden was a literal place with a historical context, but there still exists the unknown identity for the "sons of God," the progenitors of "Adam and Eve" – O'Brien's Anunnaki creator gods who built and managed the Eden settlement. There can be little doubt that these "men of renown" and "heroes of old" were the remnants of an older, more sophisticated civilization. Among numerous others, both John Anthony West as well as Marija Gimbutas believed so, although in different ways. It is a highly debated and interpretative issue, but the evidence for their physical existence has been discovered in Egypt, Mesopotamia, the Levant, modern day Turkey, as well as regions in southwestern Iran. The most mysterious of which is the megalithic ruins of Baalbek, near Beirut, Lebanon, where three 1200-ton slabs form the foundation of a temple. There are also the rich, ancient agricultural societies of Jericho and Çatalhöyük for which James Mellaart could not find a legacy in later cultures of the Near East.

Yet, what became of this culture is not so much a mystery, as it is a willingness to believe the oral and mythical traditions passed on from the people who witnessed history's making. A cataclysm of unparalleled proportion must have occurred late in prehistory to spur the numerous flood myths. They exist for nearly every culture of the Mediterranean. It would explain why there were giants in those days before *and after* the flood. The flood was not global, but to a civilization that was decimated by it, it would surely seem so. Despite thousands of years of religious dogma, and through the endless generations of telling tales, the stories in the early chapters of *Genesis* are literally true, but for so long have been hidden in history behind such mysterious words as *the Sons of God and Daughters of Men.*

End Notes

Chapter 1: Mound Builders of the Ohio Valley

1. Dinosaurs: Scientific Evidence that Man and Dinosaurs Walked together, Carl E. Baugh, Promise Publishing, Orange CA, 1987, pictorial p. Q.
2. Ibid., p. 60-61.
3. Ibid., p. 61
4. Ibid.
5. The Unexplained, Karl P. Shuker, Barnes and Noble Inc., 1997.
6. "Giants," television documentary.
7. Ancient American [Volume 6, Issue 41], p. 9, originally published in *The Daily Telegraph*, Toronto, Ontario, Wednesday, August 23, 1871, p. 1.
8. "Holocaust of Giants: The Great Smithsonian Cover-up", Ross Hamilton, Self-Published 2001, Hamilton cites The History of Brown County, Ohio, complied from past accounts, 1883, see http://greatserpentmound.org/articles/giants3.html.
9. History of Ashtabula County, Ohio with Illustrations and Biographical Sketches of its Pioneers and most Prominent Men, Philadelphia, PA, Williams Brother, 1878, p. 17.
10. Ibid., p. 19.
11. "A Tradition of Giants", Ross Hamilton, Self-Published 2000, http://greatserpentmound.org/articles/giants.html.
12. Ibid.
13. History of Monroe County, Ohio, H.H. Hardesty & Co., Publishers, dated 1882, articles from various newspaper files, and items written by interested individuals. Collating and printing of the history was made possible by the efforts of Mr. Harold P. Haley, secretary of the Woodsfield Chamber of Commerce, Woodsfield, OH. Booklet compiled in Woodsfield during the year 1969. [Dick Henthorn, http://members.aol.com/RYouCuz/monroeco.html]
14. Ibid.
15. "A Tradition of Giants".
16. History of Morrow County and Ohio, Chicago, O. L. Baskin & Co., Historical Publishers, 186 Dearborn Street, 1880.
17. "Tradition of Giants".

18. Ibid.
19. Ibid.
20. History of Erie County, Pennsylvania, Chicago, IL, Warner, Beers & Co., 1884.
21. "Tradition of Giants".
22. Ibid.
23. Ibid.
24. Ibid.
25. Historical Encyclopedia of Illinois, Edited by Newton Bateman, LL.D. and Paul Selby, A.M. and History of Lake County, Edited by Hon. Charles A. Partridge, Illustrated. Chicago: Munsell Publishing Company, Publishers, 1902, see http://www.northstarnet.org/wrkhome/hmca/k2.htm.
26. "A Tradition of Giants".
27. The Mound Builders, Robert Silverberg, Ohio University Press, 1968, pp. 29-49.
28. Ibid., p.213.
29. From Black Land to Fifth Sun: the Science of Sacred Sites, Brian Fagan, Perseus Books, 1998, p. 187.
30. "Holocaust of Giants: The Great Smithsonian Cover-up" Ross Hamilton, Self-Published 2000, http://greatserpentmound.org/articles/giants3.html, original cite: 12th Annual Report of the Bureau of Ethnology to the Secretary of the Smithsonian Institution 1890-1891 (published in 1894).
31. Ibid.
32. Ibid.
33. The Mound Builders, p. 195.
34. Ibid., p.176, 204.

Chapter 2: Giants of Native American History

1. Red Earth – White Lies: Native Americans and the Myth of Scientific Fact, Vine Deloria, Jr., Fulcrum Publishing, Golden Colorado, 1997, P. 192.
2. Indian Legends of the Pacific Northwest, Elle E. Clark, University of California Press, Berkeley, California, 1953, P. 83.
3. Red Earth – White Lies: Native Americans and the Myth of Scientific Fact, Vine Deloria, Jr., Fulcrum Publishing, Golden Colorado, 1997, P. 153.
4. Sketches of Ancient History of the Six Nations, David Cusick, Recorder Print, Fayetteville New York, 1823, pp. 10-11.
5. "A Tradition of Giants", see also "The Problem of Ohio Mounds", Cyrus Thomas, full text available online at http://www.flora-source.com/library/1411-1.html, Hamilton cites Jones, James Athearn, Traditions of the North American Indians. London, Colburn and Bently, 1830.

6. The upper Mid-West was largely undocumented in the early 1800s. This collection of journal writings, published in 1821, describes the area between Detroit and Sault Ste. Marie as recorded by Henry Schoolcraft. This explorer and Indian agent includes vivid descriptions of the topography and natural history of the area. Researchers will also find information regarding the mineral wealth of Minnesota and Wisconsin, including the lead mines at Dubuque. For researchers seeking to understand the country their ancestors settled, this can be a helpful source of information.
7. "A Tradition of Giants".
8. Ibid., Hamilton cites Heckewelder, John, History, Manners, and Customs of the Indian Nations, The Historical Society of Pennsylvania, 1876 (originally published in 1819).
9. Ibid.
10. The Prehistoric World: or Vanished Races, E. A. Allen, Central Publishing House, Nashville, 1885, the source used was the Project Gutenberg Etext version, see Chapter 12 – The Prehistoric Americans.
11. Ibid.
12. Ibid., Allen quotes Du Pratz, "History of Louisiana", Vol. II, Lond., 1763.
13. From Black Land to Fifth Sun, p. 187.
14. The Problem of the Ohio Mounds, Cyrus Tomas, Chapter 5 - The Cherokees and the Tallegwi, See http://www.flora-source.com/library/1411-1.html
15. Ibid.
16. Sketches of Ancient History of the Six Nations, p. 3.
17. Ibid., p. 5.
18. Ibid., p. 6.
19. Ibid.
20. Ibid.
21. Ibid., p. 7.
22. Ibid., p. 8.
23. Ibid.
24. Ibid., p. 9.
25. Ibid., p. 15.
26. Ibid.
27. Ibid., p. 16.
28. Ibid., p. 29.
29. Ibid.
30. The Code of Handsome Lake, the Seneca Prophet, Arthur C. Parker, 1913, p.128.
31. Myths of the Cherokee - From Nineteenth Annual Report of the Bureau of American Ethnology 1897-98, 1900, p. 392.
32. Sketches of Ancient History of the Six Nations, p. 25.

33. Life Among the Piutes: Their wrongs and Claims, Sarah Winnemucca Hopkins, University of Nevada Press, Reno NV, 1994, p. 73-74.
34. Ibid., p. 74.
35. Ibid.
36. Ibid., p. 75.
37. Legends of the Kaw, Carrie De Voe, Franklin Hudson Publishing, Kansas City MO, 1904.
38. The Dîné: Origin Myths of the Navaho Indians, Aileen O'Bryan, Bulletin 163 of the Bureau of American Ethnology of the Smithsonian Institution, 1956.
39. Idaho's Flood-Giants Remembered, Thomas E. Farner, PhD, Ancient American Volume 6, Issue 41, page 9.
40. Indian legends of the Pacific Northwest, Ella E. Clark, University of California Press, Los Angeles California, 1953, P. 64.
41. Ibid.
42. Indian Legends from the Northern Rockies, Ella E. Clark, University of Oklahoma Press, Norman OK, 1966, P.64.
43. Ibid.
44. Ibid.
45. Ibid.
46. Ibid., P. 113.
47. Ibid.
48. Ibid. P. 137.
49. Ibid., P. 140.
50. Ibid., P. 141.
51. Indian legends of Canada, Ella E. Clark, McClelland and Stuart, 1960, P. 104

Chapter 3: Men of Renown - Heroes of Old

1. Joshua 5:6
2. The Works of Josephus- Complete and Unabridged, Translated by William Whiston, A.M., Hendrickson Publishers, 1981, pp. 110-111.
3. Numbers 13:31-33.
4. The Works of Josephus, p. 111.
5. The Book of Joshua only describes these cities as being destroyed. See Joshua 6:24 for Jericho, 8:19-20, 28 for Ai, and Joshua 11:11 for Hazor.
6. Joshua 13:1.
7. First Samuel 17:4-11.
8. Second Samuel 21:15-22 and also First Chronicles 20:4-8.
9. First Samuel 6:17
10. Is the Bible True? – How Modern Debates and Discoveries Affirm the Essence of the Scripture, Jeffery L. Sheler, Harper San Francisco Zondervan, 1999, p. 98.

11. See the Table of Nations, Genesis chapter 10.
12. Numbers 13:29.
13. Job 41:6 & Proverbs 31:24.
14. From Black Land to Fifth Sun: the Science of Sacred Sites, Brian Fagan, Perseus Books, 1998, p. 78.
15. Genesis 13:18.
16. See Genesis 14:5-6.
17. Deuteronomy 2:10-11.
18. The Jewish Encyclopedia, 1901-1906, Rephaim pp.656-659, Zuzim pp.706-707, Emim p. 152, Horite p. 462, see also http://www.jewishencyclopedia.com.
19. Deuteronomy 9:2.
20. Joshua 14:12,21.
21. Joshua 21:11.
22. Genesis 6:1-4 (New International Version).
23. "Deuteronomy 32:8 and the Sons of God", Michael S. Heiser, unpublished academic position paper, see http://www.michaelsheiser.com/mshcv.htm or http://www.facadenovel.com/positionpapers.htm.
24. Ibid.
25. Ibid.
26. Deuteronomy 33:14.
27. Genesis 5:24.

Chapter 4: Enoch the Scribe

1. The Canon of Scripture, E.F. Bruce, Intervarsity Press, 1988, pp 39-40.
2. The Jewish Encyclopedia, "Angelology - Biblical, Talmudical, and Post-Talmudical", p 181.
3. The Book of Enoch, Translated by R.H. Charles, SPCK, Holy Trinity Church, London, first published in 1917, 27th impression, 1997, Chapter 6, verses 1-3, pp. 34-35.
4. Ibid., Chapter 6, verse 4-7.
5. The Jewish Encyclopedia, "Angelology - Biblical, Talmudical, and Post-Talmudical", p 583.
6. The Book of Enoch, Chapter 69, verse 11, p. 90.
7. Ibid., Chapter 7, verse 1, p. 35; Chapter 8, verses 1-3, pp. 35-36; Chapter 69, verses 6-7, pp. 89-90.
8. Ibid., Chapter 69, verse 9, p. 90.
9. Ibid., Chapter 69 verse 11, p. 90.
10. Ibid., Chapter 7, verses 3-6, p.35.
11. Ibid., Chapter 9, verse 9, p. 36.
12. Genesis 6:5,13.

13. The Book of Enoch, Chapter 10, verses 9-10, p. 37.
14. Ibid., Chapter 10, verses 1-3, p. 37.
15. Genesis 6:8-9.
16. The Book of Enoch, Chapter 10, verse 3, p.37.
17. Jubilees 4:16.
18. The Book of Enoch, Chapter 106, verses 1-2, pp. 150-151.
19. Ibid., Chapter 106 verses 3-7, p. 151.
20. The Complete Dead Sea Scrolls in English, Geza Vermes, Penguin Books, New York, NY, 1998, pp.449-450.
21. Ibid.
22. Leviticus 16:6-10.
23. Genesis 27:9.
24. Leviticus 17:6-7.
25. Strong's Concordance, Hebrew word #8163.
26. The Book of Enoch, Chapter 10, verses 3-9, p. 37.
27. Ibid., Chapter 12, verse 4, p. 39.
28. Ibid., Chapter 15, verse 2, p.42.
29. Dead Sea Scrolls 4Q203, 1Q23, 2Q26, 4Q530-532, 6Q8.
30. Book of Jubilees 4:17.
31. Ibid., 4:19-20.
32. The Genesis Apocryphon, Dead Sea Scroll 1Q20.
33. Hebrews 11:5.
34. The Book of Enoch, Chapter 69, verse 6, p. 89.

Chapter 5: Roots of Genesis

1. Joshua 24:2.
2. Genesis 11:27-32.
3. Genesis 12:1-4.
4. Earliest Civilizations of the Near East, James Mellaart, McGraw-Hill, New York 1965, p. 63.
5. Ibid., p. 64.
6. Ibid., p. 68.
7. "The Tower of Babel", David Rohl, see http://www.nunki.net/PerDud/TheWorks/Express/TowerBabel.html, originally published in "The Express", Thursday, May 13, 1999.
8. The number of days of the Flood story does not add up correctly. At one point, Noah takes two of each animal; at another point, he takes two of some, seven of others. Joseph is sold into slavery to Ishmaelites in one verse, to Midianites a few verses later. The Mountain of Revelation is sometimes called Sinai and sometimes Horeb. Moses' father-in-law is sometimes called Yitro and sometimes Ruel, and so on.

9. Several stories are repeated, with different characters or different emphasis (called "doublets"). For instance, there are two creation stories (Gen 1 and Gen 2). There are three stories of a patriarch traveling among pagans and pretending his wife is his sister. There are two stories of Moses striking a rock to produce water. There are two versions of the Ten Commandments (one in Exodus, one that Moses recaps in Deuteronomy) with slightly different wording. There are, in fact, a lot of these doublets.
10. Exodus 3:13-14.
11. "The Tower of Babel".
12. Ibid.
13. Online Matthew Henry Bible Commentary.
14. Enmerkar and the Lord of Aratta, Enmerkar and Ensuhkeshdana, Lugulbanda and Enmerkar, Lugulbanda and Mount Hurum.
15. The Hebrew word "Eden" (5731) is derived from the prime root "adan" (5727) which means Soft and pleasant. See Abingdon's Strong's Exhaustive concordance of the Bible, Hebrew and Chaldee Dictionary, p. 85.
16. Ezekiel 28:13, a tabret is a timbrel or tambourine, generally played by women.

Chapter 6: The Garden of Eden

1. The Dragons of Eden, Carl Sagan, Ballantine Books, New York, 1977, p. 99.
2. Ibid.
3. Ibid.
4. Genesis 2:8-14.
5. "In Search of Eden", Television Documentary, written and produced by David Rohl, 2002, Based on the book, Legend: the Genesis of Civilization, Century, London, 1998.
6. Ibid.
7. Ibid.
8. Ibid.
9. Ibid.
10. Genesis 4:26.
11. The Book of Enoch Chapter 8, verses 1-3, pp. 35-36; Chapter 69, verses 6-12, p. 89-90.
12. Dolichocephalic means to have an abnormally long head. The condition of being dolichocephalic is known as dolichocephaly. Compare dolichocephalic to brachycephaly, which is a short head. A normal, medium sized head is known as mesocephalic. Dolichocephalic comes from the Greek word "dolichos" meaning "long", the Greek word "kephale" meaning "head", and the Greek word "ikos" meaning "pertaining to". Put the words together and you have "pertaining to a long head". Technically, a dolichocephalic head is defined as having a skull with a cephalic index below 75. The cephalic index is

a rating scale that is used to measure the size of the head. The rating on the cephalic index is obtained by multiplying the maximum width of the head by 100, and dividing that number by the maximum length of the head. A cephalic index between 76 and 80 is considered normal. Dolichocephalic is also known as dolichocranial, dolichocephalous, cymbocephalic, cymbocephalous, tectocephalic, scaphocephalic, and scaphocephalous.

13. Archaeobotanical Archive Report, Christine Hastorf and Julie Near, Catalhoyuk 1997 Archive Report, See http://catal.arch.cam.ac.uk/catal/Archive_rep97/hastorf97.html.

14. Animal Bone Report, Louise Martin and Nerissa Russell, Catalhoyuk 1997 Archive Report, (See http://catal.arch.cam.ac.uk/catal/Archive_rep97/martin97.html).

15. "Figurines", Naomi Hamilton, Catalhoyuk 1997 Archive Report. (see http://catal.arch.cam.ac.uk/catal/Archive_rep97/hamil_fig97.

16. In the Land of the Mothers, Anita Louise, Awakened: the Journal of Women's Spirituality, August 2, 2000.

17. Earliest Civilizations of the Near East, James Mellaart, McGraw-Hill, New York, 1965, p, 77.

18. Ibid., p. 79.

19. The Genius of the Few: The Story of Those Who Founded the Garden of Eden, Christian & Joy O'Brien, Turnstone Press LTD, 1985.

20. From the Ashes of Angels: The Forbidden Legacy of a Fallen Race, Andrew Collins, Bear & Company, Rochester VT, 1996, p. 205.

21. Ibid.

22. Ibid.

Chapter 7: Cro-Magnon Civilizations

1. Becoming Human – Evolution and Human Uniqueness, Ian Tattersall, Harcourt, Brace & Company, 1998, p.10.

2. Ibid., p. 9.

Chapter 8: Cro-Magnon Art & Technology

1. Ibid., p. 10.

2. The Mind in the Cave, David Lewis-Williams, Thames & Hudson, 2002, p. 77.

3. Ibid.

4. Becoming Human, p. 13-14.

5. "The Earliest Images", Randall White, Expedition, Journal of the University Museum, University of Pennsylvania.

6. The Cave of Lascaux, French Ministry of Culture and Communication website, see http://www.culture.fr/culture/arcnat/lascaux/en/.
7. Ibid.
8. Ibid.
9. Ibid
10. The Mind in the Cave, David Lewis-Williams, p.17.
11. The Cave of Chauvet Pont D'arc, French Ministry of Culture and Communication website, see http://www.culture.fr/culture/arcnat/chauvet/en/.
12. Pech Merle Prehistory Center, see http://www.quercy.net/pechmerle/visite_fr.html.
13. Ibid.
14. "Ice Age Chemists," Archeology, Online News, Norman Hammond, November 23, 1999.
15. Ibid.
16. Becoming Human p.176.
17. The "Venus Figurines" – Textiles, Basketry, Gender, and Status in the Upper Paleolithic, O. Soffer, M. Adovasio, D.C. Hyland, Current Anthropology, Volume 41, Number 4, August-October 2000, p.528.
18. "Woven cloth dates back 27,000 years", BBC News Online, Dr, David Whitehouse, June 14, 2000.
19. "World's Oldest Hats Discovered? 'Venus Wear' Reveals 27,000-Year-Old Fashion", Jennifer Viegas, ABCNEWS.com, May 9, 2002.
20. The "Venus Figurines" – Textiles, Basketry, Gender, and Status in the Upper Paleolithic, p.520.
21. Ibid.
22. Ibid. p. 518.
23. Ibid. p. 522.
24. Ibid. p. 524.

Chapter 9: Prehistoric Beliefs And Religion

1. The Creative Explosion: An Inquiry Into The Origins Of Art And Religion, John E. Pfeiffer, Harper & Row: New York, 1982, p.213.
2. The Mind in the Cave: Consciousness and the Origins of Art, Thames & Hudson, 2002, p. 127.
3. Ibid.

Chapter 10: Mysteries of Cro-Magnon

1. The "Venus Figurines" – Textiles, Basketry, Gender, and Status in the Upper Paleolithic, p.526.

2. Grammaire de la Langue Basque (d'apres celle de Larramendi), S.H. Blanc, Lyons & Paris, 1854.
3. "The Races of Europe", W.Z. Ripley, D. Appleton & Co., New York, 1899.
4. The Roots of Witchcraft, Michael Harrison, Citadel Press, Secaucas, N.J., 1974.
5. "Europe's Mystery People", Evan Haddingham, World Monitor, p. 34, September 1992. Cr. A. Rothovius.
6. From Science Frontiers #15, Spring 1981, 1981-2000 William R. Corliss.
7. "Gods, Bears, Stones, and Stars", Suizan Eram, Iowa Alumni Magazine-December 2000.
8. Ibid.
9. "Conflicting Identities: A Comparative Study of Non-commensurate Root Metaphors in Basque and European Image Schemata", Roslyn M. Frank and Mikel Susperregi, for Institute for Basque Studies Symposium, July 5, 2000, p. 13.
10. Ibid., p. 6.
11. Ibid., p. 10.
12. Ibid., p. 9.
13. Ibid., P. 16.
14. Ibid., p. 12.
15. Ibid., p. 3.
16. Becoming Human – Evolution and Human Uniqueness, Ian Tattersall, Harcourt, Brace & Company, 1998, p.10.
17. Becoming Human, p.10.
18. Ibid., p. 180.
19. The Mind in the Cave, p. 99.

Chapter 11: Ancient Engineers of the Amazon

1. "Atlantis Found", Produced and Directed by Peter Getzels and Harriet Gordon, For the BBC/ Discovery Channel, 2002.
2. Ibid.
3. Ibid.
4. "The Pristine Myth: The Landscape of the Americas in 1492", William M. Denevan, Department of Geography, University of Wisconsin, 1992.
5. Ibid.
6. "The Myth About Pristine America", Stewart Truelsen, The Voice of Agriculture View, For the week of June 17, 2002.
7. "Atlantis Found".
8. "Pre-Columbian Roads of the Amazon", Clark L. Erickson, Expedition 43(2):2 1-30–2001.

9. "Prehispanic Earthworks of the Baures Region of the Bolivian Amazon", A Project of the Instituto Nacional de Arqueologia de Bolivia Arqueologist Wilma Winkler Verlarde and the University of Pennsylvania Museum, Dr. Clark L. Erickson.
10. Ibid.
11. Ibid.
12. Ibid.
13. "An Artificial Landscape-Scale Fishery in the Bolivian Amazon", Nature 408, 190 - 193, Macmillan Publishers Ltd., Clark L. Erickson, 2000.
14. Ibid.
15. Ibid.
16. Ibid.

Chapter 12: American Paleolithic

1. "The Solutrean Connection Question", Dr. Cyclone Covey, Professor Emeritus of Ancient History, Wake Forest University, Winston-Salem, NC, unpublished. See http://www.wfu.edu/~cyclone/THE SOLUTREAN CONNECTION QUESTION.HTM. Covey cites "The Antiquity of Man in America," Natural History XXVII/3 (1927), pp. 232-34. Although Dr. Covey's paper appears to be hastily written, it contains a wealth of information and sources, and is fully documented. The original references of Dr. Covey will be cited.
2. "The Solutrean Connection Question", Covey cites: "Folsom Culture & its Age," in "Proceedings of the New York Meeting," Bulletin of the Geological Society of America XL (1929), p. 128.
3. "The Solutrean Connection Question", Covey cites: "A Folsom Complex: Preliminary Report on Investigations at the Lindenmeier Site in Northern Colorado", Smithsonian Miscellaneous Collections XCIV no. 4 (20 June 1935), pp. 1-3.
4. "The Solutrean Connection Question", Covey cites: "Additional Information on the Folsom Complex", Smithsonian Misc. Colls. XCV no. 10 (1936), 1-38; see also N.C. Nelson's review, "Notes on Cultural Relations between Asia & America," Am. Antiquity II/4 (April 1937), p. 267.
5. "The Solutrean Connection Question", Covey cites: Wilmsen & Roberts, Lindenmeier, 1934-1974: Concluding Report on Investigations, Smithsonian Contributions to Anthropology no. 24 (1984).
6. Ibid., pp. 179-180.
7. Ibid p. 175.
8. "The Solutrean Connection Question", Covey cites: John Lambert Cotter, "The Occurrence of Flints & Extinct Animals in Pluvial Deposits Near Clovis, New Mexico. Part IV, Report on Excavation at the Gravel Pit, 1936,"

Proceedings of the Academy of Natural Sciences of Philadelphia 1937, 1-15; Edwin Wilmsen, Lithic Analysis & Cultural Inference: A Paleo-Indian Case (U. Ariz. 1970), 22, 78-79; & James Hester, Ernest Lundelius, Jr., & Roald Fryxell, Blackwater Locality No. 1; A Stratified Early Man Site in Eastern New Mexico, Ranchos de Taos, Ft. Burgwin Research Center #8 (SMU 1972).

9. "The Solutrean Connection Question", Covey cites: Figgins, "A Further Contribution to the Antiquity of Man in America," Proceedings of the Colorado Museum of Natural History XII (1933), 4-8; C. Vance Haynes, Jr , "Fluted Projectile Points: Their Age & Dispersion," Science CXLV/ 3639 (25 Sept. 1964), p. 1408.

10. "The Solutrean Connection Question", Covey cites: Green, "The Clovis Blades: An Important Addition to the Llano Complex," Am. Antiquity XXIX/ 2 (Oct. 1963), pp. 145, 149-50, 152, 154, 157.

11. "The Solutrean Connection Question", Covey cites: Warnica, "New Discoveries at the Clovis Site," Am. Antiquity XXXI/ 3 (Jan. 1966), pp. 345-57.

12. "The Solutrean Connection Question", Covey cites: "Fluted Projectile Points," pp. 1408-13.

13. "The Solutrean Connection Question", Covey cites: Fiedel, "The Peopling of the New World: Present Evidence, New Theories, & Future Directions," Journal of Archaeological Research VIII/ 1 (March 2000), p. 53.

14. "The Solutrean Connection Question", Covey cites: "Fluted Projectile Points," p. 1008.

15. "The Solutrean Connection Question", Covey cites: "A Mammoth Ivory Semifabricate from Blackwater Locality No. 1, New Mexico," Am. Antiquity LC/ 1 (Jan. 1990), 112-16; Green, "Comments on the Report of Worked Mammoth Tusk from the Clovis Site," ibid. LVII/ 2 (April 1997), 331-37; & Haynes, Sanders, & Agogino, "Reply to F.E. Green's Comments on the Clovis Site," ibid. 338-44.

16. "The Solutrean Connection Question", Covey cites: "Sandia Man," Scientific American CLXIII/ 1 (July 1940), p. 15.

17. "The Solutrean Connection Question", Covey cites: Douglas Byers, "Concerning Sandia Cave," Am. Antiquity VII/ 4 (April 1942), pp. 408-409.

18. "The Solutrean Connection Question", Covey cites: "A Chronological Problem Presented by Sandia Cave, New Mexico," Am. Antiquity V/ 3 (Jan. 1940), 200-01, including inserted page of photos, front & back.

19. "The Solutrean Connection Question", Covey cites: Donald Brand, "Regarding Sandia Cave," ibid. V/ 4 (Oct. 1940), 339; Hibben, "Sandia Cave," ibid. VI/ 3 (Jan. 1941), 266; Bliss, "Sandia Cave," ibid. VI/ 1 (July 1940), pp. 77-78.

20. "The Solutrean Connection Question", Covey cites: Covey - "Association of Man with Pleistocene Mammals in the Sandia Mts., N.M.," Am. Antiquity II/4 (April 1937), pp. 260-263.

21. "The Solutrean Connection Question", Covey cites: Anon., "Sandia Man," TIME XXXV (6 May 1940), 67, & Hibben, Evidences of Early Occupation in Sandia Cave, New Mexico, and Other Sites in the Sandia-Manzano Region, Smithsonian Miscellaneous Collections XCIX no. 23 (1941), p. 8.

22. "The Solutrean Connection Question", Covey cites: "Sandia Cave" (July 1940), p. 77.

23. "The Solutrean Connection Question", Covey cites: "An Association of Man," 263 & fig. 2 opposite.

24. "The Solutrean Connection Question", Covey cites: William Roosa, Reply to Mason, p. 263.

25. "The Solutrean Connection Question", Covey cites: Reply to Mason, p. 257.

26. "The Solutrean Connection Question", Covey cites: "Human Artifacts in Association with Horse & Sloth Bones in Southern South America," Science LXXXVI/2219 (9 July 1937).

27. "The Solutrean Connection Question", Covey cites: Pleistocene-Recent Boundary in the Rocky Mt. Region, Geological Survey Bulletin 996-A (Gov't Printing Office 1953).

28. "The Solutrean Connection Question", Covey cites: Sandia Cave: A Study in Controversy, Eastern New Mexico U. Contributions in Anthropology VI/1, ed. Cynthia Irwin-Williams (E.N.M.U. Paleo-Indian Institute 1975), pp. 35-36.

29. "The Solutrean Connection Question", Covey cites: "Ancient Man in America," Geographical Review XXVII (1937), 507-09, & "Correlation of the Deposits of Sandia Cave, New Mexico, with the Glacial Chronology," appendix to Hibben, Evidences of Early Occupation in Sandia Cave.

30. "The Solutrean Connection Question", Covey cites: "Age of the Sandia Culture," Science CXXVI/3268 (16 Aug. 1957), pp. 305-306.

31. "The Solutrean Connection Question", Covey cites: "Radiocarbon Dates for Sandia Cave, Correction," Science CXXV/3241 (8 Feb. 1957), p. 234.

32. Ibid., p. 235.

33. Ibid.

34. "The Solutrean Connection Question", Covey cites: "Age of the Sandia Culture," p. 305.

35. "The Solutrean Connection Question", Covey cites: University of Michigan Radiocarbon Dates I," ibid. CXXIV/3223 (5 Oct. 1956), p. 670.

36. Ibid. / 3224, 664-72; Hibben, "Specimens from Sandia Cave & Their Possible Significance," ibid. CXXII/3172 (14 Oct. 1955), 688-89; & Crane, "Antiquity of the Sandia Culture: Carbon-14 Measurements," ibid. 698-90; Krieger, "News & Notes," Am. Antiquity XXII/4 (April 1957), 435-36; & Stevens &

Agogino, Sandia Cave, 18-22. Subsequent sources debating Sandia dates added no new data.

37. "The Solutrean Connection Question", Covey cites: Roosa, "The Lucy Site in Central New Mexico," Am. Antiquity XXI/ 3 (Jan. 1956), p. 310.

38. "The Solutrean Connection Question", Covey cites: Reply to Mason, p. 263.

39. "The Solutrean Connection Question", Covey cites: "The First 38 Sandia Points Industry," Am. Antiquity XI/ 3 (Jan. 1946), 257-58; & Evidence of Early Occupation in Sandia Cave, p. 32.

40. "The Solutrean Connection Question", Covey cites: Ancient Man in North America, 91. Cf. Roy L. Carlson (who seconded Krieger's view of Sandia points as enigmatic), "The Far West," chap. 6 in Early Man in the New World, ed. Shutler, p. 83.

41. "The Solutrean Connection Question", Covey cites: Emerson, "The Paleolithic and the New World," p. 60.

42. "The Solutrean Connection Question", Covey cites: "The First 38 Sandia Points Industry," pp. 257-258.

43. "The Solutrean Connection Question", Covey cites: "The French Connection," P. 67.

44. "The Solutrean Connection Question", Covey cites: Preston, "The Lost Man," p. 76.

45. "The Solutrean Connection Question", Covey cites: Quoted in Burne, "Goodbye Columbus, Hello Solutreans," p. 3.

46. "The Solutrean Connection Question", Covey cites: "The Peopling of the New World, p. 83.

Chapter 13: Breaking the Clovis Barrier

1. The Significance of the Bluefish Caves in Beringian Prehistory, Jacques Cinq-Mars, February, 2001, This is a translation of a paper originally published, in French, in *Revista de Arqueología Americana*, No. 1, (1990): pp. 9-32. But for a few minor corrections and the presentation of upgraded illustrations (Fig. 1-5) and faunal list (Table 1), this Web version is essentially the same as the original one, see http:// www.civilization.ca/ academ/ articles/ cinq1_1e.html.

2. Ibid., p. 1-3.

3. Ibid., p. 4.

4. Kennewick Man, James C. Chatters, Smithsonian Institution website, From Northern Clans, Northern Traces: Journeys in the ancient circumpolar world, see http:// www.mnh.si.edu/ arctic/ html/ kennewick_man.html, 1997.

5. Ibid.

6. Ibid.

7. Confederated Tribes of the Colville Reservation, Confederated Tribes of the Umatilla Reservation, Confederated Tribes and Bands of the Yakama Indian

Nation of the Yakama Reservation, the Nez Perce Tribe of Idaho, and the Wanapum Band. See http://www.pbs.org/wotp/kennewick_man/.

8. Dennis Stanford, Curator of Archaeology at the Smithsonian's National Museum of Natural History; Robson Bonnichsen, director of the Center for the Study of First Americans at Oregon State University; D. Gentry Steele, an anthropology professor at Texas A&M University; C. Loring Brace, a curator at the Museum of Anthropology at the University of Michigan; George Gill, an anthropology professor at the University of Wyoming; C. Vance Haynes Jr., an anthropology professor at the University of Arizona, and Richard Jantz, an anthropology professor at the University of Tennessee at Knoxville. See http://www.pbs.org/wotp/kennewick_man/.

9. "Putting a New Face on Prehistory", The Washington Post, Boyce Rensberger, Tuesday, April 15, 1997; Page A01, See http://www.washingtonpost.com/wp-srv/digest/daily/april/24/nevada.htm.

10. "Paleoamerican Origins", Smithsonian Institution, Anthropology Outreach Office, 1999. See http://www.si.edu/resource/faq/nmnh/origin.htm.

11. "Monte Verde Archeologist Prevails In Dispute Over Settlement's Age", The Scientist, 4[2]:1, Jan. 20, 1990.

12. "Chilean Field Yields New Clues to Peopling of Americas", The New York Times on the Web, John Noble Wilford, August 25, 1998.

13. "The South American Twist - Clovis First Doesn't Fit the Rich Prehistory of the Southern Continent", Ruth Gruhn, Scientific American Discovering Archeology Magazine, January/February 2000, pp.51-53.

14. "Chilean Field Yields New Clues to Peopling of Americas", The New York Times on the Web, John Noble Wilford, August 25, 1998.

15. "Early New World Settlers Rise in East", Bruce Bower, Science News Online, Week of April 15, 2000; Vol. 157, No. 16.

16. Ibid.

17. "Cactus Hill Update", Archeology Online, Newbriefs, Mark Rose, April 10, 2000.

18. "The Topper Site: Beyond Clovis at Allendale", James M. Chandler, Mammoth Trumpet Volume 16 No.4 - Sept 2001.

19. Ibid.

20. Ibid.

Chapter 14: Digging Deeper

1. "The Solutrean Connection Question", Covey cites: A photo made newspapers internationally at the time. Kerby Smith's photo appears in Thomas Y. Canby, "The Search for the First Americans," National Geographic CLVI/3 (Sept. 1979), p. 350.

2. "Anatomy of an Anomaly", Mark Owen Webb and Suzanne Clark, Disputatio Magazine online, May 1999. See http://www.terravista.pt/Nazare/5474/Articles/art61.html.

3. Ibid.

4. "The Hueyatlaco Dilemma", Science Frontiers ONLINE, No. 21: May-Jun 1982, William R. Corliss.

5. "The Solutrean Connection Question", Covey cites: "Early Man in the New World," in Early Man in the New World, ed. Shutler, p. 133.

6. "The 50,000-Year-Old Americans of Pedra Furada", Science Frontiers Online, No. 87: May-Jun 1993.

7. Ibid.

8. "The Solutrean Connection Question".

9. "Deflating a Paradigm: Brazil's Pedra Furada", Science Frontiers #108, William R. Corliss, NOV-DEC 1996.

10. "The Solutrean Connection Question", Covey cites: Guidon & G. Delabrias, "Carbon-14 Dates Point to Man in the Americas 32,000 Years Ago," Nature CCCXXI/6072 (19 June 1986), 769-71; Guidon, "Les Premières Occupations Humaines de l'Aire Archéologique de São Raimundo Nonato-Piauí-Brasil," L'Anthropologie XXXXVIII/2 (May 1984), 263-71, "On Stratigraphy & Chronology at Pedra Furada," Current Anthropology XXX/1 (Dec. 1989), 641-42, "Las Unidades Culturales de São Raimundo Nonato—Sudeste des Estado de Piauí—Brasil," in New Evidence for the Peopling of the Americas, ed. Bryan, 157-71; "The First Americans: Cliff Notes," Natural History XCVI/8 (Aug. 1987), 6, 8, 10, 12; Robert G. Bednarik, "On the Pleistocene Settlement of South America," Antiquity LXIII/2 (March 1989), 101-07; Paul Bahn, "Dating the First American," New Scientist CXXXI (22 July 1991), 26-28; Warwick Bray, "Finding the Earliest Americans," Nature CCCXXI/6071 (19-25 June 1986), 726; Fiedel, "The Peopling of the New World," 51, & Prehistory of the Americas (Cambridge U 1987), 79; Meltzer, Adovasio, & Dillehay, "On a Pleistocene Human Occupation at Pedra Furada, Brazil," Antiquity LXVIII/261 (Dec. 1994), 695-714; Guidon, A.-M. Pessis, Fabio Parenti, Michel Fontugue, & Claude Guérin, "Nature & Age of the Deposits in Pedra Furada, Brazil: Reply to Meltzer, Adovasio & Dillehay," ibid. LXX/268 (June 1996), 408-21; Guidon & B. Arnaud, "The Chronology of the New World," 167-78; etc.

11. "The South American Twist - Clovis First Doesn't Fit the Rich Prehistory of the Southern Continent", Ruth Gruhn, Discovering Archaeology Magazine.

12. "The Solutrean Connection Question", Covey cites: Adovasio, A.T. Boldurien, & Ronald C. Carlisle, "Who Were These Guys?" Americans Before Columbus: Ice-Age Origins, Smithsonian symposium 26 Sept. 1987), ed. Carlisle, Anthropological & Ethnological Monographs 12 (U. Pittsburgh 1988), 45-61; Adovasio, Jack Donahue, & R. Stukenrath, The Meadowcroft

Rockshelter Radiocarbon Chronology 1975-1988. Some Ruminations (Society for Am. Archaeology 53rd annual meeting Phoenix 27 April-1 May 1988); Adovasio, Carlisle, K. Cushman, Stuckenrath, & P. Wiegman, "Meadowcroft Rockshelter & the Pleistocene/ Holocene Transition in Southwestern Pennsylvania," Quaternary Vertebrate Paleontology.. Memorial to John E. Genoways & Mary R. Dawson, Carnegie Museum of Natural History (Philadelphia) Special Pubs. 8 (1988), 347-69; Adovasio, "The Ones that Will Not Go Away," 205-15; Dincauze, "An Archaeo-Logical Evaluation of the Case for Pre-Clovis," chap. 5, Advances in World Archaeology, ed. Fred Wendorf & Angela E. Close (Academic Press 1984), III 286-87; "On the Meadowcroft Papers..," Quarterly Review of Archaeology II (1981), 3-4; Adovasio, Donahue, Stuckenrath, & J.D. Gunn, "The Meadowcroft Papers: A Response to Dincauze," ibid. II/ 3., 14-15; Adovasio, Gunn, Donahue, & Stuckenrath, "Meadowcroft Rockshelter, 1977: An Overview," Am. Antiquity XLIII/ 4 (Oct. 1974), 632-51; Adovasio, Gunn, Donahue, Stuckenrath, John E. Guilday, & Kenneth Lord, "Meadowcroft Rockshelter," in Early Man in America from a Circum-Pacific Perspective, ed. Bryan, 149-80; Richard Shutler, Jr., "Dating the Peopling of the New World," in Environments & Extinctions: Man in Late Glacial North America, ed. Jim I. Mead & David J. Meltzer, Peopling of the Americas series (U. Maine at Orono: Center for the Study of Early Man 1985), 122-23; Adovasio, Carlisle, Kathleen A. Cushman, Donahue, Guilday, William C. Johnson, Lord, Paul W. Parmalee, Stuckenrath, & Paul W. Wiegman, "Paleoenvironmental Reconstruction at Meadowcroft Rockshelter, Washington County, Pennsylvania," in ibid., 73-119; Adovasio, Donahue, & Stuckenrath, "The Meadowcroft Rockshelter Radiocarbon Chronology 1975-1990," Am. Antiquity LV/ 2 (April 1990), 348-53; Adovasio, Donahue, Cushman, Carlisle, Stuckenrath, Gunn, & Johnson, "Evidence from Meadowcroft Rockshelter," chap. 13 in Early Man in the New World, ed. Shutler, 163-89; etc. ad inf.]. Marie Wormington's survey of a decade's scholarship adjudged Meadowcroft investigations "very impressive" {"Early Man in the New World: 1970-1980," in Early Man in the New World, ed. Shutler, 194; etc.

13. "The Solutrean Connection Question", Covey cites: Adovasio, "The Ones that Will Not Go Away: A Biased View of Pre-Clovis Population in the New World," chap. 15 From Kostenki to Clovis, 206 fig. 2; 212 fig. 6; & 214.

14. "The Solutrean Connection Question", Covey cites: "Clovis Technology: A Comparative Study of the Kevin Davis Cache", Texas (U. Texas 1999), 180. Overshot, common of Clovis blades, was a fracture that split a flake from parent core clean across, taking away part of the far edge.

15. "The Solutrean Connection Question", Covey cites: "Early Man in the New World," ed. Shutler, p. 133.

16. "The Solutrean Connection Question", Covey cites: Adovasio et al., "Evidence from Meadowcroft Rockshelters," p. 165.

17. "The Solutrean Connection Question", Covey cites: Adovasio et al., "The Meadowcroft Rocshelter Radiocarbon Chronology," 349 & chart350.

18. "The Solutrean Connection Question", Covey cites: "The Earliest Americans," Science CLXIV #3906 (7 Nov. 1969), p. 714.

19. "The Solutrean Connection Question", Covey cites: "Fluted Projectile Points," p. 1411.

20. "The Solutrean Connection Question", Covey cites: Adovasio, "The Meadowcroft Rockshelter Radiocarbon Chronology", p. 353.

21. "The Solutrean Connection Question", Covey cites: Shutler, "Dating the Peopling of North America" 123; Adovasio et al., "Evidence from Meadowcroft Rockshelter," p. 188.

22. "The Solutrean Connection Question", Covey cites: "The Ones that Will Not Go Away," p. 207.

23. "The Solutrean Connection Question", Covey cites: "Is It Really that Old?" A Comment about the Meadowcroft Rockshelter 'Overview,'" Am. Antiquity XL/ 3 (July 1980), pp. 579-582.

24. "The Solutrean Connection Question", Covey cites: Prehistory of the Americas, p. 53.

25. "The Solutrean Connection Question", Covey cites: "Pre-Clovis Occupation South of the Ice Sheet," chap. 5, Early Man in the New World, ed. Shutler, pp. 65-72.

26. "The Solutrean Connection Question", Covey cites: Evidence from Meadowcroft Rockshelter," pp. 170-171.

27. "The Solutrean Connection Question", Covey cites: "Comments on the Meadowcroft Radiocarbon Chronology & the Recognition of Coal Contamination," Am. Antiquity LVII/ 2 (April 1992), pp. 321-326.

28. "The Solutrean Connection Question", Covey cites: -"Never Say Never Again: Some Thoughts on Could Haves & Might Have Beens," Am. Antiquity LVII/ 2 (April 1992), p. 327.

29. Garrett G. Fagan, Assistant Professor of Classics and Ancient Mediterranean Studies and History, Penn State University.

Chapter 15: Tiahuanaco and the Lake Titicaca Basin

1. "An Answer to Graham Hancock", Garrett G. Fagan, Assistant Professor of Classics and Ancient Mediterranean Studies and History, Penn State University, see
http://www.thehallofmaat.com/maat/article.php?sid=18&page=1.

2. "Atlantis in the Andes", Produced and Directed by Lisa M. Hutchison, Of Like Mind Production, 2001.

3. Ibid.
4. Fingerprints of the Gods, Graham Hancock, p.84.
5. Notes on a Lecture by Graham Hancock,
   http://www.luckymojo.com/hancocklecture.html, Catherine Yronwode,
   1995.
6. Atlantis in the Andes".
7. Ibid.
8. "Evidence from Lake Titicaca sheds light on sudden global climate changes",
   Stanford Report, Mark Shwartz, January 25, 2001.
9. Ibid.
10. Ibid.
11. Ibid.
12. "Ancient temple found under Lake Titicaca", BBC Online, August 23, 2000.
13. "Pilgrimage Route Uncovered at South America's Lake Titicaca", National
    Geographic News Online, Hillary Mayell, June 4, 2001.
14. Radiocarbon Database for Bolivia, Equador and Peru, Mariusz S. Ziólkowski,
    Mieczyslaw F. Pazdur, Andrzej Krzanowski, Adam Michczynski, Polbooks s.c.,
    ul. Dembego 14/12, 02-796 Warsaw, Poland, 1998. On the web see
    http://www.uw.edu.pl/uw/andy/LABIA-E.HTM.
15. Mummies 101, Public Broadcasting System, See
    http://www.pbs.org/wgbh/nova/chinamum/mummies101.html.
16. "Atlantis in the Andes".
17. "Did the Incas Build Machu Picchu?" David Hatcher Childress, World
    Explorer Magazine, Vol. 3 No. 6.

Chapter 16: Andean Genesis

1. History of the Incas, Pedro Sarmiento De Gamboa, translated by Clements
   Markham, Cambridge: The Hakluyt Society 1907, pp. 28-58.
2. Ibid.
3. Myths and Myth-makers: Old Tales and Superstitions Interpreted by
   Comparative Mythology, John Fiske, Electronic Text Center, University of
   Virginia Library, original publisher - Houghton, Mifflin and Company,
   Boston and New York, 1900, pp 153-154.
4. Valley of the Spirits: a Journey into the Lost Realm of the Aymara, Alan
   Kolata, John Wiley & Sons, 1996, pages 65-72.
5. Ibid.

Chapter 17: The Iberian Connection

1. "Paleoamerican Origins", Anthropology Outreach Office, Smithsonian Institution, 1999. See http://www.si.edu/resource/faq/nmnh/origin.htm.
2. "The Solutrean Connection Question", Covey cites: "Pre-Clovis Occupation South of the Ice Sheet," chap. 5, Early Man in the New World, ed. Shutler, pp. 65-72.
3. "The Solutrean Connection Question", Covey cites: Quoted in Parfit, "Hunt for the First Americans," p. 61.
4. Quoted in "Did First Humans in America Come from East Europe?" p. A6.
5. "First Americans from Europe? - Study Clouds Asian Land Bridge Theory", Joseph B. Verrengia, The Associated Press. See http://abcnews.go.com/sections/scitech/DailyNews/firstamericans991101.html.
6. Ibid.
7. "Texas Site Suggests Link With Europe's Upper Paleolithic", George Wisner, Mammoth Trumpet Vol. 15, No. 1, 2000.
8. See http://www.primtech.net.
9. Ibid.
10. "The Solutrean Connection Question", Covey cites: cf. Olga Soffer, "Upper Paleolithic Adaptations in Central & Eastern Europe & Man-Mammoth Interactions," chap. 4 in From Kostenki to Clovis, ed. Soffer & Nikolai Dmitrievich Praslov (July 1989 symposium at Leningrad with subsequent revisions) (Plenum Press 1993), 45; & Paul Dolukhanov, "The Pleistocene-Holocene Boundary: Environmental Processes & Social Adaptations," chap. 14 in ibid., p. 195.
11. "The Solutrean Connection Question", Covey cites: Michael Jochim, "Late Pleistocene Refugia in Europe," chap. 20, The Pleistocene Old World: Regional Perspectives, ed. Soffer (Plenum 1987), 321-22; Soffer & Praslov, "Fluted Points & Female Figurines–Understanding Late Paleolithic People of the New & Old Worlds," chap. 1, From Kostenki to Clovis, 4; & L.G. Straus, "Solutrean Settlement of North America? A Review of Reality," American Antiquity LXV/2 (April 2000), pp. 220-221.
12. "The Solutrean Connection Question", Covey cites: Quoted in Sharon Begley & Andrew Murr, "The First Americans," Newsweek (26 April 1999), 57; & cf. Karen Wright, "First Americans," Discover XX/2 (Feb. 1999), 52-63; Sasha Nemecek, "Who Were the First Americans?" Scientific American CCLXXXIII/3 (Sept. 2000), 83; Kenneth B. Tinkersley, "Who Were th0e First Americans?" Archaeology LIII/5 (Sept./Oct. 2000), 72-75; Frédéric Sellet, "The French Connection: Investigating a Possible Clovis-Solutrean Link," Current Research in the Pleistocene (Center for the Study of Early Man, U. Me.) XV/x 1998), 67-68; Mark K. Stengel, "The Diffusionists Have Landed," Atlantic Monthly CCLXCV/1 (Jan. 2000), 35-48; Robson Bonnichsen & Alan L. Schneider, "Battle of the Bones," The Sciences XL/4

(July-Aug. 2000), 40-46; Constance Holden, "Were Spaniards Among the First Americans?" Science CCXXCVI/ 5444 (19 Nov. 1999), 1467-68; Douglas Preston, "The Lost Man," New Yorker (16 June 1977), 76; Jerome Burne, "Perspectives: Goodbye Columbus, Hello Solutreans, " Financial Times (London) (2 Sept. 2000), 3; Anon., "Who Was Kennewick Man?" Wilson Quarterly XXIV/ 4 (Autumn 2000, 112-13; Anon., "Did First Humans in America Come from East Europe?" Seattle Times (21 March 1992), A6 & reprinted AIAR Institute Newsletter VIII/ 3-4.

13. "The Solutrean Connection Question", Covey cites: Donald Cyr, "A Short Summary of the Vailian Canopy Theory," Midwestern Epigraphic Journal IX/ 1 (1995), 23-25, "Hidden Halos of Stonehenge" & "The Hidden Halo Hypothesis," Stonehenge Scrolls (Stonehenge Viewpoint 1987), 67-102, & "The Crystal Veil: Avant-Garde Archaeology," Stonehenge Viewpoint 1995), 160 ff, combining articles serialized 1986-87.

14. "The Solutrean Connection Question", Covey cites: "Solutrean Settlement of North America?" op. cit., pp. 219-226.

15. "The Solutrean Connection Question", Covey cites: "The North Atlantic & Early Man in the New World," Michigan Archaeologist VI/ 2 (1960), 19-39; "The Upper Paleolithic & the New World," Current Anthropology IV/ 1 (Feb. 1963), 42, 53, 61, 86; & Reply to Mason, "The Paleo-Indian Tradition in Eastern North America," ibid. III/ 3 (June 1962), 253; Félix Mascaraux, "Les Silex de Montaut (Landes)." Revue Anthropologie XXII (1912), 156-64, & Station Humaine et Gisement de Silex Taillés à Montaut (Landes) (Dax: H. Labeque 1890).

16. "The Solutrean Connection Question", Covey cites: "A Fluted Point from the Old World," Am. Antiquity XXVIII/ 3 (Jan. 1963), pp. 397-399.

17. "Does skull prove that the first Americans came from Europe?", Steve Connor, Science Editor, The Independent. See http:/ / news.independent.co.uk/ world/ science_medical/ story.jsp?story=3580 01

18. "Paleoamerican Origins", Smithsonian Institution, Anthropology Outreach Office, 1999.

19. "The Solutrean Connection Question", Covey cites: "Dental Evidence for the Peoplng of the Americas," chap. 11 in Early Man in the New World, ed. Shutler, pp. 147-157.

20. "The Solutrean Connection Question", Covey cites: C.L. Brace & D.P. Tracer, "Craniofacial Continuity & Change: A Comparison of Late Pleistocene & Recent Europe & Asia," in The Evolution & Dispersal of Modern Humans in Asia, ed. T. Aleazawa et al. (Tokyo: Hokusensha Publishing 1992), 439-72; D.G. Steele & J.F. Powell, "Paleobiological Evidence of the Peopling of the Americas," in Method & Theory for Investigating the Peopling of he Americas, ed. Bonnischen & Steele (Ore. St.

U: Center for the Study of the First Americans, Dept. Anthropology 1994), 261-73; Claude Chaucat & Jean Paul Lacombe 1984; Paul Ossa 1973, 1978; Chaucat 1988; etc., ad inf.

21. "The Solutrean Connection Question", Covey cites: "Does skull prove that the first Americans came from Europe?", Steve Connor, Science Editor, The Independent.

22. Life Among the Piutes, P. 6-7.

23. Indian legends of the Pacific Northwest, Ella E. Clark, University of California Press, Los Angeles California, 1953, p. 53.

24. Black Elk Speaks-Being the Life Story of a Holy Man of the Oglala Sioux, John G. Neihardt, University of Nebraska Press, 1932, P. 23.

25. Red Earth – White Lies: Native Americans and the Myth of Scientific Fact, Vine Deloria, Jr., Fulcrum Publishing, Golden Colorado, 1997, P. 61.

26. Ibid.

27. Ibid.

28. Ibid., P. 64.

29. Mammals and Land Bridges, George Gaylord Simpson, 1940, P. 153, see http://www.wku.edu/~smithch/biogeog/SIMP940B.htm.

30. Ibid., P. 155.

31. Red Earth-White Lies, P. 91.

32. "Archaeology Finds New Picture of Paleo Indians", Robert Suriano, The News Herald, Panama City, Florida, May 16, 1996.

33. "Secrets of the Bog People: Windover", Film Documentary, A Brighton Films/ Horsebridge Productions/ Electric Sky Co - Production for DCI, aired on The Learning Channel (TLC), August 14, 2003

34. "The Dawn of Humans: Hunt for the First Americans", National Geographic Magazine, Michael Parfit, December 2000, p. 66.

35. Ibid., P. 61.

36. Ibid., P. 65.

37. Ibid., P. 67.

38. Ibid., P. 63-64.

Chapter 18: Paleolithic Worldview

1. Shamanism: Archaic Techniques of Ecstasy, Mircea Eliade, Princeton University Press, 1972, p.11.

2. Ibid. p. 260-261.

3. Ibid. p. 264.

4. Ibid. p. 266.

5. Ibid. p. 266.

6. Ibid. p. 271.

7. Ibid. p. 272.

8. Ibid. p. 272
9. Ibid. p. 273-274.
10.Ibid. p. 9-10, 160.
11.Ibid. p. 33.
12.Ibid. p. 168.
13.Ibid. p. 266.
14.Ibid. p. 5-6.
15.Ibid. p. 88-95.
16.Ibid. p. 168-175.
17.Ibid. p. 149-152.
18.Ibid. p. 167.
19.Ibid. p. 158-163.
20.Ibid. p. 161-162.
21.Ezekiel, Chapter 37
22.Shamanism: Archaic Techniques of Ecstasy, Mircea Eliade, Princeton University Press, 1972. p. 274-278.
23.Ibid. p. 133-134.
24.Ibid. p. 68-71.
25.Ibid.
26.Ibid. p. 67.
27.Ibid. p. 99.
28.Ibid. p. 265-266.
29.Ibid. p. 282-286.
30.Ibid. p. 267-268.

Chapter 19: A Clash of Cultures

1. Terence McKenna: Mushrooms Sex and Society: Interview by Philip H. Farber, New History magazine, June 1993.
2. Food of the Gods: The Search for the Original Tree of Knowledge, Terence McKenna, Bantam Books, New York, 1993, P.39.
3. Ibid. p. 70-73.
4. Ibid. p. 79.
5. Ibid. p. 83. McKenna cites James Mellaart, Catal Huyuk: A Neolithic Town in Central Antolia (McGraw-Hill, New York, 1967, pp. 221-222).
6. Ibid. p.85.
7. Ibid. p.87.
8. Ibid. p. 88-89.
9. Ibid. p. 89.
10.Ibid. p. 89.
11.Ibid. p. 123-124.

12. Ibid. p. 83. McKenna cites Riane Eisler, The Chalice and the Blade: Our History, Our Future (San Francisco: Harper and Row, 1987.

13. Ibid. p. 123-124.

14. Ibid. p. 137.

15. Ibid. p. 120.

16. "Learning the Language of the Goddess", an interview with Dr. Marija Gimbutas, October 3, 1992, see http://www.levity.com/mavericks/gimint.htm.

17. "The Age of the Great Goddess: An Interview with Kell Kearns", Marija Gimbutas, Sounds True Recordings, Boulder CO, 1992.

18. "Learning the Language of the Goddess".

19. Ibid.

20. Ibid.

21. Ibid.

22. Ibid.

23. "Birthing as Shamanic Experience", Leslie McIntyre, Awakened Woman, February 20, 2000, see http://www.awakenedwoman.com/birth_story.htm.

24. Ibid., "The Age of the Great Goddess: An Interview with Kell Kearns.

25. "Learning the Language of the Goddess".

26. "The Age of the Great Goddess: An Interview with Kell Kearns.

27. Ibid.

28. Ibid.

29. Field Report, Peter Akkermans and Marie Le Miere, American Journal of Archeology, Volume 96 No. 1, January 1992, see http://www.ajaonline.org/archive/96.1/akkermans_peter_mmg_.html.

30. Rocking the Cradle, Andrew L. Awler, Smithsonian, May 2004, pp. 40-48.

31. The Giza Power Plant, Christopher Dunn, Bear & Company, 1998, p. 170.

Chapter 20: Symbolism of the Serpent

1. The Goddesses and Gods of Old Europe, Marija Gimbutas, University of California Press, Berkeley, 1974 p. 93.

2. The Languages of the Goddess, Gimbutas, Marija Harper, San Francisco, 1989, p. 134.

3. Seals were most often made of stone but also sometimes of bone, ivory, faience, glass, metal, wood, or even sun-dried or baked clay. A recessed inscription was carved onto the cylinder, which produced a raised impression when rolled on a clay tablet or envelope. Cylinder seals were used to protect vessels, clay envelopes and storeroom door latches from tampering. They guaranteed authenticity, marked ownership, indicated participation in a legal transaction and protected goods against theft.

4. NABU: His epithets: Supreme Messenger Herald of the Gods. Divine Scribe. Director of the World. Wielder of the Wand of Divination. Opener of the Wells. Far Traveler. - His character: Nabu, son of Marduk and grandson of Ea, is by origin a water divinity. His power over human existence is immense. He engraves the destiny of each person as the Gods together have decided it on the tablets of the sacred record; and he himself can increase or diminish at will, the length of any person's life span. Nevertheless this divine messenger is a deity worthy of grateful devotion. He and his consort Tashmetum together invented writing ad bestowed it upon the world; also, as his titles imply he is lord of the arts of divination and particularly of the discovery of water by means of dowsing. He is patron of all learning, both overt and occult. His emblems are the stone tablet and writing chisel and the winged dragon, which is initially his father's. He wears a cap adorned with curving home of power, and stands with hands clasped before him in the ancient gesture of priesthood. Kudurru of Melishihu, Taken from Babylonia to Susa, Kassite period (1202-1188 BC), Grey Limestone, H 0.65 m; W 0.30 m, Sb 22. The kings of Babylon from the Kassite dynasty made generous gifts to their vassals. Record of this was, in principle, kept on the boundary posts, the kudurru of the lands that had been made over. In actual fact it was inscribed on great slabs, or standing stones, kept in the temples. These lists of donations were placed under the protection of the greatest possible number of gods, most often represented in their symbolic form and arranged according to the hierarchy of the pantheon. However, at the top, are symbols of the three heavenly gods; Sin (moon), Shamash (sun) and Ishtar (Venus), in order of their position in the heavens, rather than their importance. They were surpassed by the supreme triad; Anu (sky), Enlil (air) symbolized by their horned crowns and Ea (fresh water from the abyss), symbolized by a kind of sceptre carried by a goat-fish. Below we find the emblems of several other gods; that of Marduk, patron-god of Babylon, is identifiable as a pointed hoe placed on a stand and the serpent-dragon, which guards the underworld of the god. The same dragon carries the scribe's stylet, which is the emblem of Nabu, Marduk's son. These emblems were difficult to interpret, even for the ancients who sometimes inscribed the name of the gods symbolized next to the symbols themselves. See http://www.louvre.fr/anglais/collec/ao/sb0022/txt0022.htm.

5. The Sumerians: Their History, Culture, and Character, Samuel Kramer, University of Chicago Press, 1963, pp. 112-113.

6. Ibid., p. 118.

7. Myths of Enki, the Crafty God, John Maier and Samuel Kramer, Oxford University Press, New York, 1989. pp. 28-30.

8. Inanna-Queen of Heaven and Earth: Her Stories and Hymns From Sumer, Diane Wolkstein and Samuel Kramer, Harper & Row, 1983: p. 8.

9. See http://www.3ho.org.
10. The Return of the Serpents of Wisdom, Mark Amaru Pinkham, Adventures Unlimited Press, Kempton Illinois, 1996, p.1.
11. Ibid.
12. Ibid. p. 3.
13. Serpents of Wisdom: An Interview with Mark Pinkham, The New Times Magazine, by James Kumle, July 1997, See http://www.newtimes.org/issue/9707/9707-snakes.html.
14. The Gnostic Gospels, Elaine Pagels, Vintage Books, 1989, P.XVII.
15. Ibid. p.XIX.
16. The Columbia Encyclopedia, Sixth Edition. 2001. Irenaeus, Saint: c.125–c.202, Greek theologian, bishop of Lyons, and Father of the Church. Born in Asia Minor, he was a disciple of St. Polycarp. Irenaeus went to Rome to plead for leniency toward the Montanists (see Montanism) and for those Eastern Christians who were threatened with excommunication because they did not observe the Roman date for Easter. He remained in the West and died in Gaul. He was the earliest Father of the Church to systematize Christian doctrine and is cited frequently by later theologians. Only two of his works survive—neither in the original Greek. Against Heresies establishes Christian doctrine against the Gnostics and incidentally supplies much information on Gnosticism. Polycarp, Saint: c.A.D. 70–A.D. 156?, Greek bishop of Smyrna, Father of the Church. He was a disciple of St. John, who appointed him bishop. Thus he linked the apostles and such 2d-century Christian expositors as St. Irenaeus. St. Polycarp was a close friend of St. Ignatius of Antioch. As a very old man, Polycarp went to Rome to discuss the problem of dating Easter. He died a martyr in Smyrna. His one surviving work, the Epistle to the Philippians, has been the subject of controversy. Some scholars have maintained that the letter is really two—one written c.115, enclosing St. Ignatius' epistles, and the other written c.135 to warn the Philippians against the teachings of Marcion. He was in his time the mainstay of Christianity in Asia Minor.
17. Jewish Encyclopedia, p.407-408.
18. Encyclopedic Theosophical Glossary, Theosophical University Press, 1999, Collation of Theosophical Glossary, See http://www.theosophy-nw.org/theosnw/ctg/om-oz.htm.
19. Serpent in the Sky, John Anthony West, Quest Books, 1993.
20. Ibid., p.59.

Chapter 21: Adam's Path

1. Genesis 2:6.
2. Genesis 1:30.

3. Genesis 2:17.